D1235673

WILLIAM McGUFFEY

WILLIAM McGUFFEY

MENTOR TO AMERICAN INDUSTRY

Quentin R. Skrabec, Jr.

Algora Publishing
New York

Library of Congress Cataloging-in-Publication Data —

Skrabec, Quentin R.
  William McGuffey: mentor to American industry / Quentin R. Skrabec, Jr.
    p. cm.
  Includes bibliographical references and index.
    ISBN 978-0-87586-726-7 (soft cover: alk. paper) — ISBN 978-0-87586-727-4 (hard
cover: alk. paper) 1. McGuffey, William Holmes, 1800-1873. 2. Educators—United
States—Biography. 3. Moral education—United States—History. 4. Readers—History.
I. Title.
    LA2317.M2S57 2009
    370.92—dc22
    [B]
                              2009021188

Front cover:
Nathan Hale Schoolhouse © Lee Snider/Photo Images/CORBIS
William Holmes McGuffey © Bettmann/CORBIS

Printed in the United States

For our Lady of Prompt Succor

and my daughter Marybeth Skrabec Shamrock

Acknowledgements

The Henry Ford Museum and Greenfield Village were crucial in the preparation of this book. I started the book by visiting McGuffey's birth home and school at the village. At The Henry Ford-Benson Research Center, I had the outstanding assistance of Carol Whittaker and Kira Macyda and the whole staff at the Benson Research Center. I've worked with archival staffs all over the country and there is no better than that of the Benson Ford Research Center. The displays at The Henry Ford and Greenfield Village provided hours of inspiration and insight into William Holmes McGuffey as well as many of my Pantheon of American capitalism. With each trip to the village and Benson Research Center, I learned more. Furthermore, I would like to thank the staff of Miami University and the McGuffey Museum for their help and guidance. I would like also to thank the staff at the Carnegie Library of Pittsburgh and the John Heinz Historical Center. Reference librarians are often the forgotten people behind a successful book; and at the University of Findlay, we are blessed with Rebecca Quintus. I would like to thank Clarence Guthrie, Services Librarian, and Robert Schirmer, Library Director. I would also like to thank the University of Findlay, for their help in funding the research, particularly,

TABLE OF CONTENTS

> "There seem to be more and more of us who in these days inquire what it was McGuffey did and how he did it; if by respectful elevation of his name we can induce serious investigation, we may see his fundamental influence rise into a flame again."
> — From "The Mind of McGuffey," 1937

For fifteen years I have been researching America's industrialization. I set out to create a literary pantheon of great Americans that contributed to America's industrial rise. In particular, it was to be a pantheon of American capitalism and exceptionalism. McGuffey in that pantheon must be considered for the seat of the Goddess of Wisdom — Minerva, who was also the Goddess of Commerce. As I researched and wrote biographies on presidents such as William McKinley and industrialists such as George Westinghouse, Henry Clay Frick, Henry Ford, Andrew Carnegie, Edward Libbey, Michael Owens, and H. J. Heinz, the name William Holmes McGuffey kept popping up. William McGuffey was clearly the mentor of many of America's greatest capitalists. Almost all had used the *McGuffey Reader*, and developed their belief systems in one-room schoolhouses.

Greenfield Village has been my adopted town since eighth grade. What always struck me at Greenfield that among the restored factories of Ford, the Edison laboratories, H. J. Heinz's first factory, the old electric plants, and America's best industrial museum was William McGuffey's birthplace and a reconstructed McGuffey school. The link, I would discover, was that all of these great industrialists pointed to their early education from the *McGuffey Readers* as important in their success. It seemed necessary to add this teacher to the pantheon of American industrialists. McGuffey not only formed the minds of these industrial giants, but the minds of the millions of immigrants that forged the world's greatest industrial empire. McGuffey created an American culture to transform the old ideas of Europe into a new society. McGuffey taught of a moralistic and religious utopia. It was the perfect approach for the time and place. McGuffey was not an idealist; he was well aware of the faults of men, but he chose to create an ideal as the vision. His approach came with what many would see today as restrictive views, but in the 1800s it crossed political and cultural lines. It reflected McGuffey's own evolution in the crucible of American society. It embodied the frontier Scotch-Irish industry of his youth, but it also infused the ideas of the frontier Germans and New England Puritans. He was intolerant of diversity, preferring to take diversity and create a new alloy, stronger than the various individual components.

The reader should be aware that McGuffeyland is much different than today's world. McGuffey worked with many assumptions that are not valid today, but while his religious bias is clear, his politics are not. McGuffey assumed a Christian world or at least, he correctly assumed his audience was Christian. What McGuffey did was to take Christian dogma and theology out of education. He was a Presbyterian, but his books are ecumenical and non-denominational (assuming you were Christian). While his texts do not try to make Christian converts, they do oppose atheism and argue for a God throughout. But even given that, the morals he promoted were universal, such as the Golden Rule, and the lessons of the Sermon on the Mount, versus theological dogma. Many of McGuffey's friends and supporters were Unitarian or secular. He used religion liberally in his texts, but the goal was to educate in the basics of reading, writing and morals, not religion. He believed in a common vision for a struggling nation. McGuffey refused to indoctrinate in religious dogma but found common ground among the diverse religious views of the time. McGuffey saw Christian morals as a base shared by all Americans regardless of faith. Successive revisions stripped more and more Christianity, retaining the moral base. It would be hard for the modern reader to see *McGuffey's Readers* as secular, but compared to the books used earlier for schooling, such as the Bible and *New England Primer*, *McGuffey Readers* appeared almost pagan. Conservative Christians such as the Amish and Mennonites, who today cherish the *McGuffey Readers*, refused to use them in McGuffey's time. The religious right of the time were appalled by McGuffey's request for common moral ground. Yet, on a personal level, at the time McGuffey was a member of the religious right!

McGuffey was well aware that the main roadblock to common schools was religion, and his goal was the common school for America. Even more important was the need to bust up the dominant Eastern educational bias of Calvinist theology, which was not popular in the West. McGuffey was the product of a Western enlightenment that came out of the Transylvania area around Cincinnati. He was part of a circle of intellectuals that included the Beecher family and Daniel Drake, the "Franklin of the West." This circle of diverse intellectuals became the driving force for common schools and textbooks, a non-denominational approach to education, and a common language. They represented political and religious extremes, but found middle ground to advance all phases of education. It was in this crucible that McGuffey formulated his approach. His ideas were often forced in the group's many debates. This group known as the "College of Teachers" has been overlooked in most history books, but it is at the heart of McGuffey's story. Criticism and errors are hopefully corrected as well.

With a series of successive biographies, every biographer tries to advance the story. McGuffey had several early hagiographic biographies, which were typical of the early nineteenth century. They are important, but they lacked the balance required by later biographies. In McGuffey's case, several were from the extended family. One biography is that of Alice McGuffey Ruggles, the granddaughter of William McGuffey's brother Alexander and his wife Elizabeth Drake (the daughter of Daniel Drake). The biography has a bit of a bias toward the role of Alexander McGuffey in the development of the Readers, which was studied and addressed. Furthermore, Alice McGuffey Ruggles felt that her great grandfather Daniel Drake's role had been slighted. Daniel Drake was a brilliant innovator and the founder of the "College of Teachers," and every effort was made to fully credit this true genius of the West. In fact, the role of the "College of Teachers" is more fully developed than in prior biographies. Dolores Sullivan's more recent biography does an outstanding job of developing the story and his contribution as a schoolmaster. This biography takes a step beyond to look at the impact of McGuffey on American society.

Other works used were *William Holmes McGuffey and his Readers* by Harvey Minnich. Harvey Minnich was a student of the McGuffey Readers and is a required first stop for any McGuffey researcher. Minnich, a former Dean of Miami University (Ohio), did more than anyone except Henry Ford to promote the memory of William Holmes McGuffey. Another primary book source is that of *A History of the McGuffey Readers* by Henry Vail. Vail was a former McGuffey editor and provides insider views of the publishing history of the Readers. Archival primary sources include those at Miami University and the Benson Research Center at The Henry Ford. In the case of Miami University a large amount of material has been digitalized, which offers the biographer a 21st-century research tool. The Miami University Library also holds a number of special collections and unpublished works. It was in the beauty of Miami's campus that I felt closest to McGuffey, who had a special love of trees.

The intent of this biography is to fully explore the impact of William Holmes McGuffey on the American Industrial Revolution, the development of American capitalism, and American culture. The question explored in detail is: why were so many American leaders so profoundly impacted by the McGuffey? There were many surprises in this quest. McGuffey is often blamed for inspiring the Robber Barons, but the evidence supports just the opposite. While McGuffey's nationalism stood out, the suggested role as a proponent of capitalism is not direct. McGuffey promoted fundamental rights that led to America embracing capitalism, but he placed charity far ahead of making money. McGuffey's capitalism was far from survival of the fitness, so popular at the time. McGuffey felt the right of property was at the core of America, but with that right came a duty, the duty of property owners to help and care for the less fortunate. In fact, McGuffey spends a disproportionate amount of effort on the duties of capitalists to those less fortunate. McGuffey did not use Christianity to justify or promote capitalism but to modify the very soul of capitalism, in particular, to morph the root individual greed of capitalism into charity for the community, to measure the capitalist not by how much he made but how much he gave.

It is interesting that while Henry Ford was the industrialist most admired by McGuffey, he was not the best reflection of McGuffey capitalism. The best reflection would be Andrew Carnegie. Carnegie lacked the religion of McGuffey but still grasped the moral content of religion. Carnegie was a pure McGuffey capitalist in terms of giving. While some might question his ethics in the accumulation of wealth, he was the only great capitalist who eventually gave everything back. He left only enough at his death for his wife and children to live out their lives in the style he had provided. There was no transfer of family wealth like that of Rockefeller and Vanderbilt. Carnegie created community foundations which still exist today, and most of his heirs are middle class. Nothing could be more consistent with the lessons of McGuffey.

This type of focused biography required that new sources be mined, including a full review of materials available at the Henry Ford Benson Research Center. Most of the material was not included in previous biographies. In general, industrial archives of the eighteenth and nineteenth centuries at the Benson Center, the John Heinz History Center in Pittsburgh, the Ohio Historical Center in Columbus, Ohio, and the McKinley Memorial in Canton, Ohio were fully exploited. Any study of McGuffey and his Readers is a study of eighteenth-century and early nineteenth-century America. To that end much time was spent at Greenfield Village in hopes of capturing a feel for McGuffey and his times. Over thirty one-room schoolhouses were visited throughout the United States to look into the past. All of these were extremely helpful in understanding the revolution created by the McGuffey Readers. The Benson Research Center, which has the Henry Ford collection of Readers, Miami University in Oxford, Ohio, and Ohio Historical Society, offered extensive collections of the endless editions, revisions, and variations of the McGuffey Readers.

Another area of new research emphasis was in the Scotch-Irish background of McGuffey, which was shared by many of the Reader alumni. The "Scotch-Irish" or "Scots-Irish" defined early American beliefs, philosophy, and its economic success. The term Scotch-Irish designated a loose amalgamation of the Ulster Scots-Irish, lowland Scotch, Presbyterians, and a mix of Protestant Scotch and Irish in America.[1] Even some early Irish Catholics took to calling themselves Scots-Irish to avoid discrimination. The Scots-Irish dominated the colonial frontier, and the formation of the American system in all aspects. Fifteen American presidents have claimed Scotch-Irish ancestry including three of pure Ulster Presbyterian lineage: Andrew Jackson, James Buchanan, and Chester Arthur. Recent presidents include Ronald Reagan and Bill Clinton. Philosophers and other leaders included Alexander Hamilton, Patrick Henry, James Madison, John Calhoun, Daniel Boone, Jim Bowie, Sam Houston, and twenty-one signers of the Declaration of Independence. It was the American Scotch-Irish enlightenment followed the great Scotch enlightenment of the 18th century. Inventors, thinkers, and creators of Scotch-Irish flourished such as Samuel Morse, Alexander Graham Bell, Francis Scott Key, Adam Smith, Dave Hume, Charles Wilson Peale, Gilbert Stuart, and countless Scottish-born writers. The basic ideas of capitalism were embodied in the writings of Scottish philosophers. The Scotch-Irish excelled in all phases of trade and American industry, claiming the likes of Thomas Mellon, Andrew Carnegie, and Henry Ford. The Scotch-Irish started and dominated industries such as pig iron, steel, whiskey, hemp, cotton, and wool. Especially in business, these Scots-Irish recognized each other like an informal clan of Scottish reciprocity going back to frontier days. This forgotten American race, more than any other immigrant group, is responsible for our way of life.

While it is often discussed in famous biographies, no book has addressed the broader picture of this group's heritage and legacy as chronicled by William McGuffey. William McGuffey was a reflection of his Scotch-Irish heritage. His belief in property rights, thrift, common schools, moralistic education, political free education, hatred of taxes, state-rights, charity, and giving are directly traceable to McGuffey's heritage. The lessons of politics tearing the Presbyterian Church apart inspired McGuffey's non-sectarian approach to education. McGuffey's own sect of the Covenanters had opposed all political issues from being discussed in church. While McGuffey Readers were profoundly Christian, they remained non-denominational and could be used in common public schools. Understanding William McGuffey and his times requires an understanding of the Scotch-Irish American. This once dominant segment of America has now blended into the melting pot becoming the "lost tribe of America."

---

1 The term Scotch-Irish is the most inclusive, while the Scots-Irish is specifically the Ulster Presbyterian Scots.

CHAPTER 1. INTRODUCTION

> "To the end of his days, Ford, like all of his generation lived in McGuffeyland. It was a wonderful land, with never a juvenile delinquent in it, because old William McGuffey's shrewdly chosen dramatic readings plunged their morals home like hot pokers, scarring the pupils all their lives with a stiff conscience, a clear knowledge of right and wrong, and an ineradicable appetite for Fourth of July oratory.
>
> — Sidney Olson, *The Young Henry Ford*

McGuffey Readers dominated American education from the 1840s into the 1900s; even today there is a revival of their use among home schoolers. McGuffey jingles such as "Twinkle, twinkle, little star" and "Where there's a will, there's a way" remain in the vernacular even today. *McGuffey Readers* were best sellers only surpassed in America by the Bible and Webster's Dictionary. In 2008, the McGuffey Eclectic Reader was ranked with Thomas Paine's *Common Sense* and Alexander Hamilton's *The Federalist* as "books that changed the course of U.S. history."[1] Published originally in the early 1830s, by 1900 over one hundred fifty million had been sold. Even today, sales average about thirty thousand a year. Amazingly, for all the sales, William Holmes McGuffey earned a mere one thousand dollars and a small payment for revisions! The publishers fared much better, creating ten millionaires. At the peak, thirty-seven states adopted the *McGuffey Readers*.[2] No single series of books dominated America as the *McGuffey Readers* did

---

1 Charles Bryan, President of Virginia Historical Society, "Books that Changed the Course of U. S. History," Alexandria Library Company 2008 Annual Lecture.
2 Randy McNutt, "Oxford pays tribute to 'McGuffey Reader' writer," *Cincinnati Enquirer*, September 21, 2000.

from 1836 to 1900. Irvin Wyllie estimated that from 1836 to 1900: "Perhaps as many as half the children in America went to school to McGuffey."[1] In 1941, the *Saturday Evening Post* said of McGuffey's books, "For seventy-five years, his system and his books guided the minds of four-fifths of the school children of the nation in their taste for literature, in their morality, in their school development, and, next to the Bible, in their religion."

The *McGuffey Readers* brought a type of magic and enthusiasm to school in the 1800s. Ohio schoolmistress Irene Hardy reminisced of her days in a one-room school in 1850 in the state of Ohio: "Reading was a daily pleasure, and a time of real enthusiasm. It was there and then the young men and young women of the school were, without their knowledge, introduced to prose and poetry, by reading for us and with us and leading us to read rightly, appreciatively, the poems and prose extracts in McGuffey's (old) *Fifth Reader*, all or most from classical English sources. It was there and then we came to know Shakespeare, Milton, Scoot, and some of our own countrymen who had said things, and most of all, the man who daily led us by their thoughts to see into his mind, and to know, dimly as we did, the sources of his knowledge and inspiration."[2] Author Richard Mosier said: "A study of the main currents of thought in the McGuffey readers may legitimately hope to embrace some of the ideas which lie at the heart of American civilization."[3]

The texts were the source of knowledge and motivation for American industrialists such as Henry Ford, Andrew Carnegie, H. J. Heinz, George Westinghouse, Thomas Edison, and John D. Rockefeller, as well as the founder of Kroger Company-A. H. Morrill. Many American presidents, such as Lincoln, Harrison, Grant, Hayes, Cleveland, Harding, Garfield, McKinley, Truman, and Roosevelt attributed their scholarship to the *McGuffey Reader*. McGuffey approached education as a moralistic adventure. He interweaved morals, religion, and virtues into basic lessons. They promoted patriotism and nationalism through the "cult of Washington." But Washington was only one of this heroic Pantheon of greats, which included Napoleon, Daniel Webster, Patrick Henry, and John Adams. In the earliest lessons the virtues of perseverance, charity, patience, courage, industry, self-discipline, and cleanliness. McGuffey assumed an orderly life, seeing goodness as basic to all human endeavors. McGuffeyland was the ideal, but to the child it was also reality.

Henry Ford championed McGuffey and his *McGuffey Readers* until his death. In a 1936 *New York Times* interview, Ford lamented: "Observing the type of character produced in the schools of the McGuffey period, I am convinced that we must

1 Irvin Wyllie, *The Self-Made Man in America* (New York: Free Press, 1954), p. 126.
2 Louis Filler, ed., *An Ohio Schoolmistress: The Memoirs of Irene Hardy* (Kent: Kent State University, 1980), p. 131.
3 Richard Mosier, *Making the American: Social and Moral Ideas in the McGuffey Readers* (New York: Russell & Russell, 1965), preface.

seek in our educational methods the causes of some of the faults today. . . . Today there are too many frills in education . . . when this country adopted a system which put less stress on moral principles, the children grew up and seemed like ships without rudders."[1] Industrialists and leaders educated by *McGuffey Readers* created a long list. These Gilded Age leaders often had nothing more than the four readers in the McGuffey series. The most interesting factor is the shared vision of these McGuffey "trained" industrialists. Most were from the industrial cities of Pittsburgh, Cleveland, and Youngstown. David McCullough described these industrialist as: "They were early-rising, healthy, hard-working, no-nonsense lot, Scotch-Irish most of them, Freemasons, tough, canny, and without question, extremely fortunate to have been in Pittsburgh at that particular moment in history. They were men who put on few airs. They believed in the sanctity of private property and the protective tariff. . . . They trooped off with their large families regularly Sunday mornings to one of the more fashionable of Pittsburgh's many Presbyterian churches. They saw themselves as God-fearing, steady, solid people, and, for all their new fortunes, most of them were. Quite a few had come from backgrounds as humble as Carnegie's."[2] McGuffeyland was a land of economic freedom and property rights, but it was also governed by duties and responsibilities to the less fortunate.

Henry Ford credited McGuffey for his success and turned part of his personal outdoor museum of Greenfield Village into McGuffeyland. Ford so loved his *McGuffey Readers* that he became an avid collector of the many editions. He loved the memories of early schooling. In the 1930s, Ford started the quest to bring McGuffey's home to Greenfield Village. He found a debate in Washington County as to whether the Blaney or Lockhart farm was McGuffey's birthplace.[3] Ford decided on the Blaney farm and moved the log cabin of the Blaney farm to Greenfield Village in 1934. In addition, he shipped old oak logs on the site to build a model McGuffey schoolhouse beside the home at Greenfield Village. The "McGuffey" schoolhouse includes a teacher's desk used by McGuffey. While in the home township of McGuffey (Finley, Washington County, Pennsylvania), Ford got involved in an effort to save one of Pennsylvania's earliest covered bridges. He ended up bringing that bridge to Greenfield Village as well. To further enhance McGuffeyland, Ford brought his Scotch Settlement School in Detroit, where he introduced *McGuffey Readers* to Greenfield Village. He added ancillary buildings such as Noah Webster's house from New England. Greenfield Village remains today a tribute to the role of William Holmes McGuffey in educating the American industrialist. In the 1930s, Ford started his own school based on the *McGuffey Readers*.

---

1 S. J. Woolf, *New York Times Magazine,* January 12, 1936.

2 David McCullough, *Johnstown Flood* (New York: Touchstone, 1968), p. 61.

3 Harvey Minnich, *William Holmes McGuffey and His Readers* (New York: American Book Company, 1936), p. 7.

Dos Passos in his famous novel and critical review of industrial America noted: "Henry Ford had ideas about other things besides assembly lines and the living habits of his employees. He was full of ideas. Instead of going to the city to make his fortune, here was a country boy who'd made his fortune by bringing the city out to the farm. The precepts he'd learned out of McGuffey's Reader, his mother's prejudices and preconceptions, he had preserved clean and unworn as fresh printed bills in the safe of a bank." Henry Ford became a passionate collector of all types of McGuffey memorabilia.

Henry Ford was far from alone in his admiration of the *McGuffey Readers*; the list is a who's who of industrialists and leaders of America's Gilded Age. President William McKinley not only cut his teeth on *McGuffey Readers* but also used them as a schoolteacher at Youngstown, Ohio. McKinley's favorite writers, Walter Scott and Robert Burns, were introduced to him in the *McGuffey Readers*. Likewise the Readers introduced him to his favorite novel, *Robinson Crusoe*, and McKinley's favorite heroes George Washington and Napoleon. Not surprisingly, Andrew Carnegie and Andrew Mellon, who also were educated with McGuffey Readers, shared a love for these very same writers, books, and heroes. McGuffey's positive and readable stories of Napoleon made him the favorite of many Gilded Age industrialists. The shared heroes and beliefs of *McGuffey Reader*-trained industrialists are striking but not surprising when one studies from the *McGuffey Readers*. Carnegie's *Gospel of Wealth* has been argued by many historians to be a mirror of McGuffey principles.

It was no accident that Thomas Edison chose a William Holmes McGuffey rhyme to be recorded first on his phonograph. Those first recorded historic words of December 6, 1877, were:

> "Mary had a little lamb,
>   Its fleece was white as snow
> And everywhere that Mary went,
>   The lamb was sure to go."

This jingle, too, had become part of the language due to the *McGuffey Readers*, as did many sayings such as "crying over spilled milk," "tit for tat," "try, try, again," "the real McCoy," "A friend in need is a friend indeed," and "waste not, want not." The *McGuffey Readers* did much to spread many famous (if apocryphal) stories, such as George Washington cutting down the cherry tree and telling his father "I cannot tell a lie." Presidents often used lines or characters from *McGuffey Readers*. Teddy Roosevelt spoke of "meddlesome Matties," and Calvin Coolidge's famous line "I do not choose to run" was derived from a *McGuffey Readers*. America's "Father of Capitalism," Henry Clay Frick, long remembered his struggle in the 1850s to memorize the McGuffey poem "Twinkle, Twinkle, Little Star."

The *McGuffey Readers* were the foundation of generations of Midwesterners that would usher in America's industrial dominance. These simple stories were highly motivational to a young mind. Charles Lanigan of Carnegie–Mellon University put it best with this summary: "We may smile now at the notion of boys and girls reciting stories of great Americans like George Washington and ancient Romans like Cicero from their *McGuffey Readers*, but such exercises instilled in the schools' impressionable charges a common knowledge of Western culture and what it means to be American, and equipped them with a common language and basis for relating to each other — whatever their ethnic or economic background. As the industrial revolution progressed and manufacturing centers such as Pittsburgh became the engines of the new market economy." Ohio Supreme Court Chief Justice said of McGuffey: "He took the best of American and English literature and made it available to all the homes of our young American nation through the Readers which in most cases were the only books to be found in homes apart from the Bible." Writer Ralph Rush in 1925 said: "Upon the generations immediately succeeding the pioneer period the influence of McGuffey may well have been greater than that of any other writer or statesman in the West. His name has become a tradition not yet extinct."[1]

McGuffey was neither a propagandist nor social reformer; he was an educator. His themes looked for common values and beliefs in American society. His bias was a reflection of his Scotch-Irish roots, Presbyterian values, and the merged culture of the Western Reserve of Ohio. His religious bias reflected that of the times. McGuffey was an educator, not a politician. His politics were those of the Western Reserve of Ohio, the Ohio Valley, and the Scotch-Irish. It was a conservative view that reflected the Whig Party of the 1840s, but he never intended to make young Whigs out of his students. We shall see that his views were part of Ohio's diversity. There is no doubt that his Readers had political impact, but that was not his goal. His reading selections were patriotic but had less political bias than textbooks today. McGuffey's ideas were mainstream, but McGuffey's contribution was to enshrine these frontier values into American culture.

Historian Rudolph R. Reeder said best:

> The McGuffey series has probably attained the largest sale and widest distribution of any series yet produced in America. In range of subject matter, it swept almost the entire field of human interest — morals, politics, literature, history, science, philosophy. Many a profound and lasting impression was made upon the lives of children and youth by the well-chosen selections of this series and valuable lessons of industry, thrift, economy, kindness, generosity, honesty, courage, duty, found expression

---

1 Ralph Rusk, *The Literature of the Middle Western Frontier* (New York: Columbia University Press, 1925) p. 22.

in the lives of millions of boys and girls who read and reread these books, to the influence of which lessons were directly traceable.[1]

McGuffey can be credited with much of the success of the Gilded Age. Abraham Lincoln called him "Schoolmaster of the Nation." McGuffey was not a politician, but many believe that his Hamilton–Federalist–Whig stream of thinking led to the progressive republicanism of Lincoln, McKinley, and Teddy Roosevelt (all of which were trained on *McGuffey Readers*). Teddy Roosevelt would often relate to McGuffey characters, realizing all in the nation recognized them. The love of the *McGuffey Readers* also cut across party lines. William Bryan Jennings, McKinley's Democrat opponent in 1896 and 1900 also attributed his belief system to the *McGuffey Readers*. The progressive Robert Lafollette was another political liberal of the Gilded Age that said he owed a debt to McGuffey. Even post-World War presidents such as Harry Truman praised the *McGuffey Readers*. President Truman often praised the *McGuffey Readers* for "educating for ethics as well as intellect, building character along with vocabulary." Presidents see better than most the problems of society, and they realize the limitations of government in trying to correct them. McGuffey was certainly consistent with Emerson's self-reliance, but he was also consistent with Emerson's belief that education must precede politics. For both Emerson and McGuffey, politics deals the symptoms of societal problems while education deals with the root causes. The success of early American business was based on a moralistic compass that allowed for limited government intervention. McGuffey's moralistic approach went to the heart of culture by preparing a moral citizen. McGuffey prepared a generation of politicians and businessmen that at least knew what high ideals were.

But the list was not just about presidents, inventors, and industrialists, but writers, scholars, and artists. Mark Twain was one of America's greatest writers and the man who coined the term Gilded Age and a McGuffey alumnus. Mark Twain started out in his youth with the *New England Primer*, and he was bored by it. The appearance of the *McGuffey Reader* was said to have changed all that for a young Mark Twain. He loved the stories and the introduction to literature in the *Fourth* and *Fifth Readers*. It was introduced to Daniel Defoe, James Fennimore Cooper, and Louisa Alcott. While Mark Twain remained a doubtful Presbyterian, his biographer noted that the biblical sections impacted Twain's style:

> The Reader had a further effect on Sammy [Mark Twain]: it established the primacy of the Bible as a cornerstone of his intellectual edifice — indeed, of his very consciousness. Biblical verses and parables formed the essential texts of the McGuffey's earliest editions. As he [Mark Twain] learned language, Sammy internalized the idioms and metaphors of the

---

1 Dolores Sullivan, *William Holmes McGuffey* (Fairleigh Dickinson University Press, 1994), p. 151.

Scriptures as well. No reading of Mark Twain's literature can miss the inexhaustible evidence of the Bible as a source.[1]

Even its critics would not dispute the impact of *McGuffey's Readers*. Clarence Darrow, socialist, labor lawyer, and atheist was one of those impacted by McGuffey Readers. Darrow, a famous American Civil Liberties Union lawyer, is probably best known for defending John Scopes' right to teach Darwin in the "Monkey" trial. Darrow had ambiguous feelings about his childhood fascination with the Readers. Darrow would state: "I am sure that no set of books ever came from any press that was so packed with love and righteousness as were those readers. Their religious and ethical stories seem silly now, but at the time it never occurred to me that those tales were utterly impossible lies which average children should easily have seen through." Darrow's mixed feelings show his inability to repute their impact.[2]

With all the accolades of Gilded Age Presidents, industrialists, and inventors, I expected to find in the McGuffey Readers a guide to Gilded Age success. In particular, I expected heroic stories of business, but what I found seemed better suited at times for future ministers. McGuffey's principles can be classified as conservative, supporting the ethics of thrift, hard work, divine providence, industry, perseverance, moral teaching, the Ten Commandments, a doctrine of stewardship, charity, and the right of property. His conservative views, which at the time best fit the Whig Party, crossed political lines and can found wings in all American political parties today. His views reflected those of conservative Presbyterians, Methodists, and Congregationalists, but he felt dogma belonged in Church discussion not public forums. He was ecumenical in his approach to his textbooks, but the audience was the Midwestern American Protestant. He was a capitalist but economic theory was not part of his texts. The text focused on morals, assuming the rest would fall in place.

McGuffey's repetitive lessons on giving and the need for philanthropy influenced the industrialists of the Gilded Age. His Christian based approach would be problematic today but fit with the nature of the times. To his credit, McGuffey stressed Christian virtues over dogma. His strong Christian-based approach does have its critics. Some critics see the anti-semantic views of Henry Ford as being rooted in his McGuffey experiences, but there are no concrete examples to make this linkage. The fact is that McGuffey led the movement for better treatment of Jews, Catholics, and Indians, which had all been targets of nineteenth century discrimination. He did oppose atheism, and many lessons argued the existence of a higher power. Still, his use of the Christian ideal could not be viewed as exclusive. Within Christianity, the *McGuffey Readers* empathize diversity and tolerance.

---

1 Ron Powers, *Mark Twain: A Life* (New York: Free Press, 2005), p. 12.
2 Elliott J. Gorn, ed., *The McGuffey Readers: Selections from the 1879 Edition* (New York: St. Martins, 1998) p. 120.

These views went against the trend of the times and many of his associates in their lack of tolerance of Catholic immigrants.

McGuffey never saw his mission as to convert readers to Christianity but to educate in the Golden Rule. The Golden Rule being "do unto others as you would have them do unto you." The Readers were more a product of his Scotch-Irish heritage and the then American West than any fundamental philosophy. McGuffey's vision was much larger than Readers and Spellers. It was one of common public schools spreading a common view of American values and culture. McGuffey, more than anyone, provided the tools for the American melting pot. One educator noted: "Many of the truths and poetic expressions memorized from these Readers were quoted by parents, preachers, and others to counteract acts of intemperance, vulgarity, laziness, brutality, dishonesty, and lawlessness, which were altogether too common among frontier people."[1] McGuffey firmly believed moralistic education was the basis of success in life. For McGuffey, the frontier school was the gateway to the American dream.

The real impact of McGuffey cannot be measured so much by our industrialists, politicians, and artists, but by the improvement of literacy of the average citizen. One journalist suggested the letters of Civil War soldiers prove the point. "You can see, or rather hear, the successful application of McGuffey's methods and curriculum in Ken Burn's documentary *The Civil War*. Burn's narration consists largely of quotes from letters written by all classes of society and from all regions of the country. The language is alive, clear, vivid, and utterly absent of jargon. The grammar is sometimes fanciful and colloquial but rooted in experiment; the usage is rhythmic with local inflection by North and South, lower-and upper-class alike, black and white. You hear a shared American written language that is marvelously expressive. Most of these letter-writers, from the wives and soldiers and runaway slaves to the aristocrats and officers, would have had little formal education by modern standards; and most would have learned to read and write through a McGuffey Reader. Nothing like that had ever been accomplished on such a wide scale before."[2]

Mark Sullivan, author of *Our Times*, stated in 1903: "it would not be surprising if at least half the school children of America, from 1836 to 1900, drew inspiration from McGuffey Readers. When America sent expeditions of school teachers to carry American culture to the Philippines and Puerto Rico, *McGuffey Readers* were translated into Spanish; when Japan felt the urge to experiment with American ways, McGuffey was translated and carried its democratic point of view into the background of a crystallized feudalism centuries old." McGuffey forged the first united view of America. It was a common vision of culture and society. He created American heroes for Americans such as George Washington. His Read-

1 John Nietz, "Why the Longevity of the McGuffey?", *History of Education Quarterly*, Vol. 4, No. 2, 1964.
2 Michael Ventura, "McGuffey's Eclectic," *The Austin Chronicle*, October 23, 2008.

ers preached religious tolerance in a time of great discrimination. The McGuffey Reader would be the instrument to install this common vision on the nation and bring about the common public school.

John Carlisle, President of the McGuffey Society, summarized the impact in 1927: "The tremendous influence of three quarters of a century of teaching from the same books cannot be overstated. The tolerance of the selections relating to religion offended neither Jew nor Gentile, Catholic nor Protestant. The selections teaching morality, that one should do unto others as he would be done by, are many and were effective in bringing up the standard of morality. The readers brought pupil and parent alike in contact with the best literature of the day. What means had the pioneers of gaining knowledge of classic writings except those that were found in the McGuffey Readers? Absolutely none. Where could they gain acquaintance with the refinement of poetry except in the McGuffey Readers? There was no place. What would they know about Shakespeare except what they read in McGuffey? Nothing. In fact, the Readers touched upon every phase of human life to advantage."

McGuffey's legacy continues to this day with grade schools, high schools, and college halls throughout Ohio, Kentucky, Virginia, Pennsylvania, and Indiana. *McGuffey Readers* still sell a quarter million a year, with popularity growing with home schoolers. McGuffey played an integral part in the development of free public education. He and his Readers were part of an American enlightenment that swept the nation in the 1830s. But it is the legacy of a nation changed and culture that remains the main highlight of the McGuffey Readers. The William McGuffey also remains America's premier educator. C. Smith, Dean of Miami University, said in 1962: "Washington was our great liberator, Lincoln was our great emancipator, Edison our great inventor, and William Holmes McGuffey our great educator." The American frontier created McGuffey as much as McGuffey created the Western culture of the frontier.

CHAPTER 2. FRONTIER SCOTCH AND SCOTCH-IRISH

"These were the frontiersmen, ideally suited by their previous and experience to spearhead the drive against colonial frontiers."
— John F. Kennedy

William Holmes McGuffey was born in Washington County in 1800 on September 23 to Alexander McGuffey of Scotch heritage and Anna Holmes McGuffey of Scotch-Irish heritage. To fully understand the nature of William Holmes McGuffey and the evolution of American education, one must fully understand the nature of the frontier Scotch-Irish of "Ohio Country," which included Western Pennsylvania, Eastern Ohio, today's panhandle of West Virginia, and northern Maryland. Many early diaries of Scotch-Irish called the hills and valleys of Western Pennsylvania — a paradise. Unlike Scotland, which the ice age glaciers scraped to bare granite and cut deep valleys, the Ohio Valley and its tributaries — the Monongahela and Allegheny valleys — were leisurely cut on a lush plateau. While having different geological origins, Scotland and Western Pennsylvania have similar topography, but Western Pennsylvania had richer soil. While the glaciers of the last ice age had reduced the Scottish soil to a thin layer of rocky soil, known as the worst in Europe, these Western Pennsylvania valleys and hills had a rich soil. Western Pennsylvania was probably inhabited before Scotland by a strange and long lost people known today as the Monongahela people. Meadowcraft Village of Western Pennsylvania, holds a record (albeit disputed) as one of the oldest sites of man at 15,000 years ago. The site is only a few miles from the birthplace of William Holmes McGuffey.

This lost tribe of people had lived off on the richness of the land producing the "three sisters" — corn, beans, and squash. The demise of the Monongahela people remains at mystery, but most archeologists date it to the 1500s. After the passing of the Monongahela people, the land remained unclaimed. The Iroquois of New York used it as a hunting reserve in the 1700s. While lush, the area was formidable to settle with its steep hills and thick hardwood forests of hickory, oak, and walnut. The area was also a rich source of herbs and useful plants such as ginseng and sassafras. The Scotch-Irish harvested wild ginseng for trade with Europe. Some small Indian villages arose near the rich flood plains of the rivers, which offered high yields of domesticated corn and rye. When the McGuffey family arrived in Western Pennsylvania, it was a rich forest with Indian tribes preserving the area as shared hunting lands. Tribes such as the Shawnees were being pushed in from the south; and from the east, the Delaware were being pushed west whites.

The animal life reflected the rich diversity of the vegetation. Large herds of wood buffalo, elk, and deer roamed the area in the 1600s. Wolves, panthers, wildcats, and bears were common as well. Streams (called "runs" by the early Scots-Irish) and the stream valleys (known as "hollows") were home to beavers, muskrat, foxes, and many species of fish. Now-extinct passenger pigeons darkened the skies for hours at time, and turkeys roared throughout the area. John Audubon painted his famous rendition of the passenger pigeon in this primal countryside, and the area remained a bastion for hunters of this species into the 1870s.[11] The now extinct Carolina parrots also were abundant. Poisonous copperheads and rattlesnakes were numerous, but the early Scots-Irish seemed to fear the boundless mosquitoes more. By far, the species of mammal that most left its mark on Western Pennsylvania were the Scots-Irish of Ulster.

The Scots-Irish (earlier term) or Scotch-Irish were best represented by the immigrants of Presbyterian Ulster Scots, who a hundred years earlier, had migrated to Ulster, Ireland, but also included many pure Scots suffering from British rule. The West coast of Scotland was about 30 miles away. Western Pennsylvania today remains the best linguist legacy of the Scots-Irish with strong accent of the population and the unique vocabulary, such as hollows, burghs, and runs. The accent of Western Pennsylvania combines the burr of the Scots with the brogue of the Irish and adds the gutturals of Germany. Many words and expressions remain in the local language, such as "you-uns" or "ye-uns" for "you (plural). Other expressions include "redd up" for clean up and "slippy" for slippery and "still" for steel. Street names of the area still include the word "diamond" for town squares. Pittsburgh has its Diamond Street and Diamond markets. Typical Scotch-Irish family names include Jackson, Taylor, Irwin, Allison, Houston, McLaughlin, McDonald, McKee, McDowell, Alexander, and Davison.

The dominance of the Ohio and Monongahela valleys by the Scots-Irish had been a slow process with deep roots in Scottish and English history. The term Scots-Irish, or Scotch-Irish as already noted, is a mix of Scots-Irish, Scotch, and later combinations of Scotch and Irish in the colonies. These valleys were considered frontier at the time during and after the American Revolution. Scotch-Irish is uniquely American with no such term existing in Ireland or Scotland. In fact, prior to 1830, the term "Irish" generally meant Scotch-Irish. Surveys of Western Pennsylvania suggest a very complex mix indeed and very reflective of America's mixing pot. There remains much debate as to the make up of Scotch-Irish. In many ways, the Scotch-Irish may be considered the first of the new Americans. On the frontier, the Scotch-Irish of Ulster readily mixed with German, English, Scotch, and Indian. While at times considered uncivilized by urban dwellers, they were the "upper class" of the frontier. Many nationalities seemed willing to assimilate into a Scotch-Irish communities and villages.

By 1730, these Presbyterian Scotch-Irish dominated the trade and agriculture of Western Pennsylvania. By the revolution, the Scotch-Irish dominated the politics and were the earliest recruits to the Continental Army. Driven from the deep belief in Calvinistic destiny, the Scotch-Irish were the nation builders. They had an inherent hatred of the British and taxation, going back to their days in Ulster. The new American government soon learned their hatred for taxes in the 1790 Whiskey Rebellion, which was the first challenge to the Federal government. They well remembered the heavy burden of British taxes in Scotland. They were fiercely independent, which naturally drew them to the wild frontier areas. While many left for Kentucky and Tennessee from the Monongahela Valley, others stayed to build banking and manufacturing empires. The values of the Presbyterian Ulster Irish would constraint Pittsburgh business into the 1870s. The Presbyterian Church did more than any Christian sect to bring education to the frontier. McGuffey's mother Anna Holmes was from a prominent Ulster or Scotch-Irish Presbyterian family.

As we have seen, to understand the domination of the Ulster Irish in Western Pennsylvania, you need to review both English and Scottish history. The Scottish immigration to the Ulster area of Ireland had been far from a success. The Scotch-Irish were finding farming the soil of Ireland not much better the Scotland. In addition, they were constantly being attacked by the local Irish and overtaxed by the British. William Penn's offer of land, no taxes, and religious freedom was a major draw. In addition, the merchants of Scotland had developed an extensive trading network from the failed colony of Nova Scotia. The colonization had allowed the lowlanders of Glasgow to develop trading interests in the New World and brought immigrants to the New World in the late 1600s. The network allowed for transportation to ports such as Philadelphia and Norfolk. As early as 1706, the Presbyterian Church had established itself and would be part of the necessary infrastructure for Scotch immigration. The failed crop of 1717 would start a trickle of Ulster emigrants that by 1720 would become a flood. By 1770, at least two hundred thousand had settled in America.[1] William McGuffey's mother's family (Holmes) came to Western Pennsylvania in this early migration. Most of these early Scots-Irish came through the ports of Philadelphia, Chester, and New Castle and then moved West through the Cumberland valley to central and Western Pennsylvania. They were sure to stay north of the disputed Maryland border (Maryland being a Catholic colony.) By 1739, the British Parliament had demanded an inquiry, as the emigration threatened to depopulate the Protestant element of Northern Ireland.

As the early Western Pennsylvania censuses suggest, there was a large influx of Presbyterian Scots (of the Calvinist Kirk Church of Scotland) at the same time. In the 1600s, Scotland was ruled politically by its own parliament and the Kirk's General Assembly, yet Scotland was a torn country. The highlanders were split with the lowlanders, and the highlanders were split along clans such as the MacDonalds and Campbells. The Campbells represented English-speaking highlanders who were loyal to the Kirk. The MacDonalds were representative of the Gaelic-speaking highlanders loyal to the Catholic and Episcopalian Church. The McGuffey (Macfie) clan was a highlander clan from the islands of Oronsay and Colonsay. The Union with England in 1707 caused a further split in Scotland over religion. The union called for allegiance to the Anglican Church. The highlander clans represented by the Kirk refused and went to practicing their faith in secret, as did the Ulster Irish, which were also loyal to the Kirk and Calvinism. The McGuffeys belonged to the early dissenters known as "Covenanters," which had a long history of persecution by England. The Covenanters formed the Reformed Presbytery of Scotland. Families with Covenanter ancestry tended to be extremely conservative and opposed both government and church structure. The British government as well as the Catholic Highlanders opposed the Covenanters. Covenanters were deeply conservative and biblical, believing that moral education, not political activism, was the way to right injustice. Covenanters opposed the evils of drinking, even while popular with many Scots. The Covenanter background would be seen in the future textbooks of William Holmes McGuffey. So the emigration of the Ulster Irish and Covenanters for religious reasons came at the same time as the first small wave of highlanders. The union with the English church also created a new practice of taxing residents. The Covenanters were particularly opposed to such church taxes. Protestantism seemed to be the bonding agent of all Scottish heritages in America. Only the highlander Catholics appear to lack the bond.

The most unusual thing about the Scotch Presbyterians was their fierce belief in education. John Knox's 1560 *Book of Disciplines*, called for a national system of

---

1   Arthur Herman, *How the Scots Invented the Modern World* (New York: Three Rivers Press, 2001).

education through the church. Knox wanted every boy and girl to be able to read the bible. In 1696, in Scotland the government Kirk passed the "School Setting Act." The act required each parish to establish a school. The act so established that a parish had to pay a minimum established salary to a parish schoolteacher. The education was to be free to all in the parish. The education supplied was extremely basic, but achieved outstanding results. By 1720, Scotland had the highest literacy rate in Europe at fifty-five percent.[1] Many believe that the real root of the American education system of public schools can be found in the Scottish "School Setting Act." The motivation to read became explosive, and by 1750 every town had a lending library. The Presbyterian Church brought this highly successful system to America in the early 1700s. This Scottish success would auger the textbooks of McGuffey and the free library of the Scotch American, Andrew Carnegie.

The Kirk lowlanders and Kirk highlanders, which were the roots of the Ulster Scots and all the Scotch-Irish, were part of the large first wave of immigration to America in the 1710s and 1720s. This first wave was fully united by their Calvinistic faith and hatred of the British and Episcopalians. Highly individualistic, these migrants had no love for the strong control of the Scottish Kirk either. They lived on harsh ground and hills similar to that of Western Pennsylvania. They believed in independent living, free of government and centralized church, always preferring the rural frontier to urban centers. They believed in the importance of reading the Bible, which evolved into an extensive educational network. The Bible was considered a basic guide for living. The highlanders brewed a malt whiskey that was part of their culture. They would quickly adapt Western Pennsylvania corn and Monongahela rye to their art. There was, however, a smaller sect, which the McGuffeys belonged to, known as the Covenanters that opposed drinking. Their warlike roots gave rise to William Wallace and Robert Bruce, who were considered as patron saints, and their stories would be used in future *McGuffey Readers*. While the Scotch-Irish had the Irish love of whiskey, they were very strict in other social morns. Drunkenness was frowned upon, and the Scotch-Irish could "hold their whiskey." Working on the Sabbath was a major crime. The strict obedience of the Sabbath was applied without exception by Pittsburgh businesses until the 1870s. The "blue laws" of Western Pennsylvania are a direct result of Scottish influence. The highlander Scots tended to be stricter than their Ulster cousins, who had moderated after decades in Ireland. The troika of pragmatic Scotch-Irish values was belief in the individual, the importance of the Sabbath, and rigid biblical morals.

Both Philadelphia and Norfolk took on large populations of Scotch-Irish and Scots, but most of them pushed inland to the west and south. Scotch immigra-

---

1 Arthur Herman, *How the Scots Invented the Modern World* (New York: Three Rivers Press, 2001) p. 38.

tion was a chain process, with the Irish Ulster Scots leading the way followed by Scotch highlanders and lowlanders, which developed settlements, and the Presbyterian Church as the Ulster Scots moved out. Many Ulster Scots had ties going back centuries to the lowland Scots, and the Scots-Irish quickly aligned with the lowlanders in Scotland for an international trade network. The majority of the Ulstermen headed to central Pennsylvania, then on to Western Pennsylvania. The Ulster Scots led the Scottish spear of immigration inland, but found what they were searching for in the hills of Western Pennsylvania, West Virginia, Maryland, and Kentucky. The Ulstermen were poor farmers, preferring fur trade and whiskey production. While fiercely religious, they were freewheeling and moved into areas lacking formal churches. Their farms were poorly kept and consisted of a few sheep on the Pennsylvania frontier. Western Pennsylvania was ideal for the Ulstermen, since it was disputed territory free of government control. Even the Indian nations had no ancestral claims on the Monongahela valley. The trade network for illegal colonial product had been in place by Glasgow merchants since the 1690s. The Indian hunting tribes offered resistance, but the Scots-Irish were warriors at heart and would fight for trade. Pennsylvania had offered land but not ownership, forcing the Scotch-Irish to frontier. By the 1750s, the Scot-Irish Ulstermen dominated the valleys of the Monongahela, Allegheny, and Ohio rivers commercially. Even the loyal British colonists of Virginia depended on the Scot-Irish to hold back the French who were migrating from the Great Lakes into the Ohio and Monongahela valleys.

Still, these enterprising Scotch-Irish brought many problems to the colonial governments. Proper English colonies such as Virginia viewed them as salvages. After the death of William Penn in 1718, his secretary Thomas Logan lamented the bringing of the Scotch-Irish. He and his assistants referred to them as "idle," "worthless," or "indigent." After seeing six ships of Scotch-Irish arrive in ten days in 1728, Logan publicly protested their arrival. They moved rapidly across Pennsylvania, leaving their settlements and legacy across the state. They built alliances with the Germans and Indians but would swear alliance to any English government. Logan soon realized that the strategy of replacing the Indians with Scotch-Irish achieved no measure of control; in fact, the Scotch-Irish often proved more difficult.

The Scotch-Irish formed cooperative communities with the frontier Indians. This is somewhat surprising considering some of the bloody battles that arose between the Scotch-Irish and the Indians. The Indians and Scotch-Irish seemed to have a natural affinity. They were economically united in trade. Both were restless subsistence farmers that preferred to be traders. They both believed in a type of property rights. They both had a love of whiskey. They were both free spirits with a dislike for formal government. Both liked the formation of clan type communities versus urban centers. Both were fighters and warriors by nature. Scotch and the Scotch-Irish often re-united in the American colonies. This reunification represented William Holmes McGuffey's parents. The Scotch-Irish and immigrant Scotch were really the same race, both being Scotch. The Scotch-Irish opened their communities to German immigrants who benefited by the educational opportunities in the Scotch-Irish community.

By the 1750, the Indians, Scotch-Irish, and lowland Scots formed a powerful fur trade empire in America. In 1752, over fifty percent of Pennsylvania exports to London were furs.[1] Even in the agricultural states such as South Carolina, fur was about fifteen percent of the exports. The Scots controlled the fur trade and the supply chain logistics to Europe. The Scotch-Irish hunted and traded with the Indians for furs. The Scotch Presbyterians reinforced the supply chain with a string of settlements across Pennsylvania. The furs were assembled and transported to the seaports by trading networks of Scots, such as George Croghan, who had wagon trains and riverboats throughout the colonies. Croghan utilized the many Scotch settlements to get his wagon trains across the Appalachian Mountains. Croghan represented the major logistics chain from the fur country to American ports, and Scots also controlled the ports. Men like Croghan and Daniel Boone expanded into the ginseng trade through the fur trade network. The Scotch-Irish were natural capitalists.

The Scots had the largest fleet of trading vessels in the 1700s. Early in the 1700s, they became the carriers of colonial tobacco with almost four hundred ships engaged in it. In fact, the Scottish imports of tobacco from America exceeded that of London and all English ports by 1745. Scotch shipping dominated the ports of New York, Philadelphia, Alexandria, and Baltimore. The control of tobacco shipping was well over fifty percent, giving the Scots domination of the Virginia colony. Not surprisingly, Glasgow Scots such as Lord Dinwiddie often were selected as British governors of Virginia. The warehouses of Glasgow had more tobacco then Virginia at any point in time. Importing, warehousing, and exporting were the specialty of the lowlanders. The lowland heritage of the Ulster Scots made for old clan and family ties in Scotland for shipping and warehousing furs. Since the frontier Ulster-Irish had family in the Scotch lowlands from centuries ago, it was easy to setup a network. The Scots shipped fur to all European and Asian ports from these Glasgow warehouses. As a Scot, Adam Smith observed the Scots had developed the world's best banking system to support their trading empire. The Scots enjoyed a colonial trading monopoly, and this system was readily adaptable to the fur and alcohol trade of the frontier Ulster Scots and Scotch-Irish.

---

1 Jane Merritt, *At The Crossroads* (Chapel Hill: University of North Carolina Press, 2003) p. 38.

A great deal of the Scotch-Irish (as the colonists began to call them) political power came with their role as a Rosetta stone for Indian communications and trade. Pennsylvania employed them as Indian agents and the Virginians used them for trade. The most important of the Scotch-Irish frontier politicians was George Croghan, who would be Pennsylvania's Indian agent for the decades preceding the American Revolution. Croghan became the "King of Traders," and his Scotch-Irish trading network rivaled that of all of New France. By the late 1740s, his network not only included the Pennsylvania frontier but most of present day Ohio with key trading posts on the Miami, Monongahela, Sandusky, Ohio, Walsh, and Cuyahoga Rivers. By early 1750, he was pushing up against the French in Detroit and the northern Great Lakes. Some of these outposts were the farthest points of white colonization, deep in the wild and well beyond any forts or any type of civilization. He had developed close relations with the Delawares of Pennsylvania, most of the Ohio valley tribes, and the Six Nations Iroquois, who claimed rule over the Ohio and Monongahela Valleys. Like many Scotch-Irish traders, he married an Indian, a daughter of a Mohawk chief. The intermarriages of the Scots-Irish became so common they were known as the "white Indians." This relationship cemented close ties with the Iroquois Confederacy, which held authority over the Pennsylvania frontier. The network covered not only the frontier, but also the Philadelphia ports. More than any group, the Scotch-Irish brought capitalism to America.

The future site of Pittsburgh was the key to Croghan's empire. He depended on river travel via canoe for a supply chain management. The rivers allowed Croghan to penetrate as far West as the Mississippi River for fur collection and to ship down river to the port of New Orleans. Croghan was the first to realize the importance of this site. One of the earliest documents of Western Pennsylvania, Bedford County's Deed Book No. 1, shows a deed in 1749 to Croghan for a parcel of land on "the south side Monongahela River, beginning at a Run nearly opposite to Turtle Creek [the 1754 site of the battle of Braddock] and down the Monongahela to its junction with Ohio." He failed to interest the Quaker Assembly of Pennsylvania in a fort at the junction. Croghan chose then to run his empire from the Allegheny River at Aughwick Creek near present day Etna. He was also a resident of the Indian camp of Logstown (Ambridge), a few miles from present day Pittsburgh.

Croghan played a balancing act throughout the 1750s in Monongahela and Ohio country. The Delawares claimed the land and the Pennsylvania Quakers favored those claims. Croghan and the Scotch-Irish settlers favored the Iroquois alliance, which left the fur trade open. The Quakers had little of the fur trade, and what little the Quaker merchants had was through the Delawares. The Quaker Assembly started to call the Scotch-Irish traders-"blood thirsty Presbyterians." William Penn's sons also had little personal respect for the hard-drinking Croghan as well. To complicate matters, the French were establishing trade posts throughout the Ohio Valley. Croghan hoped for a military alliance of the British, Iroquois, Shawnee, and even the Delawares to battle back the French. The French were the real threat to the Scotch-Irish fur trade on the North American continent including Canada.

While Croghan started out as a Pennsylvania agent, he was soon drawn to his Scottish brethren in Virginia such as Governor Dinwiddie (governed from 1751 to 1757). Virginia had argued early on that the Monongahela Valley and West was outside the Pennsylvania charter. Dinwiddie was from the Glasgow trading destiny that had supported the Scottish Act of Union in 1707. Prior to Dinwiddie's arrival, a group of Virginians including Lawrence Washington and Thomas Lee had formed the Ohio Company to settle Western Pennsylvania and develop trade with the Indians. Upon his arrival, Dinwiddie became a major shareholder, seeing it as a means of participating in the lucrative Scottish fur trade. He already had financial interests to Glasgow banking, warehousing, and shipping. Croghan also saw the Ohio Company as a means to getting military support as the aggressive French traders were moving into the Allegheny, Ohio and Monongahela valleys in the 1750s.

The conflict with the French came to a head in 1752 as the French pushed south into the Allegheny River valley, overrunning many of Croghan's trading posts as well as other Scots-Irish traders such as John Fraser and John Findlay. Croghan lost posts and employees throughout the Allegheny and Ohio valleys as well as in Kentucky. John Fraser retreated to his home on the confluence of Turtle Creek and the Monongahela River while Croghan reinforced his headquarters on the lower Allegheny. By the summer of 1753, the Scots-Irish fur trade was shutdown. This threat to the Scotch-Irish trading empire would change the world. Virginia's Governor Dinwiddie immediately realized the threat to the Scottish and British fur trade by the French advance. He dispatched a twenty-one-year-old George Washington to take a letter of concern to the French in Western Pennsylvania with frontiersman Christopher Gist in late 1753. On November 23, Washington met with Scots-Irish traders at Fraser's Turtle Creek home and later with Croghan at Logstown. After delivering the letter, Washington returned to Williamsburg to inform Dinwiddie of the French defiance. Dinwiddie dispatched a regiment of forty-one Virginians to build a fort at the confluence of the Allegheny and Monongahela where the Ohio River formed. The Virginians teamed up with local Scots-Irish to build the first encampment at the site of today's Pittsburgh as George Croghan and John Fraser had suggested in the 1740s.

Scotch-Irish John Fraser, who immediately incorporated a trading post, christened this new fort Fort Prince George. England and the colonies would unite, and England sent General Edward Braddock and two "Irish" regiments, Sir

Peter Halket's 44th Foot and Thomas Dunbar's 48th Foot. These regiments had a mixed make up, probably the majority being Scotch highlanders and Scots-Irish. Officially, the 48th was listed as forty percent English, ten percent Scot, thirty-four percent Irish, and sixteen percent American.[1] With Roman Catholics being banned from the army, the listed Irish had to be Scots-Irish, Protestant Irish-English, and a considerable number of undeclared Roman Catholics. The poor conditions in the Scottish highlands in the 1750s made it a recruiting gold mine for the stretched British Empire. Once in America, many of these would desert to blend in the Scots-Irish population. Washington's Virginians and the Carolina Americans would join Braddock's 44th and 48th. It should be noted that these units were considered Britain's poorest as opposed to the famous Highlander regiments such as the "Black Watch." Yet, the riflemen of Scotch-Irish Daniel Morgan would demonstrate a new approach to frontier fighting that would be applied with success in the future Revolutionary War.

The road that Braddock built followed a wide trail developed for decades by Scotch-Irish immigrants through the Cumberland Valley (originally an Indian path). It was the same path many years later that the McGuffey family would follow to Western Pennsylvania. The Scots-Irish soldiers deserted along the way to find "relatives" in the woods. On July 9, 1755, with Halket's 44th, Braddock crossed the Monongahela at Fraser's trading post on Turtle Creek. The French and Indians ambushed the force. The result was the bloodiest defeat of the British on American soil. The field that day would have more future generals than any other known fight including George Washington, Thomas Gage, Horatio Gates, Daniel Morgan, Charles Lee, John St. Clair, Adam Stephen, James Craik, and James Burd. Others included Pontiac, the father of Chief Tecumseh, Daniel Boone, George Croghan, Christopher Gist, and William Shirley. Sir Peter Halket, who died that day, was a distant cousin of Scotsman Andrew Carnegie who would build his first steel mill on this very site over one hundred years later. General Braddock also died in this defeat, and the town of Braddock honors him. The battle would change the nature of battles on American soil forever. Many of the Scotch and Scotch-Irish soldiers remained in the hills and started settlements.

Braddock's defeat caused many of the frontiers to leave in fear; only the Scotch-Irish remained at their reinforced trading posts. It changed British army recruiting as well. Lord Loudon was appointed commander of American forces after the death of Braddock. He listened to Washington and Croghan forming light ranger units of American frontiersmen. He rebuilt the British regiments with pure Scottish highlanders in place of lowlanders, poor Irish, and English. The Highlanders would lead England and General Wolfe to a major victory at Montreal. Loudon's strategies were continued by his replacement Jeffery Amerherst. General Forbes would lead an expedition that took Fort Duquesne in 1759,

---

1 Stephen Brumwell, *Redcoats* (Cambridge: Cambridge University Press, 2002) p. 23.

renaming it Fort Pitt. Fort Pitt was reinforced with a regiment of Highlanders. By 1763, Fort Pitt was a Scottish enclave ruled by Highlander Redcoats and supported by Scotch-Irish traders and merchants. George Croghan and his company became the proprietors of the Indian and fur trade. With a shaky peace with the Indians and British security, yet frontier lack of laws, the Scots-Irish started to settle in the area. At the Fort they became tailors, merchants, and started light industries such as blacksmithing. Letters from soldiers and frontiersmen brought more Scottish immigrants to Fort Pitt and the Monongahela region. Its tradition of trade made Pittsburgh the world's largest inland port.

Pontiac's Uprising of 1763 brought one final challenge to the Pennsylvania frontier as well as to the Great lakes. The Indian uprising of the Ottawa Chief Pontiac once again shut down trade on the frontier. Over a thousand small farms were destroyed according to George Croghan. The climactic battle with the Indians would take place in Monongahela country at Bushy Run about fifty miles from Fort Pitt. Two Highlander regiments, the 42nd and the 77th, would lead the charge. The 42nd foot was a pure Scottish Highlander regiment known as the "Black Watch." Colonel Bouquet used non-conventional tactics including Highlander charges to give the Indians a crushing defeat. The defeat allowed the Scotch-Irish settlers to pursue more industrious enterprises in the area. The dominant Scotch-Irish settlements in the area became a magnet for East coast Scotch-Irish, who would find freedom from all British authority. The Scotch-Irish were restless and loved the personal freedom of the frontier.

The Scotch-Irish trade networks sent huge amounts of fur, whiskey, and ginseng to the Scottish cartels in Europe. The Ohio River allowed shipments of these products to New Orleans and then to the East Coast and Europe. Such trade led to the production of oak and hickory barrels as well as flat boat construction. By the 1770s, the Scotch-Irish were permanent settlers, with some estimating they were the second largest ethnic groups after the English and ahead of the Germans.

The next big immigration wave of Scotch-Irish into Western Pennsylvania came after the American Revolution. William Holmes McGuffey's father Alexander came in this migration in 1789. A 1790 survey of Western Pennsylvania including five Western counties: Allegheny, Washington, Fayette, Westmoreland, and Bedford support the assumption of much intermixture of blood.[1] The survey of 12,955 families showed thirty-seven percent English with the "Scotch-Irish" making up thirty-six percent. Of the thirty-six percent Scotch-Irish, there were 17 percent Scotch, "Scotch-Irish" were 7.5 percent, 2.7 percent were Ulster Irish, 4.7 percent were English-Irish, and 4.6 percent were southern Irish. The survey supports the blended view of the term "Scotch-Irish." This early survey is

---

1 Solon Buck and Elizabeth, *The Planting of Civilization in Western Pennsylvania* (Pittsburgh: University of Pittsburgh Press, 1967) p.233.

surprising in that it refutes the common belief of Ulster Irish controlling the area. The reason for this perception was the dominance of the Presbyterian Church as a frontier church. Presbyterian Church reflected the values and the hearts of the Ulster Irish. The Presbyterian Church bound frontier protestants into a political force. The Presbyterian Church cannibalized other frontier Christians, particularly the Protestant Irish, Scotch, and English. Another usual part of the "Scotch-Irish" legacy was they were often found in Pennsylvania and Maryland alongside protestant German settlers. The Germans not only assimilated with the Scotch-Irish but also claimed their identity to improve their social status.[1] Most frontier communities had Scotch-Irish living side-by-side with Germans. By the 1800s, the Presbyterian Church had taken in many protestant Germans as well in Western Pennsylvania, and the Scotch-Irish had taken in many German cultural traditions. The German immigrants infused a more moderate form of hyper patriotism in the Scotch-Irish with a dislike of the horrors of war.

The backcountry farms such as the McGuffey's were poor by European standards but produced crops such as flax, hemp, and rye. Backcountry industries were started by the now "Scotch-Irish," which included weaving flax into linen and hemp into rope. Rye was used in place of Scotch barley to make whiskey, and Monongahela Rye was becoming world famous. The Ohio River allowed shipments of these products to New Orleans and then to the East Coast and Europe via Scotch-Irish world trade networks. Such trade led to the production of oak and hickory barrels as well as flat boat construction. By the 1790s, the Scotch-Irish were permanent settlers, with some estimating that they were the second largest ethnic groups after the English and ahead of the Germans. The Scotch-Irish now represented a broader term of Ulster Scots, Scottish, Irish, and mixed blood. The Scotch-Irish would make up more than one-third of the Revolutionary War soldiers and about the same in the War of 1812. The Scotch-Irish proved fiercely patriotic and held a particular hatred of the British.

The "Whiskey Rebellion" of the Western Pennsylvania Scotch-Irish in the 1790s would be the root of American domestic politics and reflected a hatred of government and taxes. The Monongahela Valley was filled with the smoke of whiskey stills in the 1790s. Rye whiskey was a mainstay of the area's Scotch-Irish and Washington County as well as iron production, which was also being taxed. As a British colony, the whiskey production had been controlled and taxed, but the remoteness of the Monongahela Valley made it almost impossible for British tax collectors. President Washington and Alexander Hamilton imposed an excise tax on whiskey in 1794. One tax collector in Western Pennsylvania was Scotch-Irish General Neville, even though he had initially opposed the tax. The tax schedule varies, but it was around six to ten cents a gallon (a gallon of rye whiskey sold for a dollar). The valley Scotch-Irish mustered a militia and burnt

1 Helen Vogt, *Westward of ye Laurall Hills* (Parsons: McClain Printing, 1976) p. 39.

the estate of General Neville. It was the first test of the Federal government. A few days later their leader, General James MacFarlane, was killed. For weeks Scotch-Irish militia roamed the area. Hamilton persuaded Washington to send 13,000 troops to w`estern Pennsylvania to put down the rebellion. Before the militia had reached Pittsburgh, the uprising was diffused as the Presbyterian Church preached enforcement of the law. The Scotch-Irish, however, moved into Ohio, Kentucky, and Tennessee to produce their whiskey. The new frontier was out of the reach of the Federal tax collectors. These Pennsylvania emigrants would form the Kentucky and Tennessee bourbon and whiskey families of today. Another more conservative group not interested in whiskey making preferred the new land of Ohio. This conservative group would include the Covenanters, which the McGuffey family was part of; however, they shared hatred of taxes for any product by all Scotch-Irish Presbyterians.

The McGuffey family followed a stream of Scotch-Irish that located in Ohio's Mahoning Valley (near Youngstown) from Pennsylvania and Maryland some years later. These frontier immigrants were trying to avoid government taxation on whiskey and iron production. These immigrants of Western Pennsylvania brought their iron making, whiskey making, farming, and schools to the Ohio frontier. Alexander moved the family there, two years after the birth of his son, William Holmes McGuffey. This Scotch-Irish migration to what was then called Ohio's "Western Reserve" included the family of future president William McKinley. The McKinley family had moved from Western Pennsylvania to the Western Reserve of Ohio to avoid iron and whiskey taxes.

This Scotch-Irish movement included whiskey makers, but most were tied to the early iron makers. The Scotch-Irish iron makers were also dedicated to religion and education, which they saw as one discipline. The real heart of the Scotch-Irish empire was the Presbyterian Church that followed them. The Presbyterian Scottish roots had helped the church evolve into a unique role. Once the Scotch-Irish cleared land and established a settlement, missionary pastors were sent from the Philadelphia Presbytery. The role of the pastor was religious, educational, and social. After services, the Sabbath was for socializing and family. This social role continued in the twentieth century, making the church a favorite with capitalists and businessmen from many protestant backgrounds such as Henry Clay Frick, Andrew Carnegie, George Westinghouse, and Thomas Mellon (all of whom took classes at Pittsburgh's Duff College, one of the first frontier Scotch-Irish colleges). Another nation and church building role was grammar school education. Presbyterian schools were the first in Western Pennsylvania and supplied highly educated teachers to the frontier. William McGuffey's mother, Anna, had received her education in these Western frontier schools. The excellent educational opportunities and social events drew in Germans as well as Scotch-Irish. Many of these Scotch-Irish teachers traveled from community to community. The families paid their salary, and the Bible and Noah Webster's Blue Back Speller were their standard textbooks. The system would create many of the American leaders of the nineteenth century.

Ultimately, the Scotch-Irish of the Ohio Valley would create an American industrial empire led by men such as Andrew Mellon, William McKinley, and Andrew Carnegie who cut their teeth on *McGuffey Readers*. This industrial valley would arm America in the War of 1812, the Civil War, World War One, and World War Two. Politically, the Ohio Valley and Pittsburgh's Monongahela Valley would change Jefferson Agrarianism into Republican industrialism. The Republican Party would be founded there. The valley would become the bulwark of Ulster Presbyterianism. There an old story that says John Knox prayed, "O! Lord give me Scotland," and God granted it, throwing in Pittsburgh for good measure. And the Scotch-Irish made the Western Pennsylvania and Eastern Ohio the heart of frontier higher education establishing colleges such as the University of Pittsburgh, Washington and Jefferson College, Duff's College, University of Cincinnati, Miami University, Ohio University, Transylvania University, Allegheny College, Geneva College, Grove City College, and Westminster College. The earlier Presbyterian college of Princeton trained many of the areas' educators and spread Princeton alumni across the Ohio frontier. The area brought forth musicians such as Stephen Foster and inventers such as Robert Fulton. Linguistically, the rivers valleys of Western Pennsylvania and Eastern Ohio remain Scotch-Irish even to this day, and culturally, the valley still prides itself on "worship on Sunday and whiskey on Monday." The valley has produced more steel than any other place on earth and probably drank more whiskey, too. It was the cradle of elementary education. It is clearly the fatherland of the American Scotch-Irish, and the Scotch-Irish are the DNA of today's American.

The Scotch-Irish have left their mark on American society. Fifteen American presidents have claimed Scotch-Irish ancestry including four of pure Ulster Presbyterian lineage: Andrew Jackson, James Buchanan, Benjamin Harrison, and Chester Arthur. Philosophers and leaders included Alexander Hamilton, Davy Crockett, Patrick Henry, James Madison, John Calhoun, Daniel Boone, Sam Houston, and twenty-one signers of the Declaration of Independence. Their greatest gift, however, might have been their schools and educational system. Far from the frontier hillbillies they are often pictured as, the Scotch-Irish believed in book learning. Like their stills, their log cabin schools dominated the frontier. The mixed and pragmatic American college curriculum was a result of the Scottish educational system. The system built liberal arts across the curriculum into an integrated approach such as "writing across the curriculum."

CHAPTER 3. A RICH HERITAGE

"To America, one schoolmaster is worth a dozen poets"
— Benjamin Franklin

The McGuffey family genealogy can be defined primarily as Scotch Presbyterian. William Holmes McGuffey's grandparents, William "Scotch-Billy" McGuffey and Ann McKittrick were both born in Scotland, and were married in the hometown of Wigtownshire (Galloway District), Scotland in 1747. Some have suggested the name McKittrick was Irish or possibly Scotch-Irish in origin, but Ann was born in Scotland.[1] Others have suggested the McGuffey clan goes back to the Danish invasion of the British isles. McGuffeys were originally from the northwest highlander clan of McFies who lived on the islands of Colonsay and Oronsay. The McGuffey clan, known for their support of Scottish James II (Jacobus is Latin for James), which had opposed British rule since 1600s, were Jacobites. These highlanders fought many rebellions were taking refuge in the rugged hills. In the 1740s, the Jacobites were finally subdued, but the oppression continued economically and religiously. The McGuffeys were one of the progressive Highlander clans that moved to the lowlands of Galloway to join the progressive pro-industrial Scotch Whigs in the early 1700s. The McGuffeys, however, were mainly farmers, but unskilled labor was needed in small industrial towns such as Wigtownshire. The McGuffey family took up trades such as shoe making. Wigtownshire was a small settlement on the Western coast of Scotland that separates the Irish Sea from the North Channel. Only about 50 miles of sea

---

1 Benjamin Crawford, *The Life of William Holmes McGuffey* (Delaware, Ohio: Carnegie Church Press, 1974) p. 51.

separates Ireland and Scotland at this point. The McGuffeys, while not "Ulster Scots," were of the same Galloway County family roots.

Scotland of the early 1700s was a land in turmoil. It had struggled often with England for independence. Scotland was a divided country of Catholics, Anglicans, and Presbyterians, but mostly controlled by the harsh, divided Kirk of the Presbyterians. The Scotch of the Galloway district such as the McGuffeys were strict Presbyterians. It was a divided economically with the poor clans of the Highlands and the industrial lowlands of Glasgow and south. Poor Highland farmers, such as the McGuffeys, immigrated to the lowlands of Scotland in search of better land. In the 1600s, poor Scotch farmers were motivated to Northern Ireland to take over Irish farms under the rule of the British. These Scotch immigrants to Ireland of the 1600s were originally lowlanders of Galloway. They became known as the "Ulster Scots" or "Scotch-Irish." They would find life in Ireland no better and many would migrate to America with lowland Scotch farmers. Crop failures accelerated in the 1700s that caused the Scotch to immigrant to British factories, Irish farms, or America.

William and Ann McGuffey saved to book passage to America. In August of 1774, the McGuffeys left Scotland with their three children, Alexander "Sandy" (William's father) age seven, Catherine age six, and Elizabeth age four. The Scotch had a well-defined route of immigration in the 1770s. The clannish Scots helped one another at all points of the trip across the ocean. The Presbyterian Church, in particular, managed these immigration routes and ports of entry. The McGuffeys landed in Philadelphia that August and progressed to nearby York County, Chanceford Township, to a Scotch settlement there. With saved money, they purchased a small farm. Eastern Pennsylvania at the time was the center of Scotch and Scotch-Irish immigrants. Philadelphia was the key port for the huge Scotch-trading network, taking furs and whiskey from the American frontiers and tobacco from the plantations. Philadelphia was the home of the American Presbyterian Church as well.

The American Scotch, "Ulster Scots," "Scots-Irish," and Scotch-Irish were all Scotch, and most often had shared roots in the Galloway District in Scotland like the McGuffeys. The Scotch and Scotch-Irish are a distinct lineage in the overall American colonists. They were fiercely independent, Presbyterian, well educated, and outstanding frontiersmen. They fed the political, economic, and religious tyranny of their English masters. They adapted readily to their adopted country and were true patriots. They believed in limited government, no taxes, and freedom of religion. They also brought a passion for education, which had spread the Scotch Enlightenment and the world's highest literacy rate. By the 1770s, they dominated Eastern Pennsylvania, the valleys of Western Pennsylvania and Maryland, and the Ohio Valley.

The Scotch-Irish and Scotch immigrants changed America and formed an educational foundation that surpassed anything in the world. In the 1600s, the English oppressed the Scotch and the Scotch-Irish in an effort to wipe out their Gaelic and Catholic roots. To this end, the English-controlled Scotch parliament passed the Education Act of 1616 and the Schools Act of 1696, not out of a love for education, but as a means to change a culture. The acts required that every Presbyterian parish establish a school and pay for the services of a schoolteacher. These acts led to the education of even the poor and took the level of general education in Scotland beyond any other country in the world. Scotland became the home of Europe's philosophers, scientists, economists, and teachers. The Scottish Enlightenment fueled not only the advance of education but also the commercial theory of capitalism. The best-educated population in the world was the 1700s Scotch. Even the "uneducated" Scots such as William and Ann McGuffey were able to read the Bible and spell, which most of the Western world could not.

As the Scotch-Irish fled British oppression to America in the 1700s, they brought a culture of elementary and higher level education. In Scotland, the literacy rate was an amazing 80 to 85%. The Scotch-Irish Presbyterian school system came with them to the American colony. By the time of the American Revolution, America's literacy rate was the highest in the world (second only to Scotland) at 70 to 75 percent, while England's rate was only 50 to 60 percent. France and Italy were under 40 percent. York County's Presbyterian schools were popular with the Germans as well as the Scotch because of their high standards. Presbyterians made up the majority of roving "subscription" teachers. The Western frontier, where William Holmes McGuffey would be born, had an amazing literacy rate of 65 percent.[1] This literacy rate, coupled with the high average wealth, allowed Americans to read and buy books at an amazing rate. This literacy rate turned the Western frontier of Pennsylvania and Ohio into the seed of the American empire.

The McGuffeys came to America on the brink of war. William "Scotch-Billy" McGuffey was a clobber and a small farmer. The Scotch-Irish people were some of the first of Pennsylvania to march to Lexington and Concord to relieve the embattled colonists. The Scotch immigrants had a deep seeded hatred of the British, and they wanted out of the New World. It is believed that the Continental Army was over fifty percent Scotch-Irish soldiers driven by their hatred of the British. William McGuffey joined the Continental Army on May 27, 1779. During the war, the family continued the farm and started a tavern. The tavern was visited several times by General Washington and his officers. The family would always be proud of their participation in the Revolutionary War. Young Alexander learned much from the tavern talk about the war. When William returned from the war, they continued to farm and manage the small tavern. William also branched into

---

1 Joseph Ellis, *After the Revolution* (New York, W. W. Norton, 1979) p. 141.

cobbling shoes, as the farm was far from prosperous. In 1789, William decided to move to Western Pennsylvania where the Scotch-Irish was prospering in farming, whiskey making, and iron making. Land was also cheap and available in Western Pennsylvania.

William McGuffey purchased land in the southwest corner of Washington County near Pittsburgh. The rich river valleys of Pennsylvania and Ohio had been considered the ultimate prizes for both British and American soldiers. General Cornwallis as well as George Washington were planning post-war plantations in these valleys. Washington County had early Scotch and Scotch-Irish going back to the fur trading days in the 1740s. The Scotch-Irish followed the Cumberland Gap trail to Western Pennsylvania. The trail from York County to Western Pennsylvania in 1789 required a difficult crossing of the Allegheny Mountains by Conestoga wagons also called prairie schooners. These giant freight wagons were named after Conestoga Creek at Lancaster, Pennsylvania. These wagons were water tight and used iron belts around the wooden wheels. Six to eight horse teams pulled these freight wagons. They moved in convoys of up to one hundred wagons, which included Scotch-Irish and German immigrants. William "Scotch-Billy" and Ann McGuffey sold their farm for five hundred dollars and purchased some acres in Finley Township, Washington County (near Claysville). They were able to get the land for a down payment of fifty cents an acre with a five-year mortgage (ultimate price of five dollars per acre). They left with their children Alexander, age 22, Catherine, age 21, and Elizabeth, age 18. Elizabeth died during the crossing and was buried along the trail.

Washington County had a mere 700 or so inhabitants (slaves were not counted), and nearby Pittsburgh had a population of only 376 in 1789 when the McGuffeys arrived. Of the five southwestern counties of Pennsylvania, Washington County was experiencing a population boom that would increase its population to 36,289 in 1810. Washington County was a mixture of immigrant Scotch Highlanders, poor Scotch Lowlanders and the Scotch-Irish (Ulster Scots). Washington County's early Scotch-Irish had come up from the Southern colonies and had slaves. There were 840 slaves in the county in 1789. The Pennsylvania Abolition Act of 1780 called for a gradual elimination of slavery, and these original inhabitants were looking west. The Scotch-Irish farmers of Washington County grew wheat, corn, rye, barley, buckwheat, and potatoes. Rye was used to produce its world famous "Monongahela Rye" whiskey, which was shipped to New Orleans and then on to Europe. A traveler in 1804 noted that farmers in the area: "seemed to live in ease and plenty." Another described the region in 1811 as: "The farms are well improved, and the farm-houses are, many of them, substantial, and bespeak affluence, ease, and comfort . . .. The people here appear to be as well lodged, as well fed, and well clothed, as those who live in the neighborhood of Philadelphia or New York." [1]

Washington County's Scotch-Irish and Scotch settlements were of the Presbyterian sect known as the "Covenanters," to which the McGuffeys belonged. The other Presbyterian sect was the "Seceders" that settled in Elizabeth Township between the Youghiogheny and Monongahela. The Covenanters had less structured organization and were known as the Reformed Church of Scotland, but compared to American Presbyterians, the Covenanters were strict and puritanical. The difference was not so much in dogma as in politics. The Covenanters rejected formal or Episcopal hierarchy in the church. The Covenanters generally frowned on drinking, dancing, and slavery. On a social scale Covenanters and Seceders were considered "hill people" by their mainstream Presbyterian brothers. Covenanters were often considered lower class in Western Pennsylvania on a level with Catholics and Lutherans. [2] The McGuffeys were Covenanters and strict Calvinists and extremely conservative on social issues. There was also much variation between geographic settlements of the Covenanters in their application of the Bible and social views. The Covenanters were aggressive in business and trading, and hated any type of government or even church regulation. The Covenanters tended to join mainstream Presbyterian Churches because there were often too few to build their own.

The "religious code" or covenant of the McGuffey Washington settlement could hardly be considered liberal and would foreshadow the code of the 1840s *McGuffey Readers*. The following code was signed by the McGuffey family and 114 others in the Scotch-Irish community in Washington County:

> "We, and each of us, whose names are underwritten, being chiefly the inhabitants of the inhabitants of the Western frontier of Washington County, considering the many abounding evils in our own hearts and lives, as also the open and secret violation of the holy law of God, which dishonors his name and defiles and ruins our country; such as ignorance, unbelief, hardness of heart, contempt of God and His ordinances, law, and gospel (in particular in setting our hearts upon the creature in one line or another more than upon God), breach of His Sabbath, disobedience to parents, back-bitings, entertaining bad thoughts, and receiving groundless evil reports of others, lascivious songs, filthy discourse, promiscuous dancing, drunkenness, defraud, deceit, over-reaching in bargains, gaming, horse racing, cock fighting, shooting for prizes, lying, covetousness, discontent, fretting against the dispensations of God's providence, unfaithfulness for God (in suffering sin to remain on our neighbor unreproved, denying God in neglect of family and secret worship, catechizing and instructions of our children and servants or slaves, vexations wranglings, and lawsuits, together with innumerable evils, provoking God to send down heavy

---

1 Solon Buck and Elizabeth Buck, *The Planting of Civilization in Western Pennsylvania* (Pittsburgh: University of Pittsburgh Press, 1939) p. 200.

2 Joseph Rishel, *Founding Families of Pittsburgh: Thee Evolution of a Regional Elite* (Pittsburgh: University of Pittsburgh Press, 1990) p. 28.

judgments on our land, and to withhold or draw His gracious presence, and unfit our soul for enjoying any solid happiness, which we desire to acknowledge with shame and sorrow of heart before God, and so in the strength of God depending on His Grace for support, solemnly promise (to our power, according to our various places and stations) to engage against both in ourselves and others, as providence shall give opportunity, and prudence direct."

This code is a powerful moral statement of these Scotch-Irish Presbyterians.

Washington County outside of Pittsburgh, in particular, developed as a model of Presbyterian education. Washington County had three famous Presbyterian ministers and educators in John McMillan, Thaddeus Dod, and Joseph Smith in the late 1790s. These Presbyterians created a number of log cabin schools in Washington with support of Presbyterian synods of Pennsylvania and Virginia. These schools also prospered because they were open to any denomination willing to pay. Cost was around $20 a year for a student. Curriculum consisted of grammar, spelling, arithmetic, and reading. There were also foreign language schools for Latin and Greek. These schools pioneered the publishing of their own textbooks by Pittsburgh printers. The McMillan school evolved into Jefferson College and Washington College in 1810 and was later combined into Washington and Jefferson College, which McGuffey would attend.

While prosperous, Washington County was still frontier in 1789 and was on the Eastern edge of the waging Indian wars. A loose Indian confederacy of Shawnees, Senecas, Miamis, Ottawas, Potawatomis, Ojibwas, Delawares, and small tribes were raiding settlements throughout Western Pennsylvania, Ohio, Michigan, and Kentucky. Most of the activity was to the West in Ohio, but Fort Pitt (Pittsburgh) remained a key staging area for the new American Army. While the elder William "Scotch-Billy" built a log cabin and started farming, Alexander McGuffey now longed for more adventure. The Scotch-Irish folk of the area were known as frontiersmen, and commonly the younger men joined the military operations on the frontier. Alexander loved the stories of Scotch Revolutionary heroes such as Daniel Morgan of North Carolina and George Rogers Clark of Virginia. Alexander was an excellent shot which made him valuable as a scout. Alexander signed up in 1790 at Fort Pitt as a scout with the Pennsylvania volunteers. He was assigned initially to operate in the Ohio River Valley out of a small fort at the site of today's Wheeling, West Virginia. Alexander McGuffey had joined with friend, Duncan McArthur, who would later become a general and governor of Ohio.

Alexander McGuffey served as a scout in the Army of General Anthony Wayne in the early 1790s. George Washington and Congress increased troop strength in 1790 but also reduced starting wages to two dollars a month. General St. Clair was put in charge of the effort to eliminate the Indians from Ohio territory. The initial effort of the army met defeat in southwest Ohio in the autumn of 1791. Chiefs Little Turtle and Blue Jacket routed St. Clair's 1,400-man army, killing over half of St. Clair's soldiers. The frontier was in a panic and fear went east to Washington County and Fort Pitt. In particular the newly established flatboat traffic between Pittsburgh and Cincinnati was challenged. While Congress tried again to establish a fighting army, scouts were needed in the Ohio River Valley, and this was Alexander McGuffey's first assignment. Alexander stayed with the army through 1796 and then tried his hand at farming.

In December of 1797, Alexander married Anna Holmes of Washington County. Anna Holmes had been born in 1776 into one of Washington County's wealthiest Scotch-Irish families. Anna was the daughter of Henry Holmes and Jane Roney. Anna had been educated in the frontier school system of Washington County. Alexander and Anna started their family on the Holmes farm known as "Rural Grove," which was the largest in Washington County. Their first three children were born there. Jane was born on February 9, 1799; William Holmes on September 23, 1800; and Henry on May 9, 1802. The confusion over the exact birthplace of William Holmes McGuffey results from the fact the family moved to a larger house in Washington County. Henry Ford decided that the original birthplace was the old Holmes farm.

Washington County and Pittsburgh were sometimes called the Scotch-Irish country of "Westsylvania." The Scotch-Irish of the area were being torn apart by many factors. On one hand you had the conservative Covenanters of the McGuffey family; on the other, the aristocratic Presbyterians. The Whiskey Rebellion had torn the Scotch-Irish along moral and political lines. Slavery also divided the Scotch-Irish of Washington County. The area was torn politically between the Federalists and the Jeffersonians, then known as the Democrat-Republican Party. This struggle can be seen in the novel of the area's Hugh Henry Brackenridge. Brackenridge was a legislator and writer. He tried unsuccessfully to negotiate a compromise between Scotch-Irish fragments during the Whiskey Rebellion. He did publish America's first novel, *West of the Alleghenies*, which dealt with the incongruities of the area. Brackenridge's *Modern Chivalry* (1798) was the American *Don Quixote. Modern Chivalry* became the favorite book of John Quincy Adams. *Modern Chivalry* deals with the conflict, diversity, and contradictions of "Westsylvania." It was also considered the first book written in "American English" as modified by the Scotch-Irish frontier. The McGuffey family, like many Scotch-Irish of the area, was hard to characterize. They were opposed to drinking but probably didn't care for taxation by the Federal government. Still, they were fiercely patriotic to the Federal government and would expect the government to help with things like protection and roads. For the McGuffey's as well as many Scotch-Irish, armed rebellion against the American government was wrong, especially if it was the army of George Washington. They appeared to have been ambivalent on the question of slavery, not unlike most of the Scotch-Irish.

Given the sect variations, there were strong beliefs that united all Scotch-Irish. They generally hated strong government and church. Their hatred of the British was the root of their patriotism. Taxes on individuals were considered immoral. They strongly believed less government was better. Government's function was protection, road building, and schools. Property ownership was considered a divine right to be protected by government and never interfered with by government. Accumulation of wealth was a right, but with it came a responsibility to help the poor. They believed Christianity to be the moral foundation of society. Education was a necessity because it was needed to read and discern biblical principles.

CHAPTER 4. THE EARLY EDUCATION OF WILLIAM HOLMES MCGUFFEY

"Simply put, eclectic merely meant the best in each and greater than any, and the idea captured the imagination of the polyglot mixture of creeds and nationalities comprising the population of the Ohio Valley of the time."
— *Harvey Minnich, biographer*

When William Holmes McGuffey was but two years old, his father Alexander moved the family to the "Western Reserve of Ohio" in 1802. The family moved to Coitsville Township, Mahoning County, a little East of Youngstown. In 1802, Alexander McGuffey and his family moved into their one hundred and sixty acre farm in the Western Reserve known as "Gravel Hill Farm." The grandparents of William (William and Ann) followed the family to Coitsville. The Coitsville area had been settled with Connecticut farmers in 1798. Alexander McGuffey was one of the first settlers of Coitsville in 1800, coming before the family to build a log cabin and clear land for farming. By 1807, Alexander held minor elected positions of "house appraiser" and "lister of property." This elected position made him an important part of the local school board.

The Western Reserve was the ideal place for small farmers such as McGuffey. Game was extremely abundant and offered a year round source of food. Turkey, passenger pigeon, bear, and deer made for an excellent source of protein. Fish was another abundant staple for the farmer. Wild fruits such as strawberry, raspberry, cherry, grape, huckleberry, and gooseberry were also abundant. The German influence in the area had helped improve farming methods. A variety of wild nuts such as butternuts, walnuts, and beechnuts were available to eat and use as hog feed. Indian corn, potatoes, squash, oats, and wheat were cultivated. The somewhat flatter land in then western Pennsylvania made cultivation easier.

Hogs and chickens were raised. New England immigrants taught the farmers how to tap maple trees for syrup. The rich forest made it easy for the small farmer to live comfortably.

The Western Reserve, a three million-acre piece of Northeast Ohio, included Cleveland, Akron, and Youngstown. It was actually a Western extension of the state of Connecticut. Connecticut had sent Puritan settlers to the area in the early 1700s, but Pennsylvania and Virginia had claimed the land as well. In 1789, Connecticut gave the Western Reserve to the Federal government, making it part of the nation's Northwest Territory. The Western Reserve would be America's first crucible, melting the Puritan stock of New England with Pennsylvania Germans, Quakers, and Scotch-Irish. It would become the birthplace of two presidents (McKinley and Garfield) and many early industrialists. The Western Reserve of Ohio would become the crucible of national politics. Originally, the political struggle was between the New England Federalists and the Democratic-Republicans of Jefferson, but new parties would evolve in this early frontier. It was here that the Whig and later Republican built their foundations. The steel industry, brick, and tinplate industry can all claim the Western Reserve as their birthplace. The canal system of the Western Reserve would first bring iron ore to Pittsburgh and coal to Cleveland. The crucible of American ideals in the Western Reserve would reflect those of the future William Holmes McGuffey.

For years, the Western Reserve was a type of no-man land. Indian tribes shared its hunting grounds and kept white settlers to the East. After Anthony Wayne's 1794 victory of the Indians at Fallen Timbers, the Western Reserve became popular with settlers from Pennsylvania, Virginia, and Maryland. The New Englanders could be considered the nativists of the Reserve, with the first immigration of Scotch-Irish coming in 1790s. These early settlers from Connecticut were from the Puritan church of America's first settlers. The tradition of Puritan congregations to develop their own creeds and branch off caused some evolution in their beliefs as they moved West. They brought their conservative religious views as well as their gristmill technology. The earliest Scotch-Irish were enticed by the Connecticut Land Company to settle the land for farming. The Connecticut Land Company agents focused on the prosperous middle class farmers of Pennsylvania's Washington and Westmoreland counties. The land was a real bargain, being sold at forty cents an acre, cheaper than the federal frontier lands at two dollars an acre. The agents created a land rush of Scotch-Irish, and by 1798, the Presbyterian Church sent missionaries to service the settlers. Reverend William Wick, a highly educated minister and teacher, was the first of these missionaries. Wick had come from Washington County and had been a friend of the McGuffey family. The First Presbyterian Church of Youngstown in 1799 was the first church in the Reserve. Pastor Wick played an important role in attracting immigrants from Pennsylvania's Washington and Westmoreland counties. Wick was typical of many Presbyterian ministers, being highly educated in Greek, Hebrew, and Latin.

Another factor in the migration of the Pennsylvania Scotch-Irish to the Western Reserve of Ohio was the Whiskey Rebellion of 1794. Many Scotch-Irish of Washington County operated whiskey stills as a source of income; however, not the McGuffeys who belonged to the strict sect of Covenanters. Whiskey made from grain could get ten times the profit of selling grain, which was difficult to ship in volume. The 1794 excise tax on whiskey had caused a rebellion that required the use of Federal troops. The Scotch-Irish were subdued, but many wanted to move further on to the frontier to avoid the taxman. The whiskey making Scotch-Irish tended to move to the hills of Kentucky and Tennessee and would make Kentucky bourbon. Another group of conservative Scotch-Irish, such as the McGuffeys, were not involved in whiskey making and favored the lands of the Western Reserve. The Puritan and Quaker roots of the Western Reserve would have been even less tolerant of whiskey making. The original New England colonists of the Western Reserve had built badly needed gristmills for the production of flour, making grain growing particularly profitable. The Youngstown area, in particular, already had established gristmills on Yellow Creek. Lastly, the flatter land of the Reserve had greatly reduced the wolves in the Western Reserve, which favored sheep rising for the Scotch-Irish. The Whiskey Rebellion in Washington County split the Scotch-Irish politically. The Whiskey rebels broke away from the central government Federalists of Alexander Hamilton and moved to the Jeffersonians who favored less government. The other branch of the very nationalistic Scotch-Irish remained with the Federalist Party, and this was the group that migrated to the Western Reserve. This group of Scotch-Irish Federalists would form the Whig Party and eventually the Republican Party. The split was difficult, pulling between the Scotch-Irish patriotism and their dislike of government.

In the same year of 1802 and the McGuffey migration, a fellow Scotch-Irish Pennsylvania immigrant of the McGuffeys, James Heaton, found iron ore and coal in the Youngstown area. The discovery launched another Scotch-Irish immigration from Washington and Westmoreland Counties in Pennsylvania. Over the years prior to the War of 1812, the Scotch-Irish settlers built a strong iron industry just in time to supply iron cannon and cannonballs for the army of Andrew Jackson and the navy of Commodore Perry. The war created an economic boom in the area, and Youngstown would be the foundation of America's iron and steel industry. The Scotch-Irish made Youngstown the largest city in Ohio by 1815, and it held that title until the late 1820s. The Scotch-Irish of the area responded as they had during the Revolutionary War to fill the army of 1812. Interestingly, the German settlers and Quakers of the area proved to be pacifists, and these German views over the years would help moderate the warlike tendencies of the

Scotch-Irish. The Germans of the Western Reserve came from Pennsylvania's monastic type sects such as the Mennonites, Drunkards, and Moravians. These Germans, however, proved extremely progressive, wanting to learn English and anxious to attend Scotch-Irish schools. The Germans, on the other hand, taught the Scotch-Irish how to farm the poorest of ground.

The Western Reserve crucible was a mixing bowl of three conservative traditions-New England Puritans, Scotch-Irish, and German. All three came to the Western Reserve as part of America's first internal migrations. While from conservative traditions, they were progressive and open to joining in mixed communities. These traditions found common ground in the virtues of thrift, Christian morals, industry, honesty, and perseverance. Covenanter Scotch-Irish and New England Puritans could find much in common. The mixing of the cultures created a hatred of slavery, drunkenness, and war, and a love of education. These attributes would be embodied in the evolution of the Whig Party in the Western Reserve. It would even modify such basic religious views as Calvinistic predestination. The McGuffey brand of Covenanters was softened a bit as well. Some of the Pittsburgh area Covenanters had taken a covenant of political decent refusing to vote in elections. This unusual covenant came from the disappointment of the constitution to recognize Jesus Christ as Lord over movement. The Western Reserve created more mainstream views of religion and politics, although McGuffey would never become a strong political activist. Covenanters joined mainstream Presbyterian churches and created a policy of not bringing politics into preaching. The Germans of the Western Reserve brought a hatred of war unlike the somewhat warlike Scotch-Irish. This new American view came to predominate the Western Reserve and the area of the Ohio, Mahoning, Allegheny, and Monongahela River valleys. And by the late 1800s, vision of the Western Reserve would be the shared vision of all Americans. It would form the basis of a new cultural, political, and social base, which would be reflected some years later in the *McGuffey Readers*.

Another product of this frontier crucible was the merger of two great educational traditions, the Connecticut Puritans and the Pennsylvania Scotch-Irish. The Connecticut Puritans, like the Scotch-Irish, believed in community education as fundamental to their religion. Bible literacy was a requirement in both sects. In the 1780s, the Connecticut legislature had required five hundred acres per township be set aside for schools, which applied to the then Western Reserve of Connecticut. At the time the McGuffeys moved to the Youngstown area, the town had a one-room schoolhouse operating. Most schooling was done at home, by ministers, or by "roving" contracted teachers. Most teachers were men and received a salary of $10 a month or charged $1.50 per pupil per four-month school year. The curriculum focused on Bible reading, grammar, spelling, and some basic arithmetic. Textbooks were rare and the Bible was used to teach. Bible reading at home added to the learning, and it was common for youths to memorize long passages. At the level above grammar school, sectarian ministers taught in their homes or at "academies." The academies were focused on young scholars who were looking at the ministry.

Education was started at home usually using Webster's *Blue Back Speller*. Connecticut immigrants used the *New England Primer*, which included a Puritan catechism. Children were read to from the Bible and some novels. Novels that could be found on the frontier were *Pilgrim's Progress (1688)*, *Robinson Crusoe (1714)*, and *Gulliver's Travels (1726)*. There were even a few children's books such as *Goody Two Shoes* and *Mother Goose's Melodies*. The McGuffeys probably had a speller and could borrow the other from their minister. Anna McGuffey was known to tirelessly work on the education of her children. Mothers usually honed their children in spelling while having them memorize Bible verses.

The education of William Holmes McGuffey was typical of frontier children. His mother started the process with Bible readings and memorization exercises. McGuffey was known to be able to cite long verses from memory throughout his life. The exact nature of his school education has been debated. What can be substantiated is that he received training as a young boy with Reverend William Wick, a Presbyterian minister, who had come with the Scotch-Irish of Washington County, Pennsylvania. Wick's school was in Youngstown about five miles away. William and his older sister Jane lived with the Wick family during the winter months. Most schooling was done in winter when the children were not needed for farming chores. There is some evidence William might have attended a Coitsville subscription school prior to going to Pastor Wick. Wick was known to have started young McGuffey on Latin, which was consistent with his mother's hope that he would someday become a minister. The death of Wick in 1814 seemed to have ended that initial phase of McGuffey's education at age fourteen.

What books McGuffey used in his education beyond the Bible can be readily be surmised, since the selection of texts during the period from 1802 to 1815 was extremely small. The most widely used text from New England to the Western Reserve was Noah Webster's *Grammatical Institutes of the English Language* ("Webster's Speller" or "Blue-Backed Speller) of 1783. Webster's text was later known as Webster's *Elementary Speller*. Webster's speller was a combination of primer, speller, and reader. It consisted of endless rows of words as well as a moral catechism. For the frontier family it was their only reference book as well. It was the first textbook to receive a U.S. copyright. McGuffey would have started with Webster's speller. Another popular text of grammar was Lindley Murray's *English Grammar*. This text was more advanced, and the style laid the groundwork for the study of Latin. Murray's book was popular with Presbyterian ministers, such as William Wick, for those who showed a future in the ministry. Murray's book was originally published in England in 1795; but by 1802, it was being published in New England due to its popularity. Another popular book in New England and the Western Reserve was the *New England Primer*, which was extremely popular with Puritans and is said to have educated five generations of Americans.

Today the *New England Primer* appears a dry and somber text, but its woodcut illustrations did help in learning, a point not lost on a young William Holmes McGuffey. The *New England Primer* dominated the colonial schools of America, and it gained popularity with its use by Benjamin Franklin. The *New England Primer* was Bible based and included the biblical history of the world. The approach of the *Primer* taught the alphabet through image-and-rhyme. Its opening lines were "In Adams' fall/ We sinned all," and the ending lines were "Zaccheus he/Did climb a tree/His Lord to see." The *New England Primer* taught the alphabet along with religion and morals. Certainly we can see the themes and styles of these three texts reflected in McGuffey's later Readers. A similar text known as the *Franklin Reader* (1802) was one of several which borrowed liberally from the un-copyrighted *New England Primer*. If arithmetic was taught, the textbook used was Dilworth's *Schoolmaster's Assistant*. The *Dilworth Speller* was also used in many homes of New England origin to home school and was favored highly for home schooling by the Scotch-Irish of Pennsylvania.

The most influential text for the young McGuffey was the *Blue Back Speller* of Noah Webster. In later life, McGuffey fully accepted Webster's approach to language and system of spelling, which actually increased sales of the *Speller* along with *McGuffey's Readers*. The Speller was a detailed reference in a period before Webster's dictionary was available, but it was much more. It contained moralistic stories and a moral catechism. The catechism used questions and answers to define the moral virtues of humility, industry, mercy, purity of heart, justice, generosity, gratitude, truth, charity, economy, and cheerfulness, and problem emotions and evils such as anger, revenge, and avarice. These would be the every basis of McGuffey's moral stories. McGuffey studied morals from early Catholic European Latin texts as well. McGuffey got a major jump in Latin and in biblical languages with Reverend Wick. Hebrew, Greek, and Latin were requirements for ministers of the time.

Reverend Wick's starting McGuffey on Latin early was not unusual for those who were destined to be scholars or ministers. *Orbis Sensualium Pictus or Visible World* (1658), the mother of all textbooks, was not only the first picture book for children but it taught both English (or the vernacular of the home country) and Latin. It was used in Catholic schools throughout Europe, and 244 editions were printed from 1658 to 1964. *Orbis Pictus* was, by far, the superior book in illustrations, pedagogy, and learning. Its Catholic theology eliminated it from use in most American schools, but Protestant ministers often incorporated it as a powerful learning tool to jump-start future biblical scholars like McGuffey. Ministers had found the combination of Latin and English to be easier than learning one at a time. McGuffey's personal learning from the *Orbis Sensualium Pictus* and the *New England Primer* would have been a revelation to the power of pictures in learning.

Subscription schools of McGuffey's youth were not much more than a small log cabin. The land in the Western Reserve was set aside for schools per the Connecticut Legislature Act of 1786. The first school in the Reserve was a simple log cabin in the square of Youngstown (1802). The community raised the building itself. It also built roads to the school. Alexander McGuffey is alleged to have built a five-mile road to Wick's school known today as McGuffey Road. Generally the log cabin had a fireplace, and on dark days, the students used small oil lamps. Some of these log buildings had a translucent window strip made of oiled paper or lard treated paper to let in more light. Oiled paper let in a soft mellow light but kept the weather out. Bear grease was also used to oilpaper windows. Since school was held from December to March, light was at a premium, but glass windows were rare in the early 1800s. The long desk or slanted board was on the walls facing the oilpaper windows. The students sat on long hewn logs with no back. School hours were from nine o'clock in the morning to four o'clock in the afternoon, except Saturday when school let out at noon. There was no school on Sunday. Writing paper was used sparingly, but chalk and the slate were the popular student tools of the time. Sometimes the thrifty Scotch-Irish used birch bark. Pencils such as Faber's pencils had been available since 1761, but homemade ink was cheaper. Writing was done with ink quill pens because ink could be readily made. Usually the student was expected to bring a bottle of homemade ink.

With William Wick's death in 1814, McGuffey was left in a precarious position. His family had little of the money needed to pursue the education for the ministry. The Western Reserve at the same time was experiencing an economic boom related to the War of 1812, influx of Scotch-Irish, and the growth of the iron industry. Still, the war was not as popular as one might expect. The New Federalists opposed the war with England, and the Federalist sentiment was strong in the Reserve. Scotch-Irish iron makers in the area found new wealth, making pig iron and cannonballs. The influx of Scotch-Irish into the Western Reserve again soared, and subscription schools were needed. McGuffey, while only fourteen years of age, had been well prepared to take a position as teacher. McGuffey signed to teach a subscription school at West Union, Ohio (today it is known as Calcutta, Columbiana County, near East Liverpool about forty-five miles from Pittsburgh). The school was one room in the back of a livery stable. West Union was a growing stagecoach stop in the center of iron and coal mining and not far from the Ohio River. West Union also had the area's first paper mill and a growing pottery business. McGuffey contracted to teach forty-eight students at two dollars per student per term, which was considerably above the average of the time. The contract initially was for one term, but was extended the following year. Still, McGuffey would have to board in the town as well, since it was about forty miles from the McGuffey farm.

McGuffey taught several years at West Union before going to a Presbyterian academy to continue his own education in 1818. The academy was that of Reverend Thomas Hughes in Darlington, Pennsylvania (then Greensburg) across the state line from the Youngstown area. The Presbyterian Church had erected this small academy in 1806 in Erie, Pennsylvania to train students to enter the ministry and as missionary teachers. This "Old Stone Academy" received a grant of six hundred dollars from the state of Pennsylvania in 1808. The state grant required that poor children be taught free, and the focus was to be on training professionals such as surveyors, lawyers, teachers, and ministers. Graduation from the Old Stone Academy helped students pass the required examinations to become a head schoolmaster. The Pennsylvania legislature found no problem with working with church related schools. The academy generally provided a specialized high school level course, which would lead to a college education. The curriculum consisted of Latin, Greek, religion, arithmetic, and "the usual circle of sciences." Thomas Hughes had been recruiting in the Western Reserve for students, and a young McGuffey offered potential. McGuffey lacked the money, but arrangements were made for McGuffey to work at the home of Thomas Hughes for his board. This arrangement reflected the potential seen in the young McGuffey. The largest part of the expense at the academy was room and board, which was about seventy-five cents a week. Room and board included simple meals such as coffee and buttered bread for breakfast; lunch known as dinner consisted of bread, meat, and potatoes; and supper was more bread and milk. Dinner was the larger meal in the 1800s. The growth of local academies had been part of the new culture evolving in the Western Reserve.

The cultural roots of the Western Reserve and Ohio changed much after the War of 1812. The war effectively ended the Indian threat in Ohio. Peace allowed the population of Ohio to double from 231,000 in 1810 to 581,000 in 1830. By 1830, the population nearly doubled again to 938,000. The postwar migration included another wave of Calvinists from New England and a large wave of Pennsylvania Germans. The professions of these new settlers changed from farming as well. An Ohio observer noted in 1819: "a certain class of men who are, undoubtedly, in possession of great advantages. . . . They are the land-jobbers, the speculators, the rich capitalists, the men who were wealthy when they came here — who were able to purchase large tracts and retail them out, reserving, however, every valuable privilege to themselves; men who were able to build mills, machinery, and even towns."[1] Ohio had become the forefront of the American Industrial Revolution. The diversity of the Western Reserve reflected all segments of America including education.

1   George Knepper, *Ohio and Its People* (Kent: Kent State University Press, 1989) p. 75.

The period of 1810 to 1825 was one of political formation on the Ohio frontier. The conservative Federalist Party was popular with most New England migrants and some conservative Scotch-Irish. Because of their agrarian stands, Ohio farmers favored the Jeffersonians of the period. The whiskey taxes had also pushed many Scotch-Irish into the Jeffersonian side. The area had already been on the forefront of the struggle between industry and farmers. The growing manufacturing and iron industry of the area wanted government to build roads and canals. Farmers even favored canal and road building to move their products to market. Many Scotch-Irish iron makers, experiencing a depression after the war, were demanding tariffs on iron. The Presbyterian Church leaders favored the existence of a strong government. There were new issues arising such as abolition. The New England Congregationalists tended to be very anti-slavery, as did the Quakers and some German Sects. Presbyterians were always split on the slavery issue. The Western Reserve remained culturally diverse and fluid as religious and political elements split and morphed into new directions.

This period also saw a pragmatic shift in the rigid Calvinist thinking of frontier and industrial Presbyterians. It was an old movement that had even occurred with the strict Calvinistic Puritans and was found in the Congregationalists of the Western Reserve. God's will was still supreme, but there was an acceptance that hard work could result in improvement of one's class. There was a belief that the right to own property was a divine one. The Scotch-Irish Presbyterians had always believed that it was possible to improve one's lot in life. It was a tradition that went back to the backing away from the rigid Scotch Church during the Scottish Enlightenment. For American Presbyterians, it was not a theological break but more of a social one. It also morphed into the obligation of the rich to take care of the poor. The Presbyterians and Puritans always had a greater focus on virtues and sin than theological dogma. Another factor of the period was the spreading of a "Great Awakening" or Revival, which brought Methodists ministers to the Western Reserve. The Methodists' doctrine of free will was extremely attractive to frontier Presbyterians. Presbyterians were attracted to the less rigid doctrines, winning over such Presbyterians as the ancestors of President William McKinley. Presbyterian converts to Methodism were extensive in the 1820s in Ohio, but the McGuffey family remained loyal to the conservative roots of the Covenanters, who seemed to have softened their view on Calvinistic predestination by adopting a modified Methodist free will view. One conservative view the Methodists maintained was against drinking. The Presbyterians, Congregationalists, Methodists, and German Pietists found common ground in honoring the Sabbath, drinking, profanity, gambling, public education, and prayer.

The "Old Stone Academy" reflected the developing culture of the Western Reserve but lacked the prestige of older schools and the highest level of learning available at established colleges of the time. From 1816 to 1820, there was a new influx of New Englanders into the Western Reserve due to crop failures in the East. These settlers came to Warren, Ohio, and new schools were need- ed. McGuffey applied for the job in 1820 even though the examiners preferred a Congregationalist. The examiners were Yale graduates and the rigorous test was beyond McGuffey's training, Hebrew being one of those weaknesses. This was around the same time that McGuffey started at Washington College in Wash- ington County, Pennsylvania.

The move took McGuffey back to his birthplace in Pennsylvania. Washington College (today's Washington & Jefferson) in Washington, Pennsylvania, while a new frontier college had already established itself an excellent Presbyterian col- lege. Although not as prestigious as its cross county rival Jefferson College (the two would unite in 1865), Washington College had started as a frontier Presby- terian academy in 1789 for the influx Scotch-Irish such as William H. McGuffey's grandfather "Scotch Billy." Washington College offered a strong curriculum in the biblical languages: Greek, Latin, and Hebrew. McGuffey would meet his men- tor, Reverend Andrew Wylie, who was a professor and president of the college. McGuffey came to Washington a poor man, and he would have to be a "part-time" student. McGuffey struggled to buy books and cover expenses. The country was in an economic recession and money was tight everywhere. The cost of a semes- ter was near thirty dollars, and room/board was about two dollars a week.

McGuffey returned to Washington County, the heart of frontier radicalism in the 1820s. The Whiskey Rebellion had changed the Scotch-Irish of the area into anti-Federalists and left a deep imprint on the area well into the future. Whiskey making was still a major endeavor in the area. The support for a rising politi- cian, Andrew Jackson, was strong in the area in contrast to the anti-Jacksonians of Ohio's Western Reserve. The stricter Presbyterians of the Western Reserve like McGuffey feared the rise of Jackson. The letters of a young McGuffey voice concerns over Jackson as a demagogue. Jackson's populist support worried McGuffey because, while born a Scotch-Irish Presbyterian, he was no supporter of organized churches. Furthermore, Jackson opposed the spread of capitalism as had Thomas Jefferson. McGuffey and his friends became deeply concerned at the ability of Andrew Jackson to fool church going Presbyterians as well as the masses. McGuffey attributed the rise of such demagogues to lack of education in basic American values. There is no question that the political success of Andrew Jackson acted as a motivation for McGuffey's quest for American education.

McGuffey often lamented the strong support of Jackson in Western Pennsyl- vania. Socially, however, the area remained religious and prone to advanced edu- cation. Washington College, however, remained loyal to the stricter "Old School" Presbyterians. Its sister college, Jefferson College, represented the more liberal Presbyterian wing. There were a number of academies and colleges in South- western Pennsylvania. Nearby Pittsburgh was becoming a major manufacturing center, and the largest city in the West. Pittsburgh had a booming iron rolling and nail making business, but the raw pig iron came from the iron furnaces of Washington and Westmoreland Counties.

McGuffey's tenure at Washington was a protracted one due to a shortage of money. He had to earn money tutoring, teaching, and doing work in the town. His curriculum was more of the same with studies of Latin, Hebrew, and Greek, so scripture could be read directly. Ancient history and philosophy were the other courses of importance. McGuffey entered Washington College at the age of twenty, which was about an average age, with a typical age range from ten to thirty years old. There were no entrance requirements and backgrounds varied widely. The student body was under thirty students, and most were studying to be ministers or teachers. Socially and politically, the college was very conservative. The Presbyterians of Washington County tended to support or at least ignored the growing debate within the church about slavery. The town of Washington and the county were the Eastern center of political support for the rising career of Scotch-Irishman Andrew Jackson. The McGuffey family and the Western Pennsylvania Covenanters, however, were concerned about Jackson's drinking and perceived bias against religion. Reverend Andrew Wylie found an anti-Jackson ally in Henry Clay.

The election of 1824 ended the "era of good feelings" and ushered in the real party system in America. It signaled the rise of one of America's most polarizing figures-Andrew Jackson. Andrew Jackson found enormous support with the Scotch-Irish of Washington County where the Whiskey Rebellion was still remembered. While Andrew Jackson was Scotch-Irish, to many conservative Scotch-Irish churchgoers of the Western Reserve he was the anti-Christ. Jackson was hard drinking, divorced, and some believed him to be atheistic. Jackson, in reality, was a frontier Presbyterian but was also anti-church establishment. The Jackson era would split the nation as well as the existing political parties and even the Presbyterian Church. John Quincy Adams represented the old Federalist Party while Henry Clay represented the National Republican Party, a conservative branch of Jefferson's Democratic-Republican Party; and Jackson took the liberal branch to form the Democratic Party. The Western Reserve went solidly for Henry Clay, especially with his support of federal canal building money, Adams held the New England vote, and Jackson took Western Pennsylvania's Washington County with the old Scotch-Irish whiskey rebels. The election was a three way split, requiring Clay to give his electoral votes to Adams and give Adams the election. McGuffey would have been for Adams, as Adams carried Western Reserve as well in 1824. Jackson represented a political, social, and moral problem for McGuffey's conservative views. McGuffey's views were clearly rooted in a Republican view of the old Federalists versus a Jeffersonian or Jacksonian Democracy. McGuffey even opposed the universal suffrage of Jacksonian Democracy. Finally, Jackson's morals came into question with McGuffey. The success of Jackson in the 1830s led to the Whig counter-revolution of the 1840s and 1850s. McGuffey would happily expound the Whig values.

Andrew Wylie's mentoring created a lasting impact on McGuffey. Wylie was a strict "Old Presbyterian" and a Whig politically, but like the Covenanter sect, he believed in keeping politics and denominational religion out of education. This was an extremely difficult challenge for a highly polarized society, yet it was at the heart of Wylie's core beliefs. Wylie believed that if you focused on morals, then you had to reject the Jacksonian philosophy. The premise was that Jackson's views were immoral. As for the Presbyterian split, for Wylie that was an internal church issue. This type of fairness doctrine would serve William McGuffey well in his future dealings.

Chapter 5. Transylvania

> Take any individual . . . separate him . . . and look at him, apart and alone, like
> some Robinson Crusoe in a far-off island of the ocean . . . and, even in such a
> solitude, how authoritative over his actions, how decisive of his contemplations
> and of his condition, are the instructions he received and the habits he formed
> in early life!
>
> — Horace Mann, "The Necessity of Education in
> a Republican Government"

McGuffey's early travels and wanderings in Ohio's Western Reserve, Pennsylvania's Washington County, Kentucky, and Cincinnati represent the heart of McGuffeyland and what might be called America's manufacturing polygon. Connecting lines between Pittsburgh-Charleston-Louisville-Cleveland, you can see this "iron" polygon of the 1800s. This polygon included the Western Reserve, the Ohio Valley, Transylvania (Northern Kentucky and Southern Ohio) and Westsylvania (Western Pennsylvania). This area has also been called the "Middle Border." While still agricultural, this region was struggling for economic growth though it had more farm markets than manufacturing. The National Road passed through and canals were starting to be built to support that growth. This was where the manufacturing soul of America emerged to challenge Jefferson's vision of an agrarian America. This was America's heartland and the Western Reserve was its political capital. Pittsburgh was the manufacturing center and Cincinnati was the intellectual center. It was an area that the Scotch-Irish dominated and was overwhelmingly Christian. It was the emerging manufacturing base of America in the 1820s. The iron polygon stood in contrast to the Puritanical bastion of New England and the Aristocracy of the Virginia. It also represented diversity, struggles, and opposing views: manufacturing versus farming, Jeffersonians versus Federalists, liberal Protestantism versus Calvinism, slavery versus abolition, government roads and canals versus no government intervention, and a republic versus a democracy. It was American culture in the making, and its views became those of McGuffey. McGuffey was much more the product of the iron polygon than it was of McGuffey's molding.

This area would be the stronghold of the emerging Whig Party of the 1830s and would launch the political career of Henry Clay. Furthermore, it would be the heart of the anti-Jacksonian movement that would morph the Whig Party into the Republican Party. In the Western Reserve, the roots of a liberal religious movement for the West started what was known as the "Great Awakening." It would bring the rise of the Methodist Church and split the Presbyterian Church on Calvinistic views. The Kentucky and Southern Ohio section would give rise to an intellectual movement that would sweep up educators like McGuffey.

In 1823, McGuffey took a teaching job in Paris, Kentucky while he was still studying at Washington College. His schoolhouse was a small one-room cabin in a Scotch-Irish community, which had been the smokehouse of Reverend John McFarland. John McFarland was the pastor of Paris Presbyterian Church. Paris is about 20 miles northeast of Lexington in Kentucky's blue grass region. In 1823 it was also the center of Scotch-Irish whiskey making. Hemp production, however, was the main industry. Hemp had been used for sail making and rope had and boomed during the War of 1812. Lexington had gone from a population of 1,792 in 1810 to 5,279 in 1820. The Lexington area was on the verge of a great enlightenment driven by its Transylvania University. The enlightenment created a wave of community schools with financial support. The enlightenment had caused a great deal of tension as Unitarians took control of the University from the conservative Presbyterians. Unitarianism was a very liberal form of Christianity compared to Calvin based Christianity that had gained popularity in the great eastern universities such as Harvard, Princeton, and Yale. Horace Holley brought Unitarianism to Transylvania from his ministry in Boston. The Unitarian revolution had hit Harvard and New England in 1820 as well. Many of the Unitarians looked to the West as the place to establish this very liberal style of Christianity. This struggle would deeply affect Presbyterian scholarship, which moved to a more conservative model to counter the rise of Unitarianism. Presbyterians in the Western Ohio Valley would split between "Old School conservatives" and "New School Liberals." This knew liberal wave brought with it a passion for education, which resulted in the birth of Kentucky's great Transylvania College. Conservatism would ultimately win out in Kentucky in religion, education, and politics. Henry Clay served on the board of Transylvania. Transylvania University suffered a fire and was not rebuilt as most of its enlightened Unitarians, Presbyterians, and Methodists moved to Cincinnati. Lexington's patriarch, Henry Clay, would ultimately lead a new conservative political party, the Whig Party.

While McGuffey avoided this controversy and held a middle-of-the-road approach, his teaching methods became well known in the area among liberals and conservatives. McGuffey taught morals and Christian principles, avoiding political activism. He used both Webster's *Blue Back Speller* and the *New England Primer* but added his questioning methodology to the mix. His pedagogy would be his strength. McGuffey would have the student read and the rest of the students would discuss. He constantly tried different questions to see which worked best. He coupled that with traditional memorization and hand copying stores. The location of his simple Paris school between the two central cities of the enlightenment (Cincinnati and Lexington) brought him in contact with the leaders of the enlightenment movement. One of those leaders was Reverend Robert Hamilton Bishop, the first President of Miami University in Oxford, Ohio, thirty miles north of Cincinnati. Prior to going to Miami, Bishop had been pastor of McCord Presbyterian Church near Paris and a professor at Kentucky's Transylvania University. Bishop had even taken the time to visit McGuffey's classroom. Bishop was a liberal and McGuffey a conservative, but Bishop was interested in the excellence of McGuffey's teaching. Bishop had a single idea of making his Miami University the best in the West.

Bishop also appeared to overlook McGuffey's reputation for discipline. One Paris student remembered McGuffey was "fond of making a boy take a whipping." Discipline in Ohio grammar schools was a given in the 1820s and 1830s. Many students looked back with pride in the sternness of their schoolmaster. President Rutherford Hayes fondly remembered his schoolmaster, Daniel Granger, in Delaware, Ohio in the late 1820s, even though he was an extreme disciplinarian. Hayes called his school master the "demon of ferocity," capable of flogging boys "twice his size." In another story, Hayes told of his schoolmaster throwing a jack knife within an inch of a whispering student's head.[1] Hayes was also a champion of Webster's *Blue Back Speller* and was himself a champion speller! At the time, we can believe that Hayes was a bit less enthusiastic about his schoolmaster (especially since many teachers of the time had a fondness for whiskey). While McGuffey was never known to throw knives, he was supportive of strong discipline.

Still, in 1825 Bishop asked McGuffey to take a position at the university. The offer was a professorship at $600 a year, which was higher than what Washington or Jefferson colleges offered ($400 per year). The problem was that McGuffey had not yet graduated from Washington College. To put the salary in perspective, the average laborer made less than 80 cents a day or $249 per year. A good mechanic or skilled worker could make $1.50 a day. A saddle horse cost from

---

1 C. R. Williams, *Life of Rutherford Hayes* (Boston, 1914), p. 16

$200 to $300, and McGuffey had a fine horse. A horse carriage cost from $300 to $400, and a carriage was one of the first things McGuffey purchased with his new salary. A house could cost from $800 to $2,000. Lodging at a tavern cost around sixty cents a day. Beef and pork was about six cents a pound. Whiskey was fifty cents a gallon. Eggs were thirteen cents per dozen and butter cost twenty-five cents a pound. Cotton fabric was around a dollar a yard, and silk was triple that (McGuffey favored silk). At one point parishioners complained about McGuffey's silk coat and fine horse and buggy. McGuffey, not a handsome man, still had a taste for fine clothes. Bishop wanted his professors to not only be the best but also the best paid. A salary of $600 for a professor could be considered upper middle class and was consistent with those at some of the best colleges in the East.

Robert Hamilton Bishop had come from Scotland in 1802 to teach on the American frontier in Kentucky. Bishop had spent twenty years as a professor at Lexington's Transylvania College, and built a national reputation. At the time, Transylvania was making a name as the West's best college and was the first West of the Alleghenies to have a medical college in 1810. Transylvania University had been started from the Presbyterian Church by a group of local activists. The hope was that Transylvania would lead a revolution in education, breaking away from the purely biblical curriculum of most colleges of the time. The new trustees brought in a Unitarian minister Horace Holley from New England to build the college to prominence. Holley brought in the best professors he could find, and by 1823, Transylvania was one of the best in the nation with 400 students and a 6,000-volume library. In the 1820s, it graduated an average of 500 students a year. Holley even sent an agent to Europe with $17,000 to purchase more books, which had been granted for that purpose by the state legislature. Its tuition of $30 a session (plus a $5 registration fee) with living expenses was estimated at $150 a year. Holley built a great college, but it was clearly liberal and "New School" Presbyterian. Interestingly, the local frontier Presbyterians that had funded and supported the college were conservative and "Old School" Presbyterians. Professors such as Robert Bishop leaned to the liberal side of the Presbyterian Church, but he was brought to Transylvania for his renowned teaching skills. Those skills became known nationally, ironically attracting conservative students such as Jefferson Davis who later left for West Point. The fame of Transylvania College, which attracted Eastern liberal professors, was a mixed blessing for the conservative local base. Bishop grew to become an abolitionist and a leader in the bluegrass new liberalism and quest for excellence in education.

Transylvania University was the first university to have a medical school in the West. Benjamin Rush's favorite understudy at the University of Pennsylvania, Charles Caldwell headed the medical school. Seven other University of Pennsylvania graduates such as Daniel Drake were on the medical staff at Transylvania. The medical college pioneered new surgery techniques that brought eastern doctors in as observers. The science department was just as prestigious with well-known scientists. Turkish-born Constantine Samuel Rafinesque was one of America's greatest botanists. In his seven years at Transylvania, Rafinesque published over two hundred papers. The overall fame of Transylvania started to bring considerable eastern students.

Transylvania University in Lexington was the center of a major cultural movement. A local paper described the cultural rise of the area as: "in the twenties, Lexington was the most exciting place in the West." Already the region's self-proclaimed Athens, the Blue Grass metropolis tried to offset its commercial and industrial decline with cultural expansion. Admitting that the center of economic power had moved elsewhere, its leaders declared that nonetheless Lexington was the transposed "capital of Science and Letters." [1] The corridor from Lexington to Cincinnati attracted artists, doctors, musicians, and scientists. Some referred to it as an "intellectual awakening" of the West. In 1815, Lexington had one of the nation's largest subscription libraries with over two thousand books. Lexington's intellectuals formed the Transylvania Philosophical Society. Fortesque Cuming opened a coffee house in Lexington that subscribed to forty-two different newspapers paid by sixty members. Cuming also opened Lexington's first theater. But with the cultural enlightenment came a liberalization of religion. As in the Western Reserve of Ohio, Methodists made inroads into the Presbyterian flock along the Lexington-Cincinnati corridor. Unitarians took professorships at the frontier universities and the Presbyterian Church split between conservative and liberal.

Robert Bishop considered himself part of the liberal and political activist movement in the Presbyterian Church and colleges, but his main focus was education, not politics. His political friends included Speaker of the House Henry Clay. When he took the position of President at Miami, he set his goal to make it the "Yale of the West." On July 6, 1824, Robert Bishop was appointed President with a salary of one thousand dollars per year and free rent at the university's mansion (a small red brick house). When he left Transylvania University, he was Vice-president. Bishop, like most of the university trustees, was a Presbyterian minister. Professor John Annan of Baltimore was hired at six hundred dollars per year to teach mathematics and natural philosophy. William Sparrow was hired at five hundred dollars per year to tutor languages. Miami University had started as a state land-grant school in 1809 but didn't officially open until 1824. Miami consisted of twenty-three students in the grammar school and another twenty in the college. The grammar school had found some success with a five-dollar tuition fee and a one-dollar a week board. The university, on the other hand, was struggling.

---

1 *Kentucky Reporter*, February 21, 1827

The university's trustees were young and visionary, and several were well educated. James Shields was from the University of Scotland; Daniel Symmes was from Princeton, and Joshua Wilson was from Transylvania. Overall, the trustees were a mix of liberal (new school) and conservative (old school) Presbyterians, but since Miami was a state school, there were Methodist trustees, secular trustees, and even a German socialist. Still, the split in the Presbyterian Church would have the greatest impact on Miami University as it did on the cultural environment of the West. The "old" versus 'new" school split was tough to define but these comparisons apply: traditional versus reform, conservative versus liberal, and maybe the most important, Calvinism versus free will. The trustees were however, united on the vision of Miami as a future great university. It was that vision that brought them to hire Robert Bishop, even though he was a "new school" Presbyterian minister.

The town of Oxford was incorporated in 1810 with the specific purpose of becoming a university town. A "quit" rent of all lots in the Oxford area lots went to the development of Miami University. Even the name Oxford was selected to promote a cultural image. While a state school, the area's Presbyterians rigorously supported Miami. The Presbyterian Church on the corner of Church Street and Campus Avenue was considered the "cradle of Western Presbyterian ministers." In 1824, the town of Oxford was primarily a Scotch-Irish settlement of over five hundred people. The town consisted of "six stores, three taverns, a harness shop, a tanyard, a livery stable, some log and frame houses."[1] There was also a Methodist Church, a Presbyterian Church, and another Presbyterian Church in the nearby town of Darrtown. The forest of walnut, maple, and poplars had been cleared for several buildings. One was a three-story brick called Franklin Hall. The other was a brick building called Center Building. The beautiful red bricks came from clay from a nearby Indian mound. Nearby Cincinnati had over 12,000 in 1820 and was rapidly growing (over 16,000 by 1826). Cincinnati had created the best system of local grade schools, and was becoming known as a cultural center of the West. The burning of Transylvania University in 1828 accelerated the influx of intellectuals into Cincinnati and Oxford.

Still the decision for McGuffey to take the position at Miami was a difficult one. He had not completed his work at Washington College, and the job requirements and distance from Washington College would make it difficult without a special arrangement. While there was no formal arrangement, McGuffey had a close friend in Reverend Wylie, President of Washington College. Within a year of McGuffey leaving, Washington College conferred a Bachelors Degree. One advantage appeared to be the ability to get his younger brother (ten years old) into the academy there and eventually the university. The education of his brother Alexander probably helped put his mother on the side of the move, but

---

1   William Smith, *About the McGuffeys* (Oxford: Cullen Printing, 1963), p. 43

she still wanted him to become a Presbyterian minister someday. McGuffey had been offered the position of Professor of Ancient Languages, which was an outstanding offer (he was also to function as librarian). He was replacing William Sparrow who had taken the position as Vice-President of Kenyon. Even Reverend Wylie supported McGuffey on taking the opportunity. Another friend noted: "I am happy and proud to enter you on my list of friends, has obtained a situation of such respectability and eminence; for judging from the position, funds, and present auspices of Oxford, I presume the time is not far distant when it will be one of the most respectable institutions in our country, and not improbably the foremost in the West."[1]

Sometimes it is overlooked that McGuffey was an ambitious young man with a found mission in education. He had become captivated in the educational process. Being a student and a teacher is where he had found his passion; and he, like most young men, was looking to make his mark. He wanted to improve the methodology of teaching. McGuffey had started to pioneer new approaches to rhetorical education in that Paris schoolhouse. There is no question that he was inspired by the frontier enlightenment that radiated out of Lexington's Transylvania College. Men like Bishop were part of a new movement that was attracting many young men into the arts and literature. This enlightenment had caught the nation's attention, and it was exciting to be part of it. Miami was an opportunity to be part of a national movement. The moving American frontier was not only growing the nation but also opening up a new frontier of ideas.

Miami University had about one hundred twenty students in 1826 when McGuffey arrived. The "university" was really a mix of grammar, academy, and college students from age ten to thirty. Bishop had made progress in bringing in professors, and the school was growing. Still, the school was a mix of grammar school and college when McGuffey arrived. There were seventy students registered for McGuffey's first semester. The cost was ten dollars per session with two sessions, one from May to September and another from May to September, which was the typical schedule for Presbyterian colleges. Board and room was one dollar a week. The grammar school was five dollars per session and was the equivalent of the "academies" of the East. Board was one dollar per week. The course of study would be four years of two sessions each. The first year focused on Algebra, Greek, Latin, English Grammar, Euclid's elements, and classical literature. The second year consisted of more Greek and Latin, trigonometry, geography, and history. In the third year, the student started Hebrew, continued Latin, Greek, and Bible studies, and started natural philosophy. The senior year added chemistry and astronomy, while continuing the study of the first three years. At the

---

1 Letter from John Scott, Washington, Pennsylvania to W. H. McGuffey, Oxford Ohio, June 14, 1826

end of the years, a student received a Bachelor of Arts. Students lived and studied together as a class (Freshman, sophomore, etc.).

Study began at 5:00 A.M., as students were called to study by a trumpet blast. It required an extremely high workload on a handful of professors. While Miami had hopes of becoming a "Yale," its professors like McGuffey often had to help out in the clearing of land for new buildings. A dormitory known as Washington and Clinton Hall was completed in 1830 at a cost of $7,000. Like previous buildings, it was a handsome red brick three-story building. The rooms were rent-free, but students had to supply their own bed, furniture, and cooking utensils. Rooms had large iron stoves, but the students had to purchase or cut wood. Kindling was often cut from stair rails. The campus was, from the start, designed to include trees and "botanical gardens."

McGuffey and his brother Alexander took a temporary room at McCullough Tavern. McGuffey started as a professor at the winter session, and Alexander entered grammar school. They would soon take a room at the college next to that of Professor John Annan. McGuffey and Annan would take their meals at the Oxford Hotel on East High Street. Professor Annan, a recent graduate of Dickinson College, was an up and coming professor of mathematics. Annan and McGuffey became good friends. Annan was a prolific writer and published often on a variety of subjects. Annan had been successful at making money by publishing for journals. A journal might pay as such as two dollars a page, which was not a small sum in the 1820s. Certainly, Annan was an inspiration to McGuffey to begin his writing career. Another factor was the environment of excellence created at Miami. Miami University's original vision was to be the best college in the West, and Bishop drove that vision in all aspects of the university. The early faculty had a mandate to perform and achieve on a national level, like those at Transylvania University.

McGuffey had come to Miami to teach biblical languages, but his interests were moral philosophy and literary analysis. The Miami position offered good money, but it was also known for its literary societies and intellectual environment. The literary societies were the brainchild of Robert Bishop and would become an important source for the McGuffey and his future Readers. McGuffey, however, is considered the founder of the Erodelphians Literary Society, and was a contributor to its journal, The *Literary Focus.* McGuffey contributed to the *Literary Journal* and helped to line up guests speakers. Miami University had two literary societies on campus in 1826 — the Frodelphian Literary Society and the Miami Union Literary Society. Professor Annan founded the Union Literary Society. Bishop gave the two societies meeting halls and money to discuss and debate. They pledged members, collected extensive books, and signed honorary members. They published proceedings and brought in speakers. Speakers and visitors from the "College of Teachers" often stopped over in Oxford to speak. Their debates and discussions stirred the intellectual interests of the students. Meetings became the highlight on Fridays of a long week of lecture. Their success made Miami one of America's best colleges and certainly the lead university in literature and philosophy. Many famous alumni were members in the early years such as Caleb Smith (Union Literary), Lincoln's Secretary of the Interior, and Charlie Anderson (Erodelphians), who would become Governor of Ohio. Here also William and Alexander McGuffey found a passion for literature and its educational value. Alexander took extensive notes and for a time acted as the Erodelphians Society's secretary.

One professor looked back on the importance: "No professor was so valuable to many a student as was his Literary Society; no classroom was so attractive as his Literary Hall; no wit or humor more talked of than that which flashed out during the attrition of Society debates. No position was so sought as an appointment to be one of the four speakers at the annual Exhibition." There was no better way to prepare for a career in teaching, the church, or the law. Robert Bishop called the societies: "a means of intellectual and moral improvement equal to at least two professorships." The approach was very consistent with the Lancasterian methods so popular at Cincinnati College, and part of the Western enlightenment started on at Kentucky's Transylvania College. The pomp and ritual of these societies made Miami famous throughout America. Nothing could have attracted McGuffey more than these discussions and debates. McGuffey couldn't help but see the enthusiasm and power in these rhetorical meetings of students. It was this approach of Robert Bishop that McGuffey successfully took to grammar schools.

In 1826, Bishop supported the two literary societies with permanent quarters to support their libraries and reading rooms. The halls were upgraded with cabinets and good furniture. There were comfortable chairs around fireplaces, creating a type of literary fraternity. The libraries were said to be larger than that of the university. An inspiring history of the literary societies of Miami is given by Walter Havighurst, but the impact on McGuffey is often overlooked.[1] Meetings of the two societies were on Fridays, and classes ended at noon to accommodate the societies. After lunch, the members wearing roses (white for the Union members and red for the Erodelphians) entered the respective halls. The afternoon was for the reading of compositions and discussions. Many of the readings and discussions would augur those of *McGuffey's Readers*.

Friday evenings were much awaited for by the students. This was the time for the famous candlelight debates. The topics varied from the purely academic such as "Was Brutus Justified in Killing Caesar?" to the political "Should Congress Assist in the Abolishing of Slavery?" or "Would Colonization Benefit the Negro?" By the mid-thirties, many such as McGuffey had become critical of the tendency to

---

1 Walter Havighurst, *The Miami Years* (New York: G. P. Putman's Sons, 1958), p. 67

have more political topics. Some of the debates had become the rallying points for an aggressive abolitionist movement and President Bishop encouraged abolition-ist debates. The societies incorporated in 1835 with the State of Ohio to assure their independence from administration and faculty pressure. The societies re-cruited honorary members such as Henry Clay, Andrew Jackson, Lyman Beecher, Robert Owen, and Daniel Webster. Speakers such as Daniel Drake and Lyman Beecher were also brought in. Over the years, many governors, congressmen, diplomats, writers, and poets would arise from the two societies. The societies would also publish their proceedings, compositions, and reviews, creating the country's best literary journals. Alexander McGuffey used some of the material for the *McGuffey Rhetorical Guide* and *Fifth Eclectic Reader*.

Chapter 6. The Miami Years

> "There is now less flogging in our great schools than formerly, but then less is learned there; so that what the boys get on one end they lose on the other."
> — Samuel Johnson

Miami University offered McGuffey a new perspective on the world. Prior to his appointment in 1826, most of McGuffey's time was dedicated to earning money to continue his education and being a student. In doing so, McGuffey became a master of three biblical languages. This made him attractive to universities such as Miami that needed to teach Hebrew, Latin, and Greek. Hebrew, in particular, often required a specialist, so McGuffey being able to teach all three was a real plus to the new university. The mastery of these languages was no small feat for a twenty-six-year-old professor, but he never saw his future in teaching languages. McGuffey loved teaching, and teaching at the college level was a dream. He did continue to pursue his license as a Presbyterian minister at the constant prodding of his mother. But his real passion was teaching moral philosophy and literature. The only problem was that President Bishop taught moral philosophy, and for several years McGuffey would resign himself to teaching languages. The atmosphere at Miami, however, inspired the small faculty to dream bigger dreams. There is no question that many of McGuffey's critics were right in that McGuffey believed in the "right to rise." The right to improve oneself would be proclaimed in his future *Readers*.

The road to advancement for McGuffey was paved with hard work and long days. McGuffey's early schedule included the monitoring of the library and the preparation of buildings as classrooms. Individual tutoring was also part of a language professor's life. Another duty of his was the holding of Bible school on Sunday mornings for the Miami students. In addition, McGuffey spent time preaching at local churches such as the student chapel and Presbyterian Church at nearby Darrtown. By 1829, McGuffey had started preaching on a wider Western circuit for the Presbyterian Church. His fundamental and conservative brand of Presbyterianism made him popular with church leaders facing the liberal enlightenment of the frontier. Also in 1829, McGuffey was ordained to the ministry by the Oxford Presbytery at Bethel Church at Indian Creek near the town of Millville. McGuffey excelled in public speaking and preaching. He enjoyed public speaking, which had made him successful in the classroom as well. All along McGuffey built a reputation for speaking in the Cincinnati area.

The other reputation he seems to have built was one as a fancy but conservative dresser. Some frontier Presbyterians even complained, seeing his dress as pretentious. Others saw it as overcompensating for his poor looks. One of his associates recalled: "He was a man so ugly as not to be readily forgotten; a huge mouth, a portentous nose, sandy reddish gray hair, worn so long that it curled up a little above his ears, a vast forehead heightened by baldness, keen eyes that snapped and twinkled at you."[1] He liked silk and wore silk stockings as well as a silk stovepipe hat. All recall that he was extremely neat in person. While criticized, it appears that McGuffey was proud of his position and dressed for it. It was also consistent with his belief of the importance of image in public speaking.

McGuffey would soon meet his future wife, Harriet Spining. Harriet was visiting her brother, Oxford merchant Charles Spining, when she was introduced to William McGuffey. Charles Spining was living at the fashionable estate on High Street known as the "Scott" estate. He had opened a clothing store a few years earlier in Oxford. Their father, Isaac Spining, from one of America's oldest families, was a prosperous judge and landholder in Dayton, Ohio. The family had migrated to New Haven, Connecticut in 1637 from London. The family moved to New Jersey and then on to Ohio in 1786. Judge Isaac Spining was also a well-known Revolutionary War veteran who had come to Montgomery County (Dayton) in 1801, where he held court in a log cabin. Through real estate investment, he amassed a fortune. The 960-acre Spining estate in Dayton was known as "Woodlawn," and today is part of Wright-Patterson Air Force base. Harriet was a beautiful young lady, and she and McGuffey both appear to have fallen in love immediately. They were married at Woodlawn on April 3, 1827.

They started their union boarding in a brick house on Oxford's main street, but soon McGuffey purchased a wood frame house on Spring Street. The frame house had been purchased from Merikin Bond of Cincinnati for $350. The house was two hundred yards from his classroom on campus. McGuffey would soon

---

1   Harvey Minnich, *William Holmes McGuffey and his Readers* (Cincinnati: American Book Company, 1936), p. 16

replace the house with a brick one, which when completed, had a tax assessment of $1,800. It was a very stylish two-story home with built in cabinets and shelves and six rooms. The house had stately French windows and a beautiful portico. It was considered one of the finest houses in Oxford and is today the McGuffey Museum. McGuffey hired a girl to help with the housework. The backyard was used as an experimental elementary school. The lovely Mrs. Harriet McGuffey was known on campus for her large collection of bonnets and caps, which was the fashion at the time. She did, however, have some health problems. The new home and maid helped, but William sought medical assistance. He took her to Cincinnati's famous physician, Daniel Drake, who would play a critical role in McGuffey's life and career. It was probably this meeting with Daniel Drake that brought him in contact with the "College of Teachers."

Daniel Drake had been a visionary in calling for common schools and textbooks. With McGuffey's interest aroused, he built his experimental backyard school. It is considered to be the first experimental school in the United States. The students were the children of his Miami associates, including his daughter Mary Haines. The school was graded using log benches. He worked on reading and spelling, developing new approaches. He used positive reinforcement by using a special log for top-performing students. These lessons became the core of his Readers. He did publish some of his methods in the *Western Monthly Magazine*. The editor of the magazine, James Hall, was also a prominent member of the "College of Teachers." McGuffey even tried his hand at fiction from the stories he was using at school. During this period, McGuffey's passion passed from teaching languages to teaching common school children. Of course, his ambition took him beyond teaching; he wanted to develop methods of teaching. This represented a new field, since there were no colleges of education or even college courses directed at methodology. Teachers learned from their own grammar school experiences. What few textbooks existed offered little in teaching techniques.

The early years at Miami were very happy ones for the young professor and his wife. For the first time in his life, he had money for the better things in life. Probably they even had some support for the remodeling of the house from Harriet's family. In the Presbyterian Church, McGuffey was gaining a solid reputation as a preacher. Miami's tree-lined campus remains today one of the nation's most beautiful campuses. McGuffey was known to plant maples to further enhance the landscape. One of these maples lived until 1926, when its wood was used for a gavel to be presented to the Ohio State Teacher's Association. Academically, McGuffey was gaining a reputation from friends outside the university and was active in intellectual groups in Cincinnati. Four of McGuffey's five children were born at the university home: Mary Haines on January 30, 1830; Henrietta on July 10, 1832; William Holmes on October 1, 1834; and Charles Spining on November 8,

1838. The fifth child, Edward Mansfield, was born on May 18, 1839 in Cincinnati. Sadly, William Holmes Jr. lived for only three weeks in 1834.

Miami University continued to grow in size and reputation under Robert Bishop. By 1835, Miami University had over two hundred fifty students and seven full-time professors. It had realized Bishop's vision of being the most prominent college in the West. However, Bishop and McGuffey started to have serious disagreements over student discipline, teaching, and Presbyterian dogma. McGuffey relentlessly pressured Bishop to let him teach moral philosophy, but the bigger problem was the "Old School" and "New School" split in Presbyterian dogma. Bishop represented the "New School" approach, while a slight majority of professors favored the "Old School" theology. In 1828, Bishop gained an ally in Professor John Witherspoon Scott, who came to Miami University as a graduate from Yale University. Scott had been a Chair at Washington College when McGuffey was there, but they were much different. John Scott had become a "New School" Presbyterian and an abolitionist like Bishop. The deflection of Professor Scott to Bishop's "New School" philosophy was a huge disappointment to McGuffey, who was a good friend and had helped Scott get his position at Miami. Scott seemed forced to enter the feud growing between Bishop and McGuffey, and once he entered the fray, he between a fierce opponent of McGuffey.

There were two other rigid "Old School" Presbyterian professors at Miami — Professors McArthur and MacCracken. MacCracken was also pastor of the Oxford Presbyterian Church. While these two professors had been allies of McGuffey, they would also oppose McGuffey's liberal friend, Henry Ward Beecher, from becoming the pastor at Oxford's Presbyterian Church in 1838. While the opposition ruled Lyman Beecher out as pastor, he remained friendly with McGuffey, understanding the split in the church. Miami University represented the evolving division in the Presbyterian Church and nation. The division was reflected in the student body and faculty. The bigger issue on campus would be abolition but that would also go to the liberal-conservative split in the Presbyterian Church. Robert Bishop had become an ardent supporter of abolition. While strongly opposed to slavery, McGuffey was not an abolitionist or political activist. He believed that the remedy for slavery was in moral education from the pulpit and classroom, not political activism. The debate had got its start in the border city of Cincinnati and ultimately linked up with the frontier enlightenment that was sweeping the area. The fight was not so much of the evils of slavery but how best to control, or in the case of abolitionists, to eliminate it. Men like Bishop and Beecher supported an end at any cost.

The tension in Cincinnati in 1820s reflected the nation's future. Across the Ohio River at Cincinnati was the slave-holding state of Kentucky. The Black population increased in 1829 to 2,258 from 625 in 1826. In 1829, blacks represented about ten percent of Cincinnati's population. Blacks commonly went to

Cincinnati to escape slavery and the rapid increase in blacks concerned another group. Most of the blacks resided in a segregated section of town known as "Little Africa." Liberal Presbyterians argued for the full elimination of slavery in all states. The conservative view, while opposing slavery, saw it as a state's rights issue. The Cincinnati editor Charles Hammond's view reflected the conservative view in that: "he opposed slavery but cautioned that there was no way the institution could be touched except by action of the slave states themselves." For even the liberals in the early 1820s, the influx of blacks into the area could not be sustained. President Robert Bishop was part of a more radical liberal wing that was to be the root of the abolition movement. Even while in the slave state of Kentucky, Bishop had started the Lexington Sabbath Schools for Negroes that had been refuted by the Presbyterian Church. In Ohio, Bishop was initially with the American Colonization Society but would move to the more radical stand of abolition.

The Colonization Society offered a type of compromise for liberals in Cincinnati. The American Colonization Society included some popular Americans such as James Madison, James Monroe, Henry Clay, Daniel Webster, and John Marshall. The Colonization Society secured funds to have slaves coming into Ohio to be re-colonized in Africa. The Colonization movement got its start in Ohio's Western Reserve and quickly spread to Southern Ohio and Cincinnati. The colonization movement got a boost in 1829 with the nation's first race riot in Cincinnati. The riot was caused by an effort to enforce the "black laws," which would have forced blacks out of Cincinnati. The riots ended the effort of Cincinnati to force the blacks out, creating more interest in the colonization movement. The riots did create a migration of Cincinnati blacks to the town of Wilberforce, Canada. Large amounts of money for the migration came from Quakers in the Western Reserve of Ohio and wealthy Cincinnatians. University professors and upper class enlightenment followers grew the movement. In 1827 with the help of Bishop, the Colonization Society formed a student auxiliary at Miami University. Bishop, of course, wanted the elimination of slavery immediately, but colonization offered a first step. By 1860 the American Colonization Society had managed to move ten thousand blacks to Liberia, which was a small fraction of the three million black slaves. McGuffey was not in full sympathy with the colonization movement and most certainly opposed student activism. Still McGuffey, like many conservatives, hoped colonization might defuse the issue.

By 1830, the Cincinnati riots and colonization movement had torn the Presbyterian Church into two factions. Both factions were anti-slavery but had a very different methodology to resolve the issue. The liberal wing turned to the political activism of abolition. The abolition movement got its start in the East, particularly Yale University. The movement came to Cincinnati through men like Bishop and Scott at Miami University. In Cincinnati, a new liberal school,

Lane Theological Seminary, emerged as a leader in abolition with professors like Lyman Beecher and Calvin Stowe. The students and professors at Lane organized a Sunday school for blacks as well as evening schools. Lane Seminary also set up lyceum for the discussion of the issue. Bishop hoped to see a similar activism at Miami, but McGuffey and other professors held Bishop back. Robert Bishop's campus support, however, developed into student organizations. In 1832 Miami students organized a more radical Anti-Slavery Society and had torchlight parades through the town of Oxford. President Bishop encouraged the students in these radical organizations. McGuffey, of course, opposed encouraging student activism. McGuffey not only opposed abolition, but also particularly disliked mixing politics and education. It would be the beginning of a feud between Bishop and McGuffey that would last the decade and encompass many issues. Critics note that both men were jealous of each other's fame and prestige. Certainly both men had large egos and ambition, again not unusual for the competitive world of academics. Generally, McGuffey represented the moral and conservative high ground, but McGuffey had many personal issues.

Whatever the reason for the split between Bishop and McGuffey, the timing indicates it began around 1831. Bishop and McGuffey had started out as friends and associates. Indeed, Bishop had hired him at Miami, and Bishop had played a role in his ordination in the church. While there were certainly many personal issues, clashing ambitions, politics, dogma, and personality differences, there was also the split with the Presbyterian Church that Bishop and McGuffey found themselves on opposite sides. Bishop stood with the liberal "new school," which were abolitionists, anti-state rights, liberal theologically, believers in political activism, and less strict disciplinarians. McGuffey's old school was conservative, believed strongly in states' rights, while anti-slavery believed it should be an individual decision and were rigid disciplinarians. Still, the record shows the split between McGuffey and Bishop to be more trivial than philosophical a lot of the time. To his credit, Robert Bishop tried to defuse the problem by allowing McGuffey to teach some moral philosophy.

Professor John Scott, an ally of Bishop, pointed out McGuffey's constant "grumbling." Scott's letter to the Board of Trustees in 1836, however, reflects maybe the child-like nature of the feud: "Scarcely an act of discipline or general management but was made the ground of exception and ill-natured remark against the Dr. [Bishop] . . . Indeed it seemed as if he [McGuffey] was disposed to look upon nothing which the Dr. did with a favorable eye, and to interpret nothing in a charitable manner."[1] McGuffey had his support as well as with the faculty. The student body also seemed split on McGuffey because of the rift between President Bishop and McGuffey. Thomas Millikin, a student during the period 1834 to

---

1 John W. Scott, Statement September 1, 1836 to Board of Trustees, Miami University Archives

1838, reported McGuffey to be: "a model teacher, studiously dignified and polite, elegant and accomplished in social life, critical and exact in knowledge, with unusual capacity to impart knowledge to others." Another student described him as: "conscientious, laborious, and a successful teacher with the charm of unassuming practical religion." When McGuffey left Miami, another student noted: "I feel no delacasy [sic] in saying that McGuffey going away from here is one of the greatest blessings [that] ever happened to Miami University."[1]

The main difference between Bishop and McGuffey was their view on discipline. McGuffey was a strict disciplinarian, which probably was from his grammar-school teacher background and his own conservative college background at Washington College. A frontier grammar school teacher was often hired on his ability to discipline students. McGuffey had been brought up in the strict discipline of the Covenanters and did not relate well to the middle class frontier students of Miami. College students west of Pittsburgh were known for their free spirited and fun loving attitudes. Documented criticism, however, comes from his opposition at the university. Professor John Scott (a Bishop ally) reported the following to the Board of Trustees: "I have myself observed a very great difference between the tone assumed by Mr. McGuffey respecting a young man in secret Faculty session, and when the young man himself was present before us. In one case it has sometimes been harsh, laconic & denunciatory in the extreme, in the other smooth as oil."[2] These remarks came in the heat of a battle between Bishop and McGuffey. It is hard to decipher the truth since the feud had reached legendary portions. Such prideful struggles are not unknown on college campuses, but the strength of this feud lives in the many archival records and biographical efforts.

This feud was deeply personal and professional. Much has been made that it was the tip of the iceberg in the divide in the Presbyterian Church. McGuffey was in the orthodox Covenanter wing, and Bishop the liberal wing. However, McGuffey was able to maintain close friendships with the liberal Beecher family in the "College of Teachers." McGuffey had a life long record of keeping religious arguments to church circles, which suggests the personal nature of this feud.

The personal battle between Bishop and McGuffey had many fronts and roots, including demands by McGuffey to teach moral philosophy. Bishop refused to turn over any of these classes to McGuffey until late 1834. McGuffey could be a bit childish, as he became more ambitious, and as a young professor, he did not fully appreciate the stress of administration. McGuffey, however, started his own experimental school at his home to work on his idea of a textbook for grammar schools. Family memories suggest that McGuffey had really started his

---

1 Robert H. Hollyday to his family, December 26, 1836, Miami University Archives, MSS Robert Hollyday
2 John W. Scott, Statement September 1, 1836 to Board of Trustees, Miami University Archives

textbook project when he was teaching at Paris, Kentucky. Folklore suggests he wrote out his stories on brown wrapping paper and passed them around to the students. McGuffey felt the texts such as the *New England Primer* did not apply to the frontier. Probably his ties with the "College of Teachers" helped his ideas about education to crystallize. The "College" had been early advocates of non-denominational common schools. Members such as Albert Pickett had already published a Western style Reader for schools. The "College" further advocated a Western text for Western students. It was not so much the Calvinistic theology but the lack of interesting stories that concerned McGuffey. McGuffey added numerous readings on nature and animals, which were of interest to the frontier child of the West. He also injected the mystery of exotic animals such as elephants, giraffes, and lions. Using logs as benches in his backyard, McGuffey held grammar school lessons in the early 1830s to test out his ideas.

His college teaching often drew mixed results. Most of the problem seemed to be related to his stern personality. He was totally devoid of humor in his classroom presentations. While an excellent preaching orator, his lecturing appeared very stiff, "speaking from his notes, as a rule, and marking off each topic as completed."[1] Discussions at the college level were somewhat limited compared to his grammar school approach of open discussion. Certainly the teaching of languages did not favor his style, and he was correct in wanting to teach a subject like moral philosophy, which lent itself to classroom discussion. Still, McGuffey also had a following of students that admired him. McGuffey loved to use the Socratic or rhetoric approach using questions and discussions versus pure lecture. The style was in contrast to the then "Sage on the Stage" approach that was in vogue. By 1835, President Bishop relented and allowed McGuffey to start teaching moral philosophy. His teaching of moral philosophy at Miami is where McGuffey would excel at Miami.

McGuffey's strong stand on student discipline did not help his standing with the student body, but there is evidence to suggest that things were getting out of control with President Bishop's liberal approach. Student drinking had clearly become an issue by 1834, particularly with the Southern students. The university had taken a strong stand on students' frequenting taverns in 1832, but both students and tavern owners ignored the rules. There were a number of taverns on High Street, which President Bishop had appealed to directly. The university trustees had even appealed to the state to outlaw liquor sales to no avail. McGuffey had always strongly opposed the use of liquor and the use by students was particularly gulling to him. It is no surprise that the first Reader that McGuffey was preparing at the time had two lessons dealing with the evils of whiskey. McGuffey continued to complain and grumble about the lack of dis-

---

1 Letter from M. Green to H. C. Minnich, Oxford, Ohio, November 1, 1932, Miami Digital Archives

cipline and control. By 1835, things appeared to take a turn to the worst. Some students were dismissed for drinking, and another student from South Carolina was charged with a shooting and stabbing in one of the college buildings. Several other groups of students were expelled for riotous behavior.

Professor John Scott and President Bishop considered the dismissal of the last group of riotous students too extreme. The problems and discipline became a political issue that played into the already divided faculty. The issue became a point of heated discussion at the faculty senate meeting. The last students to be dismissed were considered the college's "best" students. Bishop and Scott described the riotous behavior as a "trifling noise" outside the dorms. The faculty initially voted to dismiss the students, with President Bishop being a dissenting vote. A few days later some professors, probably under pressure from the administration, changed their vote. This, of course, only aggravated the split. President Bishop had most of the student body support and a majority of the townspeople. President Bishop, always the social progressive, pushed on, giving the students a bigger say in the running of the university. Further relaxing of regulations further angered McGuffey. McGuffey, on the other hand, had a majority support of the faculty and the support of the Presbyterian Church, which was dominated by "old school" supporters. Interestingly, McGuffey found support for college discipline throughout the geographical area.

McGuffey probably started his quest to compile a Reader in 1830, but he had been developing lessons for some years' prior. In 1829, McGuffey published a paper titled "Methods of Teaching Reading." This paper really was an outline and plan for his future work with his Readers. McGuffey had also made a study of all Spellers and Readers in use to prepare his 1829 treatise published in London. He was already preparing a manuscript for a Primer in 1831, incorporating his experiences and testing at his home experimental school. The publishing of the treatise in London was an obvious attempt to interest British publishers in a "Western" primer for America. The need for a Western primer and Reader had been a major topic at the "College of Teachers" as well. McGuffey seems to have started his First Reader simultaneously with his primer or shortly after, probably gaining interest from his 'College of Teachers" meetings. As we have seen, Albert Picket of the "College of Teachers" released his own Western Reader in 1833. Catharine Beecher had also published a book, *Suggestions on Education*, which was gaining popularity in the American West. Clearly, McGuffey's vision was a Western primer and Reader.

It may seem strange that the strict disciplinarian professor known as "Old Gruff" with his college students would be interested in elementary education. From all reports, McGuffey was much different around younger children. Friends and biographers all noted his love of children. He sympathized and empathized with the struggle of these young students to learn their lessons. While McGuffey loved the role of student, he personally often struggled with learning. He often developed his own little methods to help. He believed in the copying of texts and readings as a learning tool. He also was extremely fond of pictures and animal stories. McGuffey depended on his teachers to help him deal with the rigid "lessons" of his boyhood texts. The learning process itself became his passion as the years went on. He knew the need for a frontier text first hand.

McGuffey and his associates saw the then Western United States (Ohio, Kentucky, Michigan, Illinois, and Tennessee) as very different, requiring focused texts. McGuffey, who had taught grammar school in Eastern Ohio, Western Ohio, Pennsylvania, and Kentucky, was well aware of the shortcomings of primers and Readers in use. The *New England Primer* had several shortcomings for the West. First, the *New England Primer* was rigidly Calvinistic and Congregational throughout. The West was a growing mix of Presbyterians, Methodists, Lutherans, Catholics, German Separatists, God-believing non-church goers, and Quakers, which were far from Calvinists. Particularly, the West was experiencing a wave of Methodist conversions, which was a revolt against rigid Calvinism. Secondly, the use of non-standardized old English almost made the language foreign in the West. The *New England Primer* could not be used in common schools because of its purely sectarian structure, and common public schooling was a key goal in the West. Lastly and maybe most importantly, the *New England Primer* covered the span from beginner to then High School. This made it extremely difficult for the beginner, who in the West increasingly lacked home preparation. The *New England Primer*, other than its introduction to the alphabet, lacked any introductory reading exercises.

Other available Readers and primers of the early 1830s also offered little for Western grammar schools. *Murray's English Readers*, published in England, offered better introductory material, but still were written in "old English," which was more geared for the American East. The *Franklin Reader*, while having more introductory material, had all the limitations of *Murray's English Readers*. *Webster's Blue Back Speller*, while eliminating the sectarian concerns was a speller, not a text to teach reading. McGuffey and his associates had often discussed these shortcomings, and McGuffey tested his improvements at his experimental school. The market for textbook primers was huge. Schoolbook production in America was 750,000 in 1820, 1,100,000 in 1830, 2,000,000 in 1840 and 5,500,000 in 1850. It was estimated that six million *New England Primers* were sold from 1690 to 1830. The need for a Western Reader was big business as well with high profit margins. The growth of the West had schools cropping up around every village. The number of textbooks printed in Cincinnati during 1826 tells just how big the market was. Cincinnati printers produced 55,000 Spelling Books, 30,000 Primers, and another various texts of 20,000. McGuffey Reader within its first year would sell 500,000! Printers wanted a Western Reader as soon as they could get it. Publishers Truman and Smith were actively lobbying Ohio's "College of Teachers" for help. It was a lot of work for a college professor teaching a heavy load, but it had become a passion for McGuffey.

Albert Pickett, President of the "College of Teachers" and schoolmaster of a Cincinnati girl's school, had issued a Western style Reader in 1832. The *Pickett Reader* correctly reflected the Western student, but had other issues. The *Pickett Reader* never achieved the sales that had been predicted for a Western Reader. *Pickett's Reader* had several problems. First, it was focused on advanced Readers, which was a smaller market, and it competed with graded series of Readers. Many teachers saw it as a "girls" Reader. Finally Pickett's style and organization offered little new over competing Readers. Pickett, for example, stuck with the newer but still "Old English" of the *Worcester Reader*. It would take William McGuffey to adopt the Western preference for Websterian pronunciation. Similarly, James Hall of the "College of Teachers" produced a Western Reader. This *Western Reader* was a collaborative effort with eastern publishers and James Hall. The *Western Reader*, while published by Cincinnati publisher Corey and Fairbanks, had the same problems as the *Pickett Reader*.

Another core issue of these early Western Readers was topical. The environment of the Western frontier was much different than the east coast. The West was biblical and wild compared to the urban east. Harvey Minnich attributed a lot of McGuffey's unique success with his selection of topics. Minnich noted: "In analysis of thirty-three early readers, the topics occurring most frequently were: first, our ethics and morals; second, God; and third, death. Immortality, history, animals, Niagara Falls, education, slavery, and riches also played leading roles in every text." These were the topics that McGuffey had tested in his experimental school to fit the Western view.

McGuffey had started his Readers probably in 1833. He did have the help of a paid assistant for the project. Benjamin Chidlaw prepared the original copies of McGuffey into publishable material and was paid five dollars. McGuffey's brother, Alexander, also helped to edit and review the material. Other sections and lessons were also reviewed by members of the 'College of Teachers." The story is that while McGuffey was preparing his primer and Readers, he did not have a publisher until 1835. In 1834, a reorganized Cincinnati publishing firm of Truman and Smith offered him a contract for "a Western reader for Western children." The offer was first made to Catharine Beecher, but she suggested McGuffey. Catharine Beecher became a trusted advisor on the content of *McGuffey's Readers*. The firm of Truman and Smith had already had a textbook success with McGuffey's associate in the publication of *Introduction to Ray's Eclectic Arithmetic*. The contract was a poor one for McGuffey, but like any writer, he was more interested in getting in print. He was paid a royalty of ten percent on all copies up until ten thousand copies, after which nothing was paid and the Readers became the property of the firm. The *First Reader* sold for twelve and a half cents, and the *Second Reader* sold for twenty-five cents. Ten percent was a healthy margin, and McGuffey probably didn't envision selling much over ten thousand copies. Effectively, the contract capped McGuffey at one thousand dollars. There appears to have been an allowance for extra payments for revisions. McGuffey reached the cap rather quickly, but the firm of Wilson, Hinkle, and Company would, in later life, pay him a small annuity annually and often added Christmas gifts such as a barrel of hams. In any case, financial awards were secondary to the fame that McGuffey relished. McGuffey's *First* and *Second Readers* were published in 1836 followed by his *Primer*.

The feud between McGuffey and Bishop had started to strain the peace on the Oxford campus. It was unfortunate for Miami since both men were visionary and gifted. McGuffey could be considered a bit of an odd bird. His personality did not favor resolution or compromise. One critic said: "McGuffey utterly lacked the ability to get along with other people." Family biographer Alice McGuffey Ruggles described him as an "uncompromising logician, root-and-branch Calvinist, the sensitive Scottish temperament that never forgets and finds it difficult to forgive." Other sources confirm this view of McGuffey, but he did age well. McGuffey recruited another ally with the appointment of Albert T. Bledsoe as a professor of mathematics. Bledsoe was a Virginian and West Point graduate with a strong Southern belief in slavery and states' rights. Bledsoe immediately began siding with McGuffey. Needless to say, Bledsoe lasted only a year, but he did team up with McGuffey in a failed impeachment effort of Bishop. Bledsoe left for the University of Virginia where, some years later, he would be reunited with McGuffey. Interestingly, Albert T. Bledsoe would become assistant Secretary of War for the Confederacy and the confederate representative to England.

McGuffey had also been working on an end run with R. Schenk of the Board of Trustees. The Trustees were also effectively split over the issues between Bishop and McGuffey. Schenk was a trustee from Dayton with ties to his wife's family. Schenk talked him out of resigning with Bledsoe. McGuffey hoped to get an appointment to a vacant seat, but that effort failed also. McGuffey resigned a few months after Bledsoe as the last effort to overthrow President Bishop failed in 1836. McGuffey's failed effort meant the end of his career at Miami. Letters confirm that McGuffey had been looking at positions at other universities from 1834. McGuffey sensed that in 1834 the feud would lead to a dramatic end. He found several opportunities.

One of those opportunities was at Mississippi College in Clinton, Mississippi. In August of 1836, McGuffey received an offer for a professorship at Mississippi College with a salary of $2,500 and a rent-free brick home.[1] The large salary was

---

1 James Scully, "A Biography of William Holmes McGuffey," (dissertation, University of Cincinnati, 1967), p. 18

extremely tempting, but he was not keen on taking the family to the Deep South; and McGuffey went to Mississippi to look at the campus. He wrote his old mentor, Andrew Wylie, who was now President of Indiana University. Wylie not only advised against Mississippi but offered him a professorship in Greek at Indiana. He decided against the Mississippi position but remained hesitant to become a language professor. Finally, Daniel Drake offered him and talked him into the presidency at Cincinnati College.

Still, McGuffey did go to visit Mississippi College. He left with an offer from his friend, Daniel Drake, to take over as president of Cincinnati College with a salary of fifteen hundred dollars per year.[1] Actually, Drake had made the offer before the others but had to wait for confirmation from the Board on the salary. Drake offered McGuffey his choice of teaching professorships as well. Another part of the plan was a future of "Normal School for the Education of Teachers."[2] This possible "College of Education" would have been the first in the nation and would have been a perfect project for McGuffey. In fact, the College of Education never came to be until 1904. This possibility and his love of Cincinnati did move him to accept the Cincinnati position. It also afforded him the opportunity to stay close to his publisher and associates in the "College of Teachers."

Drake, like Robert Bishop, was a visionary. In the case of Daniel Drake, a Philadelphian, he envisioned Cincinnati becoming the "Philadelphia of the West." He had been drawn west with the Western enlightenment that had started in Lexington, Kentucky. In 1814, Drake had opened an experimental scientific college in Cincinnati known as the Cincinnati Lancastrian Seminary. The school had been modeled after the practices of British educator, Joseph Lancaster. One of these principles utilized older students to help teach. thus reducing the number of teachers needed. In 1819, Drake reorganized his school with the Medical College of Cincinnati. Drake modeled his new university after the first Western medical school at Transylvania College in 1810. In 1821, the university conferred a degree on future president, William Henry Harrison. By 1836, Drake's Cincinnati Medical School had graduated over two hundred fifty doctors. In 1836, Drake hoped to expand the role of Cincinnati College into one equal in excellence to Miami University. Drake had even attracted local investors to support his grand vision. Cincinnati College had achieved much fame in a short period, but in doing so had strained its financial resources. As president, McGuffey would be expected to lead this ambitious conversion and growth. Personally, McGuffey was attracted to Cincinnati because it was the center of the American educational enlightenment.

---

1 Letter from Daniel Drake to W. H. McGuffey, Oxford, Ohio, August 20, 1836, Miami University McGuffey Archives

2 Letter from Board of Trustees, Cincinnati College, to William McGuffey, August 20, 1836, Miami University McGuffey Archives

Chapter 7. College of Teachers

The McGuffey-Bishop feud sometimes gets a disproportional amount of historical review compared to McGuffey's work to form a public school system, and his membership in a major Western enlightenment group known as the "College of Teachers." A group of Cincinnati teachers and citizens formed a small group in 1830, which would be the DNA of the *McGuffey Readers*. The group had evolved from an earlier teacher association in Cincinnati known as "Western Literary Institute and Board of Education" and the "Western Literary Institute and College of Professional Teachers." Cincinnati had been the seed of the common schools in the 1820s. The Ohio Legislature had passed a law in 1825 that allowed for a half-mil property tax to be collected to pay for schools. Cincinnatian and state senator Nathan Guilford led that school funding bill. Cincinnati established a Board of Trustees and Visitors to oversee the Cincinnati district in 1829.

The Cincinnati area in the 1820s was replacing Lexington as the "Athens" of the West. Cincinnati's *Saturday Evening Chronicle* noted in 1828: "Need we name our two museums, both respectable-one the pride of the city; the Medical College of Ohio, preeminent in local advantages; our schools and academies, both numerous and respectable; the Academy of fine arts, yet in its incipient stage, but establishing on a firm basis; the circulating library, increasing in books and readers; the *Western Medical and Physical Journal*, a work of much promise with already 400 subscribers; and lastly the *Western Quarterly Review*." Cincinnati was rapidly becoming a Western center of culture. The nucleus of this effort led to the formation of the "College of Teachers."

McGuffey was part of this early group known as the "College of Teachers," which had evolved out of the Transylvania College enlightenment. The group was one of many intellectual bodies that formed in the Cincinnati area as part of the Western enlightenment. The group would fight for common schools, Western textbooks, the education of women, and professional teachers. The core of this group was located in the Cincinnati, but its members extended into Indiana, Kentucky, Illinois, Tennessee, and all of Ohio. Their annual meetings covered hundreds from the Western frontier. The "College of Teachers" also formed the following committees: Committee for Best Method of Introducing and Study of Anatomy; Committee on Effects on the Effects on the Progress and Character of the Learned Professions in the West; Committee for Promotion of Useful Information; Committee to Study the Subject of Emulation; Committee on Physical Education; and the Committee on the Influence of Sunday School on Common Schools,

Albert Pickett, who had been a pupil of Noah Webster, led the formation of the initial group with the help of Calvin Stowe of Cincinnati's Lane Theological Seminary. Albert Pickett would later develop a Reader and Speller of his own for his Cincinnati girls' school. The "College of Teachers," which formally became known as the College of Professional Teachers, spent time discussing the issues of teaching on the Western frontier as well as concerns about the role of religion in education. The association met monthly informally and held more formal annual meetings where the proceedings were published. Some of the group formed informal committees to work on specific issues. It was at these meetings that McGuffey met Joseph Ray of Cincinnati's Woodward College and future author of *Introduction to Ray's Eclectic Arithmetic* (1834). Alexander McGuffey was also a member of the group briefly. Alexander had graduated from Miami University at sixteen; and in 1836 joined the faculty of Woodward College, teaching English and ancient languages. Alexander continued his education at the Cincinnati Law School, graduating in 1839. Over the period, Alexander helped in the editing and review of McGuffey's early readers.

Edward D. Mansfield was a member of the "college" and friend of William McGuffey. McGuffey would be a fellow professor of Mansfield years later at Cincinnati College and would name his fifth child, Edward Mansfield, after him. Mansfield was a graduate of Princeton and an early settler in Cincinnati. Mansfield had been an earlier member of the "College of Teachers." Mansfield was a versatile writer, and his first effort in 1834 was a law text called *Political Grammar*. He published a number of biographies and histories as well as books on education such *American Education*. Mansfield was a friend and supporter of Daniel Drake's broader approach to education, and a man for all seasons. In *McGuffey's Fourth Reader*, he added two essays on the *"Value of Mathematics."* Later Mansfield would become a leader in the Whig and Republican parties. His influence had deep roots as he served as editor of the *Cincinnati Chronicle* from 1836 to 1848. He encouraged the writing of Harriet Beecher Stowe, being a motivator for the "College of Teachers."

Another early member was Daniel Drake (1785–1852) who had founded the Medical College of Ohio in Cincinnati in 1825 and had been a trustee at Miami University. Daniel Drake had come to the area first to join the Medical College of Transylvania University. Drake had studied under the famous Benjamin Rush, founder of the University of Pennsylvania. Drake's Medical College was the first in the West and would become part of the University of Cincinnati's Medical College. Drake was known in Ohio as the "Franklin of the West." Drake brought a new type of intellectualism to Cincinnati, taking intellectual discussions outside the church. Drake brought together Cincinnati's best minds in informal meetings at his home. Cincinnati's leading minister, Joshua Wilson, complained of one of these in his diary: "Spent evening at home with a group of friends, including Doc Drake, Rev. Osborne, Maj. Raffner — topic was commerce. I would be glad to hear more about the way to heaven than the way to be wealthy." By 1815, Daniel Drake owned a drugstore, which became famous as the first to offer soda water. Drake was active in many civic efforts, and as a trustee of the city, he was instrumental in the founding of a circulating library, a Western Museum, and the Lyceum. In 1815, he authored the book, *Picture of Cincinnati*, which acted as a type of "chamber of commerce" to bring immigrants to the city. The work was closer to Thomas Jefferson's *Notes on Virginia*. Drake's *Picture of Cincinnati* dealt with Cincinnati's topography, meteorology, botany, and diseases. He helped bring a branch of the United States Bank, which created an economic boom in the area. Later in his career, he became a director of the bank. Clearly, Drake exhibited the same intellectual capacity and breath of interest of a Benjamin Franklin.

Drake noted the problem with frontier education was: "lack of trained teachers, good books, and time."[1] Drake, in particular, was fascinated by the possible improvement in grammar school text, and he believed in standard approaches. Drake also believed in a non-denominational approach. Drake said the following of his early education: "I had learned to spell all the words in Dilworth, and a good portion of those in Noah Webster, Jr., whose spelling book then seemed to me a greater marvel than does his Quarto Dictionary, now lying before me." Drake would, in future years, be a contributor to the *McGuffey Readers* on the subject of free education. Daniel Drake was a follower of Benjamin Rush and his theory of free education and science based curriculum. Drake had briefly attended Benjamin Rush's College of Physicians of Philadelphia and used as a model for his Cincinnati medical college. The educational principles of Benjamin Rush became the core curriculum of the "College of Teachers" through the effort of Daniel Drake. The main courses Rush proposed were rhetoric, history, and science. Rush's vision for education was tied closely to his vision for America. Rush's educational approach included "all the means of promoting national prosperity and

---

1 Emanuel D. Rudolph, "Daniel Drake as a Nineteenth Century Educational Reformer," *Ohio Journal of Science*, Volume 4, 1985, pp 148-149

independence, whether they relate to improvements in agriculture, manufacture, or inland navigation." The "College of Teachers" formed a vision that attracted the best thinkers of the West. It was an organization that favored debate on both sides of all issues. The "College of Teachers" attracted diversity with a single vision of improved education in the West. The "College of Teachers" was far from a local organization; its members came not only from the West but from the East.

The first meetings deal with discussions for teaching improvements and the use of more standardized approaches. The group's constitution stated: "in order to promote the sacred interests of education so far as may be confided to their care, by collecting the distant members, advancing their mutual improvement and elevating the profession to its just, intellectual, and moral influence on the community, do hereby resolve ourselves into a permanent body . . . its objects shall be to promote, by every laudable means, the diffusion of knowledge in regard to education." The work of the group would soon become the passion of a young McGuffey. The biggest challenge facing the Western schools was various nationalities, but just as problematic was the lack of standardized spelling (even the alphabet varied). This involvement pulled McGuffey further away from his career as a language professor. Interestingly, McGuffey's brother Alexander married Elizabeth Drake, the daughter of Daniel Drake, in 1939.

Albert Pickett is considered the founder of the "College of Teachers," but Daniel Drake brought a type of inspiration to the organization. Another early partner of Pickett and Drake was Alexander Kinmont. Alexander Kinmont was a flamboyant Scotch scholar. Kinmont's knowledge was extensive, being a master in both the classics and mathematics. In 1827, Daniel Drake had originally offered him a professorship at Cincinnati College at $2,000, but he preferred to open his own academy in Cincinnati. Like Drake, Kinmont strongly believed in scientific education and education in the mechanical arts. Kinmont's Boys' Academy was also known as "the Academy of Classics and mathematics." Alexander Kinmont represented the true diversity of the "College of Teachers," being a member of the radical New Jerusalem Church. He believed in the patriarchal model of slavery and the "benevolent" institution of slavery. Alexander Kinmont became a passionate supporter of common schools in the "College of Teachers."

The initial mission of the "College of Teachers" was to promote common schools throughout the West. As seen, most of the immigrants to the early colonies believed in the need for schools beyond their European experience. Protestant immigrants, in particular, saw education as a necessity to promoting their faith as well as basic freedoms. In the 1600s and early 1700s churches were the center of education, particularly in New England. With its diversity, Pennsylvania preferred to move toward common state schools free to all. William Penn, Benjamin Franklin, and Benjamin Rush were the leaders of the common school movement. These men also saw education as the means to unity. Benjamin Rush said: "I conceive the education of our youth in this country to be peculiarly necessary in Pennsylvania, while our citizens are composed of many different kingdoms in Europe. Our school of learning, by producing one general and uniform system of education, will render the mass of people more homogenous, and thereby fit them more easily for uniform peaceable government." Daniel Drake was a student and apostle of Benjamin Rush. In the early 1830s, Pennsylvania, New York, Connecticut, and Massachusetts passed various bills to promote common schools.

The "College of Teachers" grew quickly in prestige and membership in the early 1830s. In 1832, Lyman Beecher and his daughter Catharine joined the group. Lyman Beecher, already America's most prominent preacher, had been persuaded to come to Lane Seminary from Boston. Lyman Beecher was a strict Calvinist and came to Cincinnati to convert the West. His daughter Catharine came with him. Catharine was an accomplished educator who had started the Hartford Female Academy in New England and opened the Western Female Institute upon her arrival in Cincinnati. Catharine was also an accomplished writer and poet as well as an accomplished writer. Catharine had published a book, *Suggestions on Education.* A few years later, another daughter of Lyman Beecher, Harriet, came to Cincinnati and joined the group. She would marry another member of the group, Professor Stowe of Lane Seminary. Harriett Beecher Stowe would become famous with the publication of *Uncle Tom's Cabin* in 1851.

The amazing diversity of the "College of Teachers" can be found in so many of the members such as Lyman Beecher. Lyman Beecher, as many in the "College of Teachers," held radical if not extreme views. Lyman Beecher had become popular with orthodox Christians by taking on the East Coast intellectually elite Unitarians, who controlled many of the universities. Unitarians, in particular, rejected the principles of Calvin. More problematic, at least in Cincinnati, was Lyman Beecher's near hatred of Roman Catholics. Lyman Beecher warned that Catholic immigration would cause the destruction of the West. In his book, *A Plea for the West*, Lyman argued: "The conflict which is to decide the destiny of the West will be a conflict of institutions for the education of her sons, for purposes of superstition, or evangelical light; of despotism or liberty." While popular with "Old School" Presbyterians, Lyman Beecher did not find majority support within the "College of Teachers." Even his family did not totally agree with his attack on Catholics.

It would be Catharine Beecher, however, that most impacted the "College of Teachers" and William McGuffey. She was an advocate for common schools and education. She would also function as McGuffey's editor for the first editions of the Eclectic Series. Catharine was also a contributor to many of the Readers. Catharine expressed the idea that common schools were fundamental to freedom, democracy, and republican institutions. In one of her essays, she expressed that belief: "The education of the common people, then, who are to be our legislators, jurymen, and judges, and to whom all our dearest interests are to be entrusted, this is the point around which the wisest heads, the warmest hearts, the most powerful energies should gather, for conservation, for planning, for unity of action, and for preserving enterprise." Catharine was also an important modifying factor in the "College of Teachers." She argued the inclusion of Catholics in mainstream society based on a simple application of the "Golden Rule." Catharine Beecher did have a few very controversial views such as that women should be the preferred teachers over men. Still, she did not believe in women suffrage, believing women were appointed to a "subordinate station."

The Beecher family brought a passion for the Temperance movement to the "College of Teachers." Both Lyman Beecher and his son Henry Ward Beecher were leaders in the early temperance movement of the 1820s. Temperance to the Beechers was part of the social gospel, which was fundamental to the Great Religious Awakening. In the 1820s, the temperance movement was concentrated in the Puritan New England States, and was being resisted in the predominately Scotch-Irish and German middle states. The Great Awakening of the 1820s and 1830s swept the middle states and with came the temperance movement. Liberal Presbyterians lost ground with the anti-drinking Methodists and Baptists. The Beecher family found an ally in William McGuffey in the "College of Teachers." In return, temperance became a prominent theme of the 1838 *McGuffey Readers*.

The Beecher family added to the movement of Western education. Scholar and Catholic Bishop, Archbishop Purcell also joined the group, giving a representative from the growing Catholic population in Cincinnati. Purcell was not alone in the "College of Teachers" with a concern about Catholics. James Hall had also pushed for a non-denominational approach that would include Catholics. The "Catholic Question" was one of heated debate in the Cincinnati, where German Catholics were pouring into the area. The Catholics were among the most hated of the new immigrants, but in Cincinnati they were over thirty-five percent of the population. Their support was needed to achieve common schools and education. To their credit, the 'College of Teachers" debated and argued their way to acceptance of Catholics, a view that McGuffey and the McGuffey Readers would reinforce. While the Catholics never fully came on board to common schools, they played a key role in their political support.

Archbishop Purcell's membership in the "College of Teachers" is testimony to the determination of the Catholics to achieve common schools. Archbishop Purcell's membership helped moderate hard line anti-Catholicism of men like Lyman Beecher. Common schools would be difficult without the support of the large catholic population in Cincinnati, and Purcell hoped to see Catholics included. Purcell, like Drake and McGuffey, was a big supporter of common schools in America. Archbishop Purcell was one of the first to visit the Beecher family school in 1833. Harriet Beecher reported the visit: "Bishop Purcell visited our school today and expressed himself as greatly pleased that we had opened such an one here. He spoke of my poor little geography lesson and thanked me for the unprejudiced manner in which I had handled the Catholic question in it. I was of course flattered that he should have known anything of the book."[1] The "Catholic question" related to anti-Catholic bias that existed. It should be noted that Lyman Beecher's daughters did not share his own anti-Catholic bias.

The huge Catholic population in Cincinnati made the "Catholic" question key to the vision of common schools. The "College of Teachers" even sponsored a debate against Protestant Alexander Campbell in Cincinnati. The "College of Teachers" had the debate printed and sold them for six cents each; and by 1833, 14,000 copies had been sold. While nothing was really resolved, the approach of common schools was modified to make it more acceptable to Catholics. In any case, the McGuffey Readers certainly helped reduce the bias against Catholics. The same goal of common schools was behind the push of the "College of Teachers" for the education of blacks as well. Furthermore, the growing Catholic population was a part of America's future, and the idea that the future leaders were in that one-room schoolhouse. Member of the "College," Samuel Lewis put it this way: "These children about your streets, some of whom cannot even speak your language, are to be your future sovereigns." It was a fundamental premise of the "College of Teachers" that no child is left out of the right to education.

For Daniel Drake, William McGuffey, and most of the "College Of Teachers," common schools were to be all inclusive in Ohio, and that would means blacks, Catholics, and Germans. The Germans were another roadblock in that they demanded German language had to be used. They also resented the use of Calvinistic materials and texts such as the *New England Primer*. In the eastern Pennsylvanian, Germans ("Pennsylvania Dutch") actually reworked the *New England Primer* using German and replacing the Calvin catechism with one of Martin Luther. This "revised" text was known as the "German ABC." In Pennsylvania, German sects such as Mennonites, Amish, and Dunkards had to be excluded from the Public School Act of Pennsylvania. For the "College of Teachers," such exclusions were counter-productive. McGuffey had experienced successful blending of education in smaller communities of Pennsylvania and the Western Reserve of Ohio. Success would depend on addressing the textbook issue head on.

Another roadblock to common schools and common textbooks, as proposed by the "College of Teachers," was the split between rural and urban views. The "College of Teachers" had a liberal view that evolved from the Cincinnati urban mix. Rural schools tended to not trust college-trained teachers. Of course, part of this was the split of the Presbyterians. Another part of it was that college trained teachers generally were graduates of eastern colleges. College trained teachers in

---

1 Anne Fields, *Life and Letters of Harriet Beecher Stowe* (Kessinger Publishing, 2004), p. 101

rural communities were considered too liberal and Unitarian. McGuffey's "Old School" Presbyterianism, however, did meet the rural requirements. The "College of Teachers" believed Western-college trained teachers would eliminate the prejudice.

The "College of Teachers" also had two influential Western editors in James Hall of *Western Monthly Magazine* and James Perkins of the *Annals of the West.* James Hall would also try his hand at a Reader in 1833 known as the *Western Reader.* James Hall had been a soldier, lawyer, poet, state treasurer, historian, editor, banker, and jurist. One biographer said of Hall, "Not only was he an elegant writer of prose, he is the author of some of the most beautiful lyrics in the English language." John Flanagan went even further in his biography of Hall, "few men had more to do with the early cultural development of the Middle West, with the artistic awakening of the region bounded on the east by the Alleghenies and on the west by the Mississippi."[1] James Hall was another strong advocate of a Western education, and in 1833 published his own *Western Reader*, which offered McGuffey many ideas for his own Reader for Western students. No such diverse literary and educational of equal existed in America. The *Western Monthly Review* and the *Western Monthly Magazine* became important literary outlets of the "College of Teachers," whose members included most of the area's poets, journalists, and authors. Besides the Beechers, there was Caroline Hentz, who ran a local grammar school and published several novels. Another novelist was Benjamin Drake, brother of Daniel, who was author of the *Life of Black Hawk.* Journalists included James Hall, who was known for defense of immigrant Catholics. Many of the journalist members were often themselves on opposing sides of issues such as abolition and immigration. This, however, was one of the strengths of the organization.

Thomas Grimke was from South Carolina and one of the Southern members of the "College of Teachers." Grimke, while one of the most distant members, was one of the most influential, and would later be featured in the *McGuffey Readers.* In an 1834 speech before the "College of Teachers," Grimke asked the group "are things the way they should be in education." He argued forcefully that there were many problems to be addressed. Grimke thought education at the time as not "American" and lacking religious conviction, an argument that by today's standards would be outrageous. Still, the "American" element was lacking in that what little literature studied was by foreign authors. In addition, most book illustrations were British. This, of course, was in total agreement with the views of Daniel Drake and William McGuffey. Grimke helped define the mission of the "College of Teachers" as an activist group. Grimke brought national leadership to the "College of Teachers." Like other members, Grimke supported reform

---

1 John Flanagan, *James Hall: Literary Pioneer of the Ohio Valley* (Minneapolis: The University of Minnesota, 1941)

in temperance, tariffs, and Sunday schools. Grimke believed in a state's right to have slavery, but his sisters Angelina and Sarah became two of America's most famous abolitionists.

Grimke acted as a senior diplomat and contributed to the body of knowledge in the "College of Teachers." His views at times could be extreme. He argued that the Bible should be part of common education, something that few in the "College of Teachers" totally agreed with, particularly Daniel Drake. However, Drake and Grimke found strong agreement on curriculum. Grimke wanted history, geography, and literature in the core curriculum. In addition, he agreed with Drake on the inclusion of a broad science curriculum including chemistry, botany, mathematics, mineralogy, and mechanical philosophy (engineering). Grimke, however, saw science as a special curriculum not to be included in the core curriculum, something that Daniel Drake did not agree with. In this respect, Grimke was the first advocate of engineering schools. Grimke went even further, believing that common school should give a student-one hour of mechanics, one hour of agricultural labor, and one hour of gardening. Grimke advocated activities that would lead to invention and technology.

Thomas Grimke was born in Charleston, South Carolina in 1786. He was a Yale educated Presbyterian, which gave him a unique perspective on the North-South slavery issue and economic issues. Grimke did give many in the "College of Teachers" a different political view. Grimke, like McGuffey, didn't believe in slavery but did believe in state rights. In the 1830s, however, the major issue between North and South was tariffs. The Southern cotton and tobacco growers opposed any tariffs on British goods, believing Britain would retaliate with tariffs on cotton and tobacco. The major portion of the South's cotton and tobacco went to Great Britain for processing. Furthermore, even the northeast representatives were torn between the textile manufacturers and the merchants, who favored free trade. The Transylvania area of Ohio, Kentucky, Indiana, and Pennsylvania strongly supported tariffs to increase industry, especially with the regional leadership of Henry Clay. Few people realized that both tariffs and slavery were leading to the ultimate divide. Grimke, being from South Carolina, knew the relationship well. Still, Grimke railed against his state when it suggested leaving the union over the issue of tariffs. On hearing Grimke, McGuffey pulled his support of tariffs because it was such a divisive issue. McGuffey and many in the "College of Teachers" with their tariff stand went against the strong regional support.

Grimke added much to the overall mission and body of knowledge of the "College of Teachers." The real strength of the "College of Teachers" was in its open discussion. The "College" encouraged open debate, often financially supporting public forms. These debates with men like Grimke helped forge a general belief. Grimke was influenced as well, becoming an apostle of teacher organizations and common schools in the South. There is no doubt Grimke influenced both William and Alexander McGuffey. The McGuffey brothers would include selections of Grimke in their first Readers.

In September of 1834, Thomas Grimke talked before the "College of Teachers" and then went on to Oxford to spend a week at Miami University. Grimke gave a speech called "The Natural and Moral Worlds" at Erodelphian Hall. One of the famous lines of the talk was: "The same God is the author of the invisible and visible worlds. The moral grandeur and beauty of the world are equally the products of his wisdom and goodness, with the fair, the sublime, the wonderful of the physical creation." Alexander and his brother were with Grimke during that week, and Alexander used the Erodelphians records to include the piece in his 1843 *Rhetorical Guide*. William used another essay of Grimke in his *Eclectic Fourth Reader*. Interestingly, after a week at Oxford, Grimke moved on to Columbus, Ohio where he died of cholera two weeks later.

One proactive member of the "College of Teachers" in the area of diverse curriculum was John D. Craig, who was a friend of Daniel Drake, James Hall, and Calvin Stone. Craig had a vision of technical training and education for engineers and technicians to support economic development. He founded the Ohio Mechanics' Institute in Cincinnati in 1828. His concept combined mechanics with a knowledge of the arts and humanities. Craig even envisioned a religious approach for mechanics to be headed up by the Reverend Robert Hamilton Bishop. In particular, he envisioned Sunday Schools for mechanics. Early classes were held at Daniel Drake's College Hall. Offerings at the institute included chemistry, geometry, mathematics, and engineering as well as religion and philosophy. The Ohio Institute became a motivator for industrial fairs and expositions, which Cincinnati became a leader in. Furthermore, John Craig promoted the addition of science to common schools.

The "College" represented a true galaxy of intellectuals in all fields. One of these was Alexander Campbell (1788–1866), who was an early leader in the "Second Great Awakening" religious movement. Campbell was a Scottish immigrant and initially a Presbyterian. Alexander Campbell, however, was concerned with the direction of Christianity on the Western frontier. This Western religious movement came out of Transylvania and promoted a more liberal Protestantism that favored the Methodists and Baptists. Campbell believed even religion in the area should reflect Western values. Campbell and Lyman Beecher came to share many ideas of the need for religious reform. Campbell found many allies in the "College of Teachers." He was featured in a number of debates by the "College of Teachers," the most famous being with Catholic Archbishop Purcell of Cincinnati on Catholic creed.

One of the most extreme members of the early "College of Teachers" was socialist James Dorsey, who was a follower of utopian socialist Robert Owen. James Dorsey served as a trustee of Miami University from 1809 to 1820. In 1816, he formed the society of the "Rational Brethren of Oxford" which wanted to turn Oxford Township into a "socialistic community." Dorsey often had Robert Owen as a speaker at Miami and the "College of Teachers." Robert Owen was the Scottish zealot that transformed the mill town of New Lanark in Scotland into a happy socialistic community and had started a similar community in New Harmony, Indiana. Owen argued against the structure of the Presbyterian Church as well as. Conservatives such as McGuffey had rejected Owen's beliefs.

Many of the "College of Teachers" were social reformers such as the Beecher family. Another social reformer was Sarah Peter of Cincinnati, who became an important inner circle member. Sarah Peter was the daughter of Ohio Governor Worthington. Sarah had a long history of working with the city's poor and founded the Cincinnati Orphan Asylum and several homes for poor women. She was also active in the development of Sunday schools. Sarah Peter supported common schools to address poverty, working with other members to form proposals to the Ohio legislature. She argued often to include Catholics in common schools and textbooks. Like most members in the "College," she was a self-activated individual with a broad array of interests including art and literature. She moved to Philadelphia where she opened the School of Design for Women in 1848, which is now known as the Moore College of Art and Design. Later in life, she joined the Catholic Church and served by helping the wounded on Civil War battlefields. In the 1870s, she traveled in Europe extensively, purchasing art for the Ladies' Academy of Fine Arts and the Art School of Cincinnati.

One the lesser-known members of the "College of Teachers" was Caroline Lee Hentz. She was born in Massachusetts but moved to the Cincinnati area in the 1830s to help her husband as a school superintendent. Hentz was a brilliant writer, but in the 1830s, she was running a girls school in Cincinnati. She was a state rights advocate and often challenged other members on slavery. Evidently, she would write the antithesis of Stowe's *Uncle Tom's Cabin*. Her novel, *The Planter's Northern Bride*, appeared at about the same time as Stowe's novel. Hentz's novel defended the Southern plantation owner for benevolence and care of the slaves. As one of the nation's earliest feminists, she argued slaves were better off than the "northern woman-worker" that society overlooked. At times she even defended the financial benefits of slavery. She certainly offered another extreme in the 'College of Teachers." Amazingly, but not unusual for the 'College of Teachers," she would become a personal friend of pro-abolitionist adversary Harriet Beecher. Certainly, this type of friendship allowed the debate of the most different issues in the "College of Teachers."

Daniel Drake became the lifeblood of the "College of Teachers" and created many subgroups that met daily and weekly. Initially, Daniel Drake held the meeting in his home's parlor. He was famous for his own brand of power breakfasts, bringing members together for informal breakfasts. The fare included his favorite baked apples with strong coffee. Maybe more important were his famous "Friday evenings." William McGuffey and his brother Alexander often attended these meetings in the 1830s, traveling thirty-three miles from Oxford. Drake did much at these meetings to promote the use of "Buckeye" for Ohioans. We have an excellent description of one of these "pioneer parties" from a later family biographer, Alice McGuffey Ruggles, granddaughter of Alexander and Elizabeth Drake McGuffey born in 1879.[1] The meetings were held at Cincinnati's "Buckeye Hall" at Drake's Cincinnati College. This particular evening the large parlor had a Buckeye in a stone jar. Buckeyes were scattered around the room. Buckeye branches were also placed in hollowed out pumpkins filled with earth. Another buckeye stump was used as a speaking podium. In a connecting room "buckeye" bowls were filled with popcorn and apples. There was another buckeye bowl with native wine. The table was adorned with native Ohio flowers. Other foods included venison jerky and corn bread.

The first formal presentation to the "College of Teachers" was titled "The Kind of Education Adapted to the West," which became a central theme of the organization. This theme certainly coincided with McGuffey's belief. The "College of Teachers" covered many topics and published its proceedings. Other published papers included such topics as "On Common Schools (Samuel Lewis)," "On the Qualifications of Teachers (E. Mansfield)," "Education of Emigrants (Calvin Stowe)," and "Reciprocal Duties of Teachers (William McGuffey)." These topics indicate that the group was on the cutting edge of education. The group did tackle the public issue of free schools, and members lobbied the Ohio Legislature. The group proved to be very diverse with liberal and conservative members. Daniel Drake presented a paper in 1834, "The Philosophy of Family, School, and College Discipline," which supported McGuffey belief in campus discipline.

The group was deeply religious but denominationally diverse. They were unified on the need for public schools, a Western textbook, teacher professional status, discipline, and female education. Politically, the group had a Whig bias and anti-slavery views but not abolitionist in the 1803s; even the Beechers were not yet abolitionists. It was the ideal form for McGuffey to test his ideas. There were also many arguments between "Old School" and "New School" Presbyterians. James Hall and William McGuffey represented the "Old School" while Lyman Beecher was "Old School" orthodox Presbyterian (at times reactionary). After a serious argument with Beecher, James Hall left for the Episcopalian Church, another testimony to the fair and balanced approach of the "College of Teachers" that Doctor Bishop and James Hall helped balance the battle of liberals and

---

1   Alice McGuffey Ruggles, *The Story of The McGuffey* (Cincinnati: American Book Company, 19500, pp. 178-180

conservatives in the Presbyterian Church. Of course, there was often debate on the "Catholic Question." These religious differences seemed to strengthen this group that loved intellectual debate. McGuffey avoided taking sides in the group on religious debates. In 1905, a writer noted the contribution of the "College of Teachers": "It accomplished much for a cause of supreme importance, and workers in educational fields in Ohio owe it a debt, which can be paid only in life-long gratitude, shown by handing on down the torch which these men lighted." If McGuffey had not been planning his Readers, this group would have inspired him to do so.

The group also was a testing ground for *McGuffey's Readers*, which McGuffey had started working on in the early 1830s. The "College of Teachers" was pushing for common public schools with Readers prepared for the West. Daniel Drake, who belonged to no church, fought hard to assure the group's charter forbid teaching any sectarian theology or dogma. William McGuffey, while a conservative Presbyterian minister, agreed that public education be sectarian free. This, of course, did not restrict McGuffey from freely using Christian and biblical references, which would be totally acceptable and even expected at the time. The highly Christian but non-denominational approach would be the model for all of *McGuffey's Readers*.

The "College of Teachers" played a pioneering role in the advance of education in America. Albert Picket, Samuel Lewis, and Calvin Stowe headed up an effort to set up public education in Ohio. Calvin Stowe went to Europe to study educational systems, particularly those of Prussia. The "College of Teachers" fought hard from 1834 to 1837 for state regulations for public schools. McGuffey would often be one of the group to make presentations to the state legislature. In 1837, Ohio passed a law providing for state and local school superintendents. Samuel Lewis became the first Ohio School superintendent in 1838. At time there were eight thousand schools with 490,000 students. Lewis started a complete survey of Ohio schools. In addition, a state school fund was setup and conditions such as a minimum of three-month terms was defined. The state allotted fourteen cents per student or about twenty-five dollars per student in today's money, for a total of $65,000 ($1.2 million today). Lewis's survey showed an additional $200,000 ($3.7 million) needed as well as five thousand additional teachers would be needed. Lewis suggested a tax on alcohol for the additional funds, but the legislature failed to act; however, districts were given the authority to raise money for schools. Lewis also advanced the profession of teaching with the state published journal – *The Ohio Common School Director*. Lewis resigned in 1839 but continued his role in the temperance movement, abolition, and the "College of Teachers."

The "College of Teachers," was by most standards, an activist group. They realized that torch light parades and riots would not change the balance of political power in moral issues but would only reinforce the status quo. Education of the

youth could, however, change the balance. The problem, of course, is an educational revolution is thirty to fifty years out. Still, education could make dynamic
shifts in public opinion. In the long run, it was not the abolitionist movement of
the 1830s that ended slavery, but the moral education of decades that changed attitudes towards slavery. In many ways the "College of Teachers" offered a model
for long-term change. For the "College of Teachers," the idea was simple; if you
wanted moral behavior in society, then you needed moral education. The impact
is not immediate but the result is decisive.

The mission and legacy of the "College of Teachers" was the formation of
common schools. It represented a rare example of intellectual compromise. Even
McGuffey's philosophical base, the "Old School" Presbyterians favored having
their own schools. Catholics, of course, wanted their own schools and feared the
Protestantism of the common schools. Lutherans opposed the perceived Calvin
bias in common schools, and both German Catholics and Lutherans wanted lessons in German. Orthodox reactionary Christians, like Lyman Beecher, wanted
to ban Catholics from common schools. McGuffey, Catharine Beecher, Daniel
Drake, and Samuel Lewis represented middle ground, but compromise was
needed. Some issues such as Catholicism were hammered out in debates and sit-
downs. A Sunday School Movement helped ease the concern of many of hard line
Christians.

The "College of Teachers" had been a big reason why McGuffey took the presidency of Cincinnati College. The Cincinnati job allowed McGuffey to become
more active in the organization. In fact, Daniel Drake had made Cincinnati College its home base. Many were calling Cincinnati, the "Philadelphia of the West,"
which Drake was fond of using. The daily meetings with Drake alone would have
been motivational for McGuffey. These were men and women promoting a new
direction for education, and his position at Cincinnati would free him from the
drudgery of teaching dead languages. McGuffey could now get involved on an
almost daily basis. This professional interaction with associates had been lacking
at Miami. Cincinnati was a true magnet at the time for Transylvania scholars and
intellectuals.

CHAPTER 8. CINCINNATI

"The prime purpose of education is making of a man, and it is impossible to make a man without giving him the purpose of being a man."
— *Bishop Fulton Sheen*

In 1836, Cincinnati was Ohio's largest city with over 30,000 people. The State of Ohio had a population of over one million. The tri state area of Transylvania (Ohio, Kentucky, and Indiana) had over three million. Cincinnati had a good blend of manufacturing, shipping, art, and trades. At the time it was known as "Porkopolis" because of its dominant business, hog slaughtering. Cincinnati had over fifty slaughterhouses. Its large German population made the city a beer-brewing center as well. Cincinnati was also blessed with heavy industry in 1836, having five steam engine manufacturers, three steamboat manufacturers, several iron foundries, and cotton-gin makers. It was also the literary center for the West as well as the publishing center of the West. In 1826, Cincinnati publishers had turned out 61,000 almanacs, 55,000 spelling books, and 30,000 primers. Cincinnati had one of the nation's best public school systems with about fifty schools operating in 1836. It was the center of the political movement for tax-supported public schools. A tax of two mills was levied in Cincinnati. The city had tax-supported school districts, and its teachers averaged $300 a year salary with a range from $200 to $500 a year. Many of the Cincinnati schools were solid two-story brick buildings, allowing for graded classes.

Cincinnati was a challenging environment for common schools and text-books. Its foreign born population was near fifty percent. Nearly a quarter of the population was German, and about fifteen percent were Irish Catholics. The Germans clustered into their own neighborhoods, as did the Irish. The Germans demanded that the German language be taught and used in common schools. The Irish Catholics had been coming since the canal building decade of the 1820s. The Catholics resented the Irish bias in the common schools. Catholics were rapidly becoming a local political factor in the expansion of common schools. In addition, Cincinnati had one of the largest concentrations of free blacks. Blacks represented from five to ten percent of the population and were isolated in ghettoes. These challenges actually helped the "College of Teachers" and McGuffey forge a non-denominational approach to common schools. Finally, Cincinnati College was challenging Transylvania to become the "Harvard of the West."

Just prior to McGuffey coming to Cincinnati, Daniel Drake had reorganized his medical college into a university. There was a medical department with eight professors, a law department with three professors, and an arts department with seven professors. Besides McGuffey, Drake had attracted some prominent professors such as O. M. Mitchell in mathematics and astronomy and Edward Mansfield in Constitutional Law and History. The reorganization of Cincinnati College would have been a challenge for even a seasoned administrator, which McGuffey was not. The Medical school was solid with a large student body, but the law and arts were overextended for a start up institution. Neither Drake nor McGuffey had the fund raising or financial expertise needed. One historian noted Cincinnati College "was endowed with genius and nothing else." Still, on a personal level, it was a great move for McGuffey, although his wife was hesitant. McGuffey was now closer to the "College of Teachers," the enlightenment movement, and the Beecher family.

Cincinnati College had many big name visionary professors. Ormsby MacKnight Mitchell, in particular, was one of those professors. Mitchell had been trained in mathematics and astronomy at West Point. He came to Cincinnati College in 1832 with much praise, and later in 1836 founded a boys' school — "Institute of Science and Languages." Mitchell hoped to make astronomy part of the enlightenment sweeping the West. Mitchell was able to build a small observatory and created much interest in the city of Cincinnati. In 1843, former president John Quincy Adams came to Cincinnati to dedicate the observatory. The Cincinnati Observatory expanded and became the most prominent in the West. Mitchell also became popular with the intellectual societies in the city and the "College of Teachers." The college also brought in a pioneer geologist, Dr. John Locke. Dr. John Locke had started Locke's Female Academy in 1823. This academy was highly experimental, applying the principles of Pestalozzi. Besides legal genius Ed Mansfield, Cincinnati recruited Timothy Walker, a graduate of Harvard. In 1837, Walker wrote one of America's first legal textbooks in *Introduction to American Law*. McGuffey was truly among scholars at Cincinnati College.

The "Academical Department" had been part of the reorganization and proved to be quite novel for the times. The scope of education proposed by Drake at Cincinnati was unequaled in the United States. The department not only expanded the science courses at the university but applied engineering and mechanics, making it one of the earliest engineering departments in the United States. Drake had envisioned a college for each of the professions: law, medicine, engineering, and education. Professor Mitchell actually taught engineering, science, mathematics, and French. Professor Charles Davies of the United States Military Academy was hired to teach astronomy. McGuffey had a great deal of autonomy, lecturing on a variety of topics such as "School Examinations," "Ethics in Education," "Common Schools," and "Malthusian Theory." He continued to be active in Temperance movements, preaching, and the "College of Teachers." McGuffey had more intellectual freedom than ever before. Longer range Drake hoped to branch off the "Academical Department" into a college dedicated to the science of teaching.

The timing for McGuffey proved to be extremely poor, however, as a financial panic was sweeping the nation. The Panic of 1837 started with the failures of banks and quickly moved to the manufacturing segments. The Panic got worse as President Andrew Jackson eliminated the national bank system that had supplied capital to the growth of cities such as Cincinnati. Cities such as Cincinnati were hit extremely hard. Cincinnati College investors and donators pulled back in the middle of planned growth. Still, as today, economic recessions often increase college applicants. Drake had oversold the college, and students arrived only to find the college lacking facilities to support them. McGuffey lacked the administrative ability to fully adjust to the mounting problems. He was in the midst of finishing up his four Readers in 1837, and work was continuing on the *Primer* and *Speller* (the *Speller* was issued under Alexander McGuffey's name in 1837). In late 1837, he had taken the presidency. The full effects of the panic did not hit until early 1839, which gave McGuffey a false sense of security as the large class of 1837 suggested an immediate success.

Personally, the McGuffey family had enjoyed the beauty of the Oxford campus and a short walk to classes. Oxford was truly an "Athens" in the forest. It was the idyllic college town. The beautiful McGuffey home on the edge of campus was a college professor's Eden. It was a great place for the McGuffey children to play and learn in safety. Cincinnati, however, was a growing city with lots of urban problems. Cincinnati had already been the first American city to experience racial riots. It was dirty and smelly with wild hogs roaming the street. The McGuffey family moved into a smaller rented home on Central Avenue. It was, however, Mrs. McGuffey who missed her Oxford home the most.

The split of the Miami faculty and McGuffey coming to Cincinnati opened up an old struggle between Oxford and Cincinnati. The intellectuals of Cincinnati had always resented the placement of a state university thirty-five miles away. The fight had never ended. In 1822, as Miami University floundered, Cincinnati politicians introduced a bill in the Ohio legislature to bring Miami to Cincinnati.

The battle and eventual vote were close, but Miami stayed at Oxford. Bishop's appointment as president had helped turn the university around, but the faculty division in the mid-1830s appeared to offer more opportunity for Cincinnati politicians. The effort never came to anything, but the rivalry continued. McGuffey was criticized for his newfound support for the Cincinnati point of view, but this could only be expected for the president of the college. The renewed effort to move Miami was also based on the deep need for funds as well. The deepening Panic of 1837 had stopped investment and banking throughout the nation.

The Panic limited Drake's hopes for expansion of the college. The strain on McGuffey grew as the last years of the decade pulled in many directions. His first textbooks appeared, and he had to personally be part of the sales effort. He and Drake were in the middle of the state's great debate over the establishment and funding of public schools. Finally, the split within the Presbyterian Church in the area continued to widen. Abolitionists were putting pressure on all parts of Cincinnati society and much of Ohio's. McGuffey was actively revising his *Readers*, *Primer*, and *Speller* through the end of the decade. He tried to steer clear of controversy, and his relations with President Bishop of Miami University actually improved during the period. McGuffey probably found a better appreciation for the problems of a college administrator. Bishop also led an effort for peace inside the Presbyterian Church, even extending a hand to McGuffey.

McGuffey had been the pastor at the Darrtown Presbyterian Church for five years but had to resign when he came to Cincinnati. He joined Cincinnati's Second Presbyterian Church of Lyman Beecher. Beecher also headed up Lane Theological Seminary. He was considered an orthodox moderate, but members of Cincinnati First Presbyterian saw him as a dangerous radical. Reverend Asa Mahan of Lane Theological Seminary was a radical. Pastor Joshua Wilson brought heresy charges in the church against both "radicals." McGuffey was torn between his conservatism and his friends' projects; he wisely avoided entering the battle. The Presbyterians were also losing members to the Methodists, which supported a more liberal philosophy, free will, and abolition. By 1850, Methodist Church was the largest Christian denomination in the United States, and by 1855, Methodists and Baptists made up seventy percent of all American Protestants (ninety percent of Black American Protestants).[1] McGuffey also appeared to moderate a bit as well because of his friends in the Beecher family and his relationship with Daniel Drake. This "liberalization" might explain his more moderate views of Calvinism that appear in his *Readers*. Certainly, McGuffey at least chose to ignore a strict interpretation of Calvinistic predestination. McGuffey also learned through these various relationships to avoid dogma conflicts. This middle of the road approach served McGuffey well in the enlightenment and church. Another concern was the growing popularity of the Methodists, who believed in free will.

---

1 Carl Richard, *The Battle for the American Mind* (New York: Rowman & Littlefield, 2004)

McGuffey realized a common school book would have to avoid rigid Calvinism. Furthermore, McGuffey made a decision to stay out of any public fights over dogma with the Readers now being sold as "non-denominational."

Besides religion, there was a growing public debate over abolition. Cincinnati and Cincinnati College had problems similar to those McGuffey had experienced at Miami. The abolitionist movement was sweeping all facets of McGuffey's life — Cincinnati College, Cincinnati, the Church, and the "College of Teachers." The Beechers were moving closer to the abolitionist movement as well as the 'College of Teachers," and the Presbyterian Church had split between North and South for all practical purposes. At the core, all of these factions saw slavery as morally wrong but differed on how to approach its elimination. McGuffey clearly learned much from these polarizing debates. McGuffey the minister went back to basics in his biblical Sunday night lectures at Cincinnati. Still, his three years at Cincinnati helped reinforce McGuffey's commitment to non-sectarian education. Daniel Drake, who belonged to no church, had the college's charter specify that no sectarian theology would be taught.

McGuffey's middle-of-the-road and non-sectarian approach was connected to and interrelated with his participation in the "College of Teachers." The "College of Teachers'" primary goal in the 1830s was the establishment of common public schools. This would require a non-sectarian textbook. Even more importantly, it would have to be apolitical. Finally, the focus was on Western schools versus Eastern schools, so the primers and Readers would have to reflect this region. The East felt comfortable with the rigid Calvinism of the *New England Primer*. In the East, Presbyterians and Puritan Congregationalists found common ground in Calvinism. The West, particularly Cincinnati, Kentucky, and Indiana, was much different. The West had many freewill Methodists, Quakers, and German Lutherans. *McGuffey's Readers*, while God and religion based, achieved acceptable neutrality. His genius was to focus on morals, which were acceptable to different sects and political views. It appears, to a large degree, he maintained similar neutrality in his personal life as well. The strong Christian bias had not been much of a problem in the 1800s.

McGuffey found much difficulty in the early 1830s, maneuvering between the liberal and conservative movements. The real struggle centered on rigid Calvinism and slavery. McGuffey personally was a rigid conservative, although he was not a rigid Calvinist. Most of McGuffey's friends in the 'College of Teachers," such as the Beechers and Daniel Drake, were liberals. When McGuffey left Miami, even his opponent Robert Bishop started to move towards the center to end the split. Bishop wrote in 1838: "Malice and guile and hypocrisy and evil speaking are the great heresies. They are to found among both the old and new school men — and they have produced and cherished all our other difficulties and evils." Certainly,

McGuffey in 1838 was starting to move to the same position. While the split in the Church was starting to heal, slavery was becoming the new dividing issue.

Politically, McGuffey and the "College of Teachers" struggled to find a home. They clearly were anti-Jacksonian, seeing his policies as breaking down traditional structures. The anti-Jacksonians formed the Whig Party in the 1830s, but it was not a perfect fit for all. The initial platform of the Whig Party was to oppose the economic policies of Andrew Jackson. In Cincinnati, William Harrison of nearby North Bend was a popular Whig along with Henry Clay of Kentucky. In 1836, Harrison carried Ohio and Cincinnati in a losing effort to President Van Buren. In 1840, the Whig Harrison carried Ohio and the nation. McGuffey certainly was always more comfortable with the conservatives of the Whigs. McGuffey personally held Whig Daniel Webster of New England in very high regard, and Webster's speeches and writings were popular in his later readers. But McGuffey was issue oriented versus party.

The slave issue had precipitated riots in the Cincinnati in the 1820s. The area was moving rapidly to anti-slavery positions and abolition. The majority of the population in the area opposed slavery on a moral basis, but the argument centered on how the nation as a whole should approach it. In 1833, Western campuses took out the issue. Early on, Miami had been a hotbed of student activism, but in 1833 the radical movement came to Lane Theological Seminary and Cincinnati College. While men like Bishop had moderated on Calvinism, they became more radical on the need for the elimination of slavery. Lane Seminary became a radical center, calling for immediate emancipation of the slaves. Efforts of Lane's trustees to stop the radicalism failed. Amazingly, Henry Beecher was then President of Lane, and while he was solidly antislavery, he was not yet committed to abolition. Many historians consider these Lane meetings to have been a key event. Historian Francis Weisenburger said: "These meetings were of tremendous importance in the development of events that were to lead to the Civil War, for they marked a turning point in the transition from mild antislavery proposals to an aggressive abolitionism."[1] Finally, they enforced a prohibition on "inflammatory" subject. The result was the loss of three-fourths of the student body, which left to become the first class of Ohio's Oberlin College. Bishop, clearly an abolitionist, favored if not encouraged similar discussions at Miami. McGuffey, while not connected to Lane, was certainly sympathetic to the administration's stand.

Miami University continued to be an antislavery campus. The campus distributed and supported the antislavery newspaper, the *Philanthropist.* President Bishop was of course supportive, but the departure of prominent professors was trying the Board of trustees. Furthermore, Miami had very strong financial support from the south and about twenty percent of the student body was Southern.

---

1   Francis Weisenburger, *The Passing of the Frontier 1825-1850* (Columbus: Ohio Historical Society, 1941), p. 368

Miami's Board of trustees enacted a rule to prohibit any discussion of slavery and sectional topics. Bishop persisted not only at the university but also at the local Presbyterian Church. In 1840, the strain between the administration and the Board reached a head. Bishop resigned as president and was reduced to a professor with a below average pay of $750 per year ($800 was average). As an ally of Bishop's, Professor Scott resigned as well. An old school pro-slavery president, George Junkin was brought in from Lafayette College. One of Junkin's daughters would marry General "Stonewall" Jackson. Junkin's tenure would not be much better then Bishop's. The student body was squarely opposed to the political views of Junkin. A strict Presbyterian, President Junkin caused an uproar in denouncing the Methodist's theology of free will. Methodist students and friends left the university, causing a major decline in enrollment. In 1844, Junkin resigned and was replaced by abolitionist Erasmus McMaster.

The antislavery spirit continued to grow in the border city of Cincinnati. Cincinnati became the birthplace of the Liberty Party, which represented abolitionists. James Birney, the editor of *Philanthropist*, was the Liberty Party's presidential candidate in 1840. While the Liberty Party was never very successful, it did develop into an antislavery wing of the Whig Party. Cincinnati College and the City of Cincinnati, while antislavery, opposed the radical abolitionists. At Cincinnati, McGuffey tried to avoid the hiring of abolitionists. Cincinnati was in the middle of the new abolition wave sweeping Ohio and the West. Cincinnati remained a divided entity, but there were really four camps. First was the pro-Southern camp, which favored slavery. Second was the state-rights group that disliked slavery morally but could tolerate its existence in the Southern states. This second group, which McGuffey belonged to, hoped that moral education would evidently eliminate slavery. Third was the anti-slavery group that opposed slavery but not to the point of war or secession. Many of McGuffey's associates in the 1830s belonged to this group such as the Beechers. This third group was also the heart of the Colonization Society to relocate Negroes. Lastly, there were the radical abolitionists calling for immediate action (even war) to eliminate slavery. Many Methodists joined the early abolitionists, as did "New School" Presbyterians. As the 1850s approached, all these groups shifted to more radical antislavery stands. The groups were tearing Cincinnati and the nation into two divisions.

The period at Cincinnati College was an extremely busy one for McGuffey. He was president of a struggling college, finishing his *Third* and *Fourth Readers* and working with the state for the establishment of public schools. In addition, his *First* and *Second Readers* were involved in a copyright lawsuit with the publishers of the *Worchester Primer*. The *Third* and *Fourth Readers* were aimed at what today are considered high school. These Readers drew heavily on biblical readings as well as his "College of Teachers" friends such as Daniel Drake, Lyman Beecher, Catharine Beecher, and Edward Mansfield. A year later in 1838, McGuffey published new revisions. McGuffey's lectures and Sunday Bible studies were extremely popular with the students and townspeople. The McGuffey Readers quickly took over the Cincinnati school system with his large network from the "College of Teachers." By 1841, the *First Reader* had sold over 700,000. His biggest struggle, however, would be the charges of plagiarism.

Samuel Worcester published the *Worcester Primer* in 1826. A few years later the *Worcester Readers* were introduced. The *Worcester Readers* had a short life, passing out of existence by the 1850s. However, Worcester filed for infringement of copyright in 1838, even before the *McGuffey Readers* were released. There was some crossover of commonly available material and the styles were similar. However, this is not surprising since the American Reader was evolved, not born. There were key differences: the *McGuffey Readers* used Webster pronunciation and orthoepy, while the Worcester adhered to British standards that were popular in New England. Still, the controversy had legs, and some Eastern academics hinted at possible plagiarism. Critics to this day still claim the possibility of plagiarism, but the use of common material among Readers was a normal practice. In addition, copyrights laws were loosely enforced and lacked the specificity of today. Samuel Worcester did not originally own many of the acknowledged plagiarized stories. In fact the lesson *"Punctuality and Punctuation"* was credited to Worcester in McGuffey's Readers, demonstrating more honesty than most during the period. Catharine Beecher came to McGuffey's defense, saying that, as editor, some general stories were selected from more than two possibilities.

There is good evidence that the controversy was a battle between Eastern and Western publishers, which even the harshest critics concede has an element of truth. Samuel Worcester had just launched a huge sales effort in the West as the 1837 McGuffey series hit the market. The Western textbook market was the major growth market in the publishing business. McGuffey was able to make the changes necessary prior to publication to void the controversy, but the publisher settled with Worcester for $2,000 versus the original $30,000. In retrospect, the question of plagiarism has little basis. The evolution of Readers from 1690 represented a confluence of similar streams of thought over 150 years. In addition, McGuffey's efforts represented a long and detailed history involving preeminent writers and teachers.

Winthrop Smith even used the opportunity to sell more books to the West by framing the debate as West versus East. In the quickly improved 1838 revision, the case is made in the preface: "The public never choose schoolbooks to please compliers. That public, then, is the tribunal to which appeals of the character ought to be made. True we might appeal to that spirit of the west, which loves to foster home talent, and home effort, and bid it uphold a choice deliberately made, and deliberately sustained." Using his sales force, Smith won the battle of the

West, but the *McGuffey Readers* never fully penetrated the New England market. The West, of course, was the much larger prize.

McGuffey's *First and Second Readers* that were released while he was at Cincinnati reflected McGuffey's personal beliefs to that point. The *First Reader* had forty-five lessons. Besides the simple beginning readings lessons about dogs and cats, McGuffey introduced many moral lessons. By the fourth lesson, McGuffey introduces God with: "It is God, my child; He makes the sun to shine, and sends the rain upon the earth, that we may have food." In lesson eleven he introduces the Bible with: "You must mind what the Bible says, for it is God's book." He persuades children not to lie, steal, and to obey their parents. Two of the lessons warned these young students of the evil of whiskey, which was very consistent with his Covenanter roots. Whiskey had also been at the root of many of his discipline problems at Miami. Three of the lessons focused on the need to give to and help the poor. There was not even a hint of theological dogma or political leanings, but Christianity was established as supreme in lesson twenty with: "He sent His Son to show you His will, and to die for your sake." McGuffey's efforts demonstrated his belief in moral education as the real agent of change and were consistent with the views of the "College of Teachers."

The *First Reader* was titled *The Eclectic First Reader for Young Children With Pictures.* The publisher who had titled Joseph Ray's book in 1834, *The Introduction to Ray's Eclectic Arithmetic*, probably selected this title as well. The word "eclectic" was an excellent choice in many ways. The Merriam-Webster definition is: "selecting what appears to be the best in various doctrines, methods, or styles." Interestingly, the word "eclectic" is from the Greek *eklegein*, meaning to select. At the time, the meaning of eclectic met drawing from a number of sources and had been in use since the late 1600s. In origin, it came from an approach of Greek philosophers that created an approach by selecting from existing philosophical beliefs. Some attribute the use of the term eclectic to the French philosophy of eclecticism and its founder Victor Cousin. This view created a philosophy based on the best of many philosophies. In any case, the term eclectic had become in vogue in many intellectual circles in the 1830s. It is Winthrop Smith, the editor, manager of Truman & Smith Publishing, and owner of the McGuffey series who gets credit for the selection of the term "eclectic" for the series. The selection of eclectic was one of many brilliant marketing ploys of Smith.

Smith used the exotic nature of the term eclectic. One researcher noted: "take the word 'eclectic' on the cover of so many millions of his Readers: eclectic was a magic word whose judicious mixture of mystery and meaning served to captivate local school boards. It is understood (if at all) as 'taking the best of all theories' — sound doctrine, or so it appeared, to an age little concerned with the fine points of philosophy."[1] In an 1838 advertisement in the *Third Reader*, Smith defined the "Eclectic System of Instruction" that: "now predominates in Prussia, Germany, and Switzerland. It is in these countries that the subject of education has been deemed of paramount importance. The art of teaching, particularly, has been most ably and minutely investigated. The Eclectic System aims at embodying all the valuable principles of previous systems, without adhering slavishly to the dictates of any master or the views of any party. It rejects the undue predilection for the mere expansion of mind to the neglect of positive knowledge and practical application."

The *Third* and *Fourth Readers* came out in 1838 and were more typical of McGuffey's rhetorical style. These Readers consisted of stories followed by discussion questions. Errors of pronunciation were also addressed in a note section. The *Third* and *Fourth Readers* targeted the equivalent of today's sixth to eight graders. These two Readers had stories, compositions, and poetry. Catharine Beecher, however, probably selected poetry since McGuffey did not fully embrace the literature of poetry. The poetry was mainly from British poets in these early additions. The *Fourth Reader*, in particular, has many biblical based stories and poetry. The *Third* and *Fourth Reader* were much larger books than the first two in the series. The *Third Reader* sold for 38 cents and the *Fourth Reader* sold for 75 cents each. Because of the lack of American woodcut print, the first editions of the *Third* and *Fourth Readers* had few illustrations. For example, the *Third Reader* had only three pictures. One criticism of the *Third Reader* was a lesson titled "Character of Martin Luther." This lesson was objected to by Catholics and would be dropped in later editions.

The *Fourth Reader* brought some minor criticism even within his "College of Teachers." The debate had started in the "College of Teachers" about overdoing direct Bible text. Many preferred a more subtle approach such as the references to the "Golden Rule." The *Fourth Reader* might have gone too far in that twenty-nine out of sixty-nine lessons (forty-three percent) were religious versus eleven out of forty-seven (twenty-three percent) in the *Third Reader*. The *Fourth Reader* appeared in the middle of the campaign by the "College of Teachers" for common schools in Ohio. There was a preference for the moral based or "Golden Rule" approach versus the highly biblical approach of the *New England Primer*. In the preface, McGuffey justified his use of biblical text with: "In a Christian country that man is to be pitied who at this day can honestly object to imbuing the minds of the youth with the language and spirit of the word of God." McGuffey went further stating: "The Christian religion is the religion of our country. From it are derived our nation, on the character of God, on the great moral Governor of the universe. On its doctrines are founded the peculiarities of our free institutions. From no

---

1   D. A. Saunders, "Social Ideas in McGuffey Readers," *The Public Opinion Quarterly*, Vol. 5, No. 4, Winter, 1941

source has the author drawn more conspicuously than from the sacred scriptures. For all these extracts from the Bible, I make no apology." Future editors, however, would tone down the religious and biblical references over the years. It may, on the other hand, explain the popularity today of the original McGuffey editions with Christian home schoolers.

During McGuffey's tenure at Cincinnati College, he was actively working with Catharine Beecher as editor on the *Third* and *Fourth Readers*. Alexander McGuffey was still reading the material first and doing text checking, but Catharine was making suggestions on the material content. There is also some evidence that McGuffey's wife helped in the initial review of materials. Catharine Beecher's impact might well have been critical in moderating McGuffey's Calvinism and belief in predestination. Catharine was not her father's daughter in religious views. She had early in life been engaged to a brilliant mathematician at Yale University, Alexander Fisher. Fisher died on a European Atlantic crossing, and Lyman Beecher refused to declare he was in heaven because of his weak faith. She had also stood in stark contrast against the anti-Catholic views of her father. Catharine revolted against the Calvinist dogma and entered the more moderate Christian movements of the West. In her book, *Suggestions on Education,* she took the stand to keep Christian dogma out of common texts and schools.

Catharine Beecher, like McGuffey, saw moral education as means of addressing the problems in American society. Beecher and McGuffey believed that education could produce a revolution that mass rallies could not. Beecher stated her views years later: "the education of the common people, then, who are to be our legislators, jurymen, and judges, and to whom all our dearest interests are to be entrusted, this is the point around which the wisest heads, the warmest hearts, most powerful energies should gather, for conservation, for planning, for unity of action, and for persevering enterprise." Catharine Beecher had founded the Western Female Institute in Cincinnati, which would also fall victim to the Panic of 1837. Catharine Beecher had some influence, having been an associate of McGuffey in the "College of Teachers." Catharine would be a leader in the education of women, but interestingly, she refused to join the political women suffrage movement. She would be a leader in the feminization of teaching.

The struggle to save Cincinnati College would not be as successful for McGuffey. The Panic of 1837 took its toll, making money extremely tight, and Cincinnati College had no church support. Drake had also over-expanded Cincinnati College. McGuffey personally became more popular and brought in new students, but he did not bring in the money. Many have suggested that McGuffey was a poor administrator, but there is little evidence to support the contention. Clearly, administration was not his passion, but he seemed to perform adequately in a difficult situation. The resolution of the Cincinnati Board offers much praise: "to accept the resignation of President McGuffey with deep regret at his presided with acknowledged ability and zeal; and, from a city in which his public efforts, as a religious and moral instructor, have been attended with so many interesting and valuable results."[1] In 1838, Ohio University asked McGuffey if he would consider the presidency of the university, and he declined. As Cincinnati faced the enviable collapse, McGuffey asked to be reconsidered in 1839. Also in 1839, McGuffey received an honorary degree of Doctor of Divinity from Indiana University where his friend Andrew Wylie was president. McGuffey commonly used the title of Doctor from that point on.

---

1 Harvey Minnich, *William Holmes McGuffey and His Readers* (Cincinnati: American Book Company, 1936), 148

CHAPTER 9. OHIO UNIVERSITY

Ohio University had a shared origin with Miami University in the Ohio Company. The university was built on land set aside by the terms of the Northwest Ordinance of 1787 with the help of Manasseh Cutler of the Ohio Company in 1804. Its location at Athens, Ohio in southeast Ohio about forty-five miles from Parkersburg, West Virginia had limited its growth. It was located in rugged hills, and was a small town in a sparsely populated segment of Ohio. Athens was an agricultural center for the nearby river valleys. Ohio University, in 1804, started as a grammar school and academy, but in 1822 had evolved into a college. When McGuffey arrived in 1839, the student body was around sixty, and the population of Athens was around seven hundred. The intellectual enlightenment had passed over this rural section of Ohio, and the Trustees of Ohio University hoped a personality like McGuffey might turn things around.

The problem was that Ohio University had been embroiled in politics and financial issues since its founding. The university had incorporated, which brought the opposition of the Jeffersonians in the Ohio Legislature. Incorporation had made landowners lessees, which had slowed population growth. The battle over educational corporations would pit Federalists and Jeffersonians. Jeffersonians argued for complete and unrestricted public control. In 1808, the university barely had the money for the construction of a two-room building. In 1816, the university was refused a loan of $8,000 for another building. The debts mounted and by 1817, the university was in debt for $18,000. Squatters and defaulters overtook the university land, and the state refused to take action against them. When McGuffey arrived, the politics and finances worsened. The student body was barely large enough to hold classes, and the poor reputation of the university had not attracted out-of-state students as had Miami University.

Ohio University had started its search for a president in 1838 to replace Robert G. Wilson, their aging president who was approaching seventy years of age. Athens' rural location had made the search a difficult one. The Trustees were determined to hire a president that could meet their vision of a great university. Ohio University's Board of Trustees approved McGuffey as President on September 17, 1839. McGuffey received an excellent salary of $1,500. The Board was anxious to bring on McGuffey because of a lack of discipline on campus, and the hope of attracting faculty, which had proved difficult because of its location. The discipline issue was one of perception compared to the radical campus of Miami. The Board at Ohio University consisted of "Old School" Presbyterians. The campus and town, however, would offer a stark contrast to the literary groups and societies of Cincinnati. McGuffey was already a success as an author with total sales over one million and contracts for revisions.

Still, even with rising sales in his Readers, having to leave Cincinnati and his circle of literary friends was extremely difficult. Biographer Minnich described his tie to Cincinnati: "Here McGuffey was deeply beloved; here were his dearest friends; here he was unanimously accorded the plaudits of the distinguished citizens of the city, the Beechers, the Mansfields, the Drakes; here his intellectual genius became the central star of an entire cultural constellation. Even the failure of the college was forgotten in the admiration of the people for its president as a man valuable in stimulating an entire city to the ideals of nobler living." Today, most Americans can relate to such a forced career change that moves you away from old friends, but in McGuffey's day such uprooting was not common. For McGuffey and his young family, Cincinnati had become home.

McGuffey's career problems grew through 1840 as he lacked the time to expand his eclectic series. Alexander McGuffey took on the job to prepare a more advanced Reader (what would become the *Fifth Reader* in the series) for publishers Truman & Smith. Alexander had been involved in all the earlier Readers and had been the sole author of a *Speller* in 1837. The *Speller* was clearly modeled after Webster's *Original Blue Back Speller*. The *Speller* adopted the Webster system and alphabet. The *McGuffey Speller* had a Christ-centered basis that made it competitive in the West with the *Blue Back Book*. In September of 1841, Alexander signed a five hundred dollar contract with Truman & Smith for an advanced *Fifth Reader*. The contract called for "a rhetorical reading book in the English language suited to the more advanced pupils in common schools to be called McGuffey's *Rhetorical Reader*." It would be published in 1844 as *McGuffey's Rhetorical Guide*. Alexander proved to be the equal in many ways to his brother. He had graduated from Miami at age sixteen and had become a distinguished professor of literature at Woodward College in Cincinnati. Alexander's passion, however, would be the law.

The sales of the basic eclectic series accelerated during McGuffey's years at Ohio University as well as the need for revisions. McGuffey was busy with revisions and additions while he served as president. The success of the first series surprised even McGuffey, but he had a number of things driving sales: a strong professional network, a Western focused product, the growth of common public schools, and a growing publisher in Truman & Smith. Truman & Smith proved to be the difference in McGuffey's quick and broad success. In particular, Winthrop Smith of the firm had a shared vision of many educators that West needed its own textbooks. The firm of Truman & Smith had been organized in 1834. Its first three books that year showed little promise, but in July 1834, the firm found some success with *"Introduction to Ray's Eclectic Arithmetic."* Smith had a background in textbooks and had been a sales agent for Eastern publishers. Smith then initiated a search for Western style series of Readers later in 1834. Truman & Smith had good equipment, and by publishing in Cincinnati, they could realize more profit by avoiding transportation costs of Eastern texts.

McGuffey's sales were surprising given the economic downturn, but textbooks were big business in 1840. Book sales had been $2.5 million in 1820 ($41 million today) by 1840, it was more than double at $5.5 million ($110 million today), and by 1850, sales measured around $12.5 million ($231 million in today's dollars). When McGuffey released his series in 1837, the "West" or the combined population of Ohio, Tennessee, Kentucky, Indiana, Michigan, and Illinois was 4,500,000 with over 1,000,000 at school age. The 1830s had also seen the technology change from hand presses at 250 impressions per hour to the steam press, which could achieve 3,000 impressions per hour. The period also represented a change in the publishing industry; whereas in 1820, seventy percent of all books sold were imported. In 1850, seventy percent of all books were produced in America. All of these factors had made the McGuffey series a major success.

W. Smith was foremost an outstanding businessman. Smith had been born in Stamford, Connecticut in 1808. He had attended a common grammar school there, and he knew the shortcomings of both the *New England Primer* and *Webster's Blue Back Book* first hand. As a youth, he worked for a New England publishing house. He left for Cincinnati in 1826 to start a career as a book agent and eventually publisher. He formed a partnership with William Truman in 1834. They opened a small publishing shop on Cincinnati's Main Street. Smith did most of the sales work at the time. The partners struggled even with the sales of McGuffey because of the high cost of investment in printing equipment. The court fight over the Readers in 1838 further stained the partnership; and in 1840, Smith bought out his partner. Smith traveled the region, pushing the McGuffey Readers and noting problems for future revisions. For Smith, the McGuffey series was his project as much as it was McGuffey's. Smith invested heavily in advertising and included advertising in the Readers themselves. He also showed brilliance as a publisher, keeping costs down with muslin binding, which he claimed was "much more durable than the thin tender leather [in reality it was thin sheepskin] usually put upon books of this class." Smith would be proven right and was far ahead of the competition.

The often-overlooked role of Winthrop Smith was that of editor. Smith had been in step with the vision of the "College of Teachers" for a unified pluralism of America. Smith had also experienced the copyright trial on the early series. He was concerned about the criticism of over religious selections in the *Fourth Reader*. Smith pushed McGuffey to maintain his original focus on morals and values. The problem was not the use of the Bible, but the possibility of its misuse in common schools. Sectarians feared that theology would be emphasized over Christianity. The *New England Primer* had proved unacceptable to Quakers, Methodists, German Lutherans, Baptists, and Catholics, all of which dominated the West, particularly, the Cincinnati area. Smith believed Christianity was best served by emphasizing Christian morals and values. McGuffey's revisions would reflect this basic approach. Smith, as the main salesman, also was sensitive to the competition and used revisions to address these needs as well.

Smith was a brilliant marketer and included ten pages of advertising in the first addition of the *Third Reader* in 1838. Smith showed this to be a series for and by teachers that additionally met the concerns of students and parents. He addressed the high cost of textbooks head on by showing the McGuffey series would be different. In the advertisement he attributed the high cost of textbooks in the variety and endless revisions (some things never change). Catharine Beecher stated in the advertisement: "The great variety and constant change of school books is an evil, expensive to parents, and troublesome to teachers and pupils. Those whose opinions may be sought as having any measure of influence in introducing such works, have some opportunity to diminish this evil by adopting the general principle, that they will examine books when solicited, and recommend only such as are decided improvements on any previous ones, and withhold any favorable opinion form such as are not."

In the ten-page advertisement, Smith further stressed that this was for, by, and reviewed by Western teachers. He listed the reviewers as Edward Mansfield, Inspector of Common Schools; Professors C. Stowe, Baxter Dickinson, and Thomas Biggs of Lane Seminary; Professors Daniel Drake, Asa Drury, and Lyman Harding of Cincinnati College; Common School Principals J. Evans, Cyrus Davenport, E. Dolph, S. Manning, M. Deming, and Darius Davenport; Professor John Hopkins of Woodward College and President B. Aydelott of Woodward College; and Catharine Beecher of the Western Female Institute of Cincinnati. Smith went on to include testimonials from Baptists, Methodists, and Presbyterians, assuring a common Christian base. These testimonials assured sales in Ohio and Kentucky from the start. Winthrop Smith was one of the first textbook publishers to supply examination copies to teachers. The *Third Reader's* success became the anchor for the overall success of the McGuffey series.

Another business innovation of Winthrop Smith was his decision to be publisher and printer of the series. Most textbooks such as the *Webster Blue Back Speller* did not have full copyright protection. Smith had initially closed that loophole, but the bigger problem was printing and distribution. Printers of Readers and Spellers usually sublet the printing out to regional and local printers. Subletting the printing created many copyright abuses, as printers took liberties with the material. Smith beefed out his warehouses and made Cincinnati the main printing operation for the West. Cincinnati was a natural transportation hub for the entire West with its Ohio River dock, canals, and a national road not far to the north. Smith did set branch partnerships with Clark, Austin, and Smith in New York; Lippincott and Company in Philadelphia; and Cobb, Pritchard, and Company in Chicago. And it wasn't just the McGuffey series; it was his whole line of "eclectic" textbooks. This proved to be a huge financial success.

Initially, *McGuffey's First and Second Readers* found little competition in the Western common schools, but the *Speller* never was successful at overtaking Webster's *Blue Back Speller*. The Readers were a different story. Besides the *Worchester Reader* from the East and the Eastern *Goodrich Reader* (printed in the West), some Western Readers had surfaced. One of those was *John Pickett's Reader*. Pickett had been an associate of McGuffey in the "College of Teachers," and had been published two years earlier. Pickett's Reader had a small following in the Cincinnati area where he was a teacher. His Reader even included a testimonial by William McGuffey. Another was *The Primary Class Book* by Thomas Lee published in 1830. Amazingly in 1840, another Eastern Reader, The *American First Class book*, competed well against *the McGuffey Readers*. The success of *McGuffey's Readers* and the implementation of common schools brought on even more competitors in 1840 such as Charles Sanders's *The School Reader*.

The *Sanders School Reader* gave McGuffey stiff competition in the early forties, as he struggled with his administrative duties at Ohio University and his revisions. The *Sanders Readers* was a progressive series that had been lagging with other competitors. The *Sanders Readers* were published in the East, but they were attractive to Western students. They had more and better illustrations then the *McGuffey Readers*. They used larger type for ease in reading. Like the *McGuffey Readers*, the *Sanders Readers* had many stories on animals, which were popular with Western students. *Sanders Readers* based morals but used less religious references. It is estimated that the series sold 13 million in the 1840s. It was the success of the *Sanders Readers* that inspired Winthrop Smith to pursue a major series revision in 1844. There had been a revision in 1841, but it addressed only errors and little content. Initially, W. Smith had used the idea of a series that would not change every year as a marketing advantage to thrifty school boards. Sanders's success, however, required new content and improved graphics. *McGuffey Readers* did win out by the end of the decade. W. Smith made the difference with his persistence and passion as a salesman.

There were probably over twenty Readers and ten Spellers on the market to compete with the *McGuffey Reader* in the early 1840s. Many of these Readers were excellent and McGuffey's product advantage was slim. Besides Smith as a salesman, McGuffey had the "College of Teachers," which, in 1837, had helped the state create a superintendence of schools; and by 1840, Ohio had over eight thousand schools. By 1850 there were around twelve thousand schools and a half million students in Ohio alone. The "College of Teachers" including McGuffey, Samuel Lewis, Albert Pickett, Joseph Ray, Edward Mansfield and Daniel Drake, had been the driving force for common schools and textbooks throughout the West. Samuel Lewis, as state superintendent, visited hundreds of schools throughout Ohio. Certainly, Samuel Lewis helped spread his friend William McGuffey's *Readers*. Lewis's essay a *"Plea for Common Schools"* would be included in the 1838 *Fourth Reader*. Lewis argued: "Patronize education, establish common stocks, and sustain them well, and you will, most assuredly, provide a place where all classes will, in childhood, become familiar, before the influence of pride, wealth, and family, can bias the mind." In addition, William Smith's sales push in Ohio, Kentucky, and Indiana pushed the Western competition of *Goodrich Readers, Pickett Readers, Porter Readers*, and *Cobb Readers*. Winthrop Smith deserves more credit for his marketing and sales strategies, which clearly bested the competition. Sales, in turn, pushed McGuffey's notoriety to new highs as well.

McGuffey's term as President of Ohio University did not go as well as his book sales. McGuffey's popularity was huge throughout the state as he arrived at Ohio University, but it had been a forced move. Attendance would double at Ohio University in his first year to 196 students. McGuffey loved the Cincinnati area and his circle of literary friends, and it was difficult to leave. Athens was about a hundred thirty miles away, a rural island in Ohio farmlands. McGuffey arrived in late fall of 1839 with his pregnant wife and children — Mary Haines, age eight, Henrietta, age seven, and Charles Spining, age four. That spring Edward Mansfield was born and shortly sickened and died. The death was a hard blow to McGuffey, who was still dealing with the failure of Cincinnati College and the move to rural Ohio. McGuffey's daughter referred to his tenure at Ohio University as "four unhappy years."

Only a few days before the death of his son Edward Mansfield, McGuffey's brother Alexander married Elizabeth Drake (daughter of Daniel Drake) in May of 1839. They moved into the wealthy East Fourth Street section of Cincinnati. While William was entering the worst period of his life, his brother was at his zenith. Alexander's *Fifth Reader* had found success with the overall series, and he had passed the Ohio Bar Exam in 1839. Alexander had risen to a chair at Woodward College. He had left teaching at Cincinnati's Woodward College to enter into

Benjamin Drake's law firm (Daniel Drake's brother). Law would be Alexander's chosen field, although he would work on some revisions through the 1840s. He would give the family some concern with his conversion to the Episcopal Church. Letters suggest that McGuffey's non-denominational approach to education did not apply to family beliefs.

McGuffey's initial months at Ohio University found some success. McGuffey reorganized the struggling university to improve the college. He abolished the academy associated with the university and went to a college preparatory school imbedded in the college. In effect, it was a type of upgraded system, which was the opposite of the graded system he supported in common schools. The model used at Ohio University for the upgraded system was derived from his experiences at Miami. He also implemented the following new schedule:

Faculty Meeting 5 A.M

Student Recitation 6 A. M.

Prayer 7 A.M.

Breakfast and relaxation 7:15 to 9 A.M.

Study/Recitation 9 A.M. to Noon

Dinner and relaxation Noon to 1 P.M.

Study and Recitation 1 P.M. to 5 P.M.

Supper and Relaxation 5 P.M. to 8 P.M.

Study 8 P.M. to 10 P.M.[1]

This is a schedule that few college students today could endure; but even for the period, it was considered extremely tough for both the students and professors. It reflected the serious approach of McGuffey toward college.

In 1840, McGuffey shook things up with the student body and faculty. Many talked about the conversion to "McGuffeyism." McGuffey addressed discipline on campus with his typical iron hand. Students were expelled for swearing, negligence, and insubordination. Two asked for permission to leave campus for a political rally, but they were refused. When they went without permission, upon their return they were expelled. Between June 15 and July 14, 1841, McGuffey expelled sixteen students in total. The result devastated the senior class, so only one out of fifteen seniors were left to graduate. McGuffey was almost as tough on his professors. Three professors resigned early in McGuffey's administration due to "McGuffeyism." Some of this was due to the cold and impersonal personality of McGuffey. The local Presbyterian Church didn't fare much better since McGuffey was also on the Board of Trustees. McGuffey went about enforcing 'Old School" Presbyterianism. Within a year, however, he had purged the University and town to fit his new system; and McGuffey's name, not his personality, became a draw for the university.

---

1 James Arnold, "A Biography of William Holmes McGuffey," (PhD diss., University of Cincinnati, 1967), p. 115

McGuffey also reorganized the university to strengthen it academically. He eliminated the academy and put the preparatory studies at the college level. He installed a modified Lancastrian system, which allowed upperclassmen to act as teachers. The system allowed him to better use his small faculty and limited resources. It reflected McGuffey's own college experience. McGuffey, however, had some success with this upgraded system at Cincinnati College. The system is somewhat analogous to today. The system was extremely attractive to well prepared students. Students seemed to like the system, and the Board of Trustees liked the lower costs, which meant more money for building. The strong start, however, would be mired with administrative issues.

William McGuffey faced a much different concern at Ohio University. He had come with high hopes of taking the university to a new level. The naming of McGuffey was met with much enthusiasm by the alumni and student body. Just prior to his arrival, the university had completed two additional buildings — the "East Wing" and "West Wing" — to facilitate the growth of the university. The problem was that money had always been a constraint for the rural university. Ohio University was five years older than Miami University, but it lacked the local support of a Miami. The Western Enlightenment had passed by this part of Ohio. Athens was farm country and lacked the cultural base of the Cincinnati area. The township had been set up for a university, going back to the 1700s; it was set aside as a land grant college, but its support was never popular. Both Miami and Ohio University came from the same land deal of John Symmes and the Ohio Company. The State of Ohio committed to the public support of Ohio University in 1803. The tax on the local farmers had never been popular in the Athens area. The financial support to the university fell on the farmers of the townships of Athens and Alexander. The farmers saw little benefit in having a college in the middle of their pastures. Many of the farmers were German and had little interest in English-speaking schools while others were from Scotch-Irish stock who had fled the East to escape taxes.

McGuffey entered into the feud almost immediately although the Trustees would have been on a collision path regardless of who was president. As president, McGuffey was to take the lead on a land reappraisal and assessment. The reappraisal was consistent with Ohio statutes to reappraise in 1840. As the word got out of the reappraisal, the farmers took to the streets in protest. They reportedly yelled and threw mud at McGuffey. As a Scotch-Irishman, McGuffey well understood the West's hatred of taxes, but he had no choice. The school was struggling for survival after barely making ends meet for twenty years. While paying a school tax, the farmers were exempt from state taxation, so in many ways they were better off. The farmers actually were not entirely struggling; crop harvests and prices had increased through the Panic of 1837, but credit and mortgages were tight and land values had probably declined. Still, no one wants their homes reassessed for more taxes, and an increase in taxes is a loss no matter what the rate is. Anger mounted with the farmers, and small disputes between the college and farmers grew. McGuffey started a simple beautification program of the college, but the farmers saw it as being insensitive to their tax burdens. Ohio University was barren in comparison to the beautiful tree lined campus of Miami University. Just prior to the re-appraisal, McGuffey added rows of elm trees (known as the McGuffey Elms to this day) and added white fencing. The farmers saw it as removing grazing land in addition to paying taxes to support the beautification program. Farmers reacted by tearing down fences. They hired a lawyer and the protest moved to 1841. McGuffey learned that the enlightenment of Cincinnati did not extend to Athens.

McGuffey did apply the same discipline he had become known for. Like at Miami, his hard line discipline was not well accepted by the students and professors. Students in 1840 were expelled for negligence, insubordination, and pranks. Several students who attended an off campus political convention after being refused permission were dismissed. He discipline sent a strong message, but at a high cost. It was noted: "This diligence and firmness just about eradicated the senior class of 1841, for only one of fifteen seniors left to graduate."[1] The combination of schedule and discipline could only be matched today by our service academies. As a Board member of the Athens Presbyterian Church, he brought discipline to the parishioners as well. Discipline was given for "profane language," dancing, "keeping vain company," and questioning scriptures. The townspeople did not fully accept this strong discipline. "McGuffeyism" had become a plague.

William McGuffey, however, continued to win over the better students and attract new ones based on his academic reputation. He taught Moral Philosophy as well as full theological curriculum. Theology was really his strength and students flocked to his classes because of his expertise. Theology of the period, particularly Protestant theology, was heavily dependent on exegesis of biblical text. McGuffey had expertise in the languages of Greek, Latin, and Hebrew, making him a true expert. McGuffey's translations and exegesis of biblical text were considered the final word. Biographer Harvey Minnich noted: "That's what McGuffey says and it's good enough for me." He also preached in the local Methodist Church with good success. Book sales were strong, and McGuffey's reputation was national. Even with the difficulties with the farmers, it should have been a good time. He seemed to find relief of administrative duties in his role of a professor. McGuffey's itinerary at Ohio was described as starting at five in the morning with a faculty meeting to study French. Then he took time to read a chapter from his Hebrew Bible followed by a class at six. Harvey Minnich described his classroom experience at Ohio University: "He was then about forty and in his full vigor and prime. He required his class to lecture on the topic of

---

1 Ibid., p. 118

received a charter from Ohio in 1831. Woodward was the first "high school" west
of the Allegheny Mountains and remains today the oldest public high school still
in operation. It had been a success from the start with a student enrollment of
over 150 in 1830s and over 250 in the 1840s. Financially strong, Woodward paid
its teachers higher than most universities. Joseph Ray had $1000 salary in 1831,
which was higher than the Presidents of Miami and Ohio University. In 1836,
Woodward was granted a new charter from the state as "The Woodward College
of Cincinnati."

While Woodward never fully achieved the status of university, Woodward's
curriculum was demanding with Greek, Latin, and endless mathematics. Woodward pioneered science and engineering education known as mechanical philosophy. Mechanics were added to the student body, making it a type of trade
school for some. The progressive "College of Teachers" and Daniel Drake had
heavily influenced Woodward in 1830s. Woodward used the same model used
by Daniel Drake at Cincinnati College. Science was a big part of the schedule
at Woodward. Woodward added courses in metallurgy, mineralogy, and physical chemistry in the 1830s, the first such courses of such east of the Alleghenies.
Woodward's faculty was a strange mix of experts, which allowed it to offer such
an unusual mix of courses.

When McGuffey arrived at Woodward College, Doctor B. P. Aydelott was
president and a close friend of Daniel Drake. Aydelotte had attended Princeton
and graduated from Chicago Medical College. Like Drake, his medical education
had led him to a love of science. Aydelott believed in the use of mechanical and
science courses along with the classics, particularly at the high school level. Both
Aydelott and Drake believed in a system of primary, secondary, and college education. Doctor Aydelott had been part of the "College of Teachers," subgroup that
believed in taking education to the working people. Doctor Aydelott's classic
line was: "We need that education which will best prepare us for our peculiar
duties as citizens of a free country." Even with his bias toward pragmatic education, Aydelott felt Christianity was the core of education. The curriculum was
not a perfect match for McGuffey, but Woodward offered interaction with some
great thinkers, many of which were active in the "College of Teachers." When
the McGuffey Readers were released, Doctor Aydelott was a major supporter
participating in advertising.

Woodward's first president, Thomas Matthews, had come from Transylvania
University in 1832 and had been active in the "College of Teachers" and its committees such as the "Western Literary Institute." Matthews was the first editor
of *The Transylvanian* literary journal. In 1832, Thomas Matthews became the first
elected president of the "College of Teachers." Matthews was, like many of the
"College of Teachers," a "man for all seasons." Matthews proved to be the perfect
fit to the broad approach to education. Matthews had expertise in civil engineer-

ing, astronomy, mathematics, literature, and business. Woodward's Joseph Ray, Doctor B. P. Aydelott, and Thomas Matthews had been old friends of McGuffey. Certainly, the presence of Ray and Matthews helped McGuffey handle the difficult transition. Ray's *An Introduction to Ray's Eclectic Arithmetic* was a companion to the McGuffey series, and would, like *McGuffey's Readers*, sell over one hundred million. Woodward was also pioneering many approaches to education such as the use of blackboards, teaching English composition, and the use of science demonstrations. From this standpoint, McGuffey was again able to get involved with the methods of teaching.

Still, the difficulty of the new position had to be a reduction in salary from the President of a university. McGuffey would also be primarily a language teacher. McGuffey had once said: "Some men are helped by a discipline of adversity; some by a discipline of prosperity. As for me, I always was best under a discipline of prosperity." McGuffey did have a national reputation, but mentally this was a low point for him. There can be no argument that McGuffey was a proud and ambitious man. He believed in the virtue of industry and the rewards that hard work could bring. He truly believed in what he wrote and preached. Now in his early 40s, he had many accomplishments including helping the formation of state schools, the advancement of the profession of teachers, as well as the eclectic series. Unfortunately, success as a university president had passed him by. Many had debated his performance as a university president and concluded he lacked administrative skills, which is at least partly true. Others have shown the other side that both Cincinnati and Ohio University had major issues as McGuffey took over.

Interestingly, about the same time Robert Bishop and John Scott had been forced to resign at Miami. They were looking at starting a "farmers and mechanics college" in the Cincinnati area. This was to come out of Pleasant Hill Academy to the north of Cincinnati. The 'College of Teachers" was determined to keep able professors of the Western enlightenment in the area. Arrangements were made to make McGuffey a professor at Woodward and possibly a church to be linked with the "farmers college." It was also clear that Winthrop Smith wanted to keep McGuffey in the area as well. Taking the position at Woodward had to be a step down and blow to McGuffey's ego, but his national fame was undiminished. His work on revisions was also continuing. His salary at Woodward was to be seven hundred dollars per year. It appears he took a side job as a preacher at the First Baptist Church. He was to preach two sermons on Sunday and one on Wednesday for five hundred dollars a year until a permanent pastor could be found.[1] It was an amazing testimony to his non-denominational appeal. In addition, William also received some compensation for his revisions of 1844.

---

1 Letter from R. Lee, Cincinnati, Ohio to W. H. McGuffey, October 30, 1844, Miami University Digital Archives.

In addition, his friends in the "College of Teachers," who wanted his help in their many common school projects, hailed McGuffey's return to Cincinnati. Catharine Beecher enlisted him as a member in a committee to form a Female Institute for Teachers. Catharine Beecher's dream had been to open the teaching profession to women. The idea of such an institute had always been a priority of the "College of Teachers." Lyman Beecher had started a national fund raising committee. The Institute had money pouring in thanks to Lyman Beecher. The plan was to recruit as many as thirty teachers to Cincinnati to train female teachers. Catharine Beecher had even written to McGuffey about the development of a special text. She even tried to persuade him to take the formal position of secretary of the committee in October of 1845.[1] Still, Catharine Beecher made her pitch in a letter: "It will give you a chance for independent action in the cause of popular education which you could not have under the thumb of a Democratic legislature and be accountable to such a population as that of Ohio or of any other state not accepting the best. It will bring you into communion with some of the most interesting men in the nation, and what I deem more agreeable a site, into the society and interests of some of the noblest, luckiest and most influential ladies in our country. It is my earnest wish that you should occupy the post." This would be a paid position but it came on the eve of several offers for McGuffey.

Another activity that consumed McGuffey while at Ohio University was his work on the revisions of 1844 on the series. His move back to Cincinnati allowed for more involvement in this key revision. The 1844 revision was to be the first major revision to go beyond mere corrections. Alexander had just finished the *Fifth Reader* in the series. Furthermore, Winthrop Smith was looking forward to a major revision in the series. The publisher Truman & Smith had now become W. B. Smith. Alexander's *Fifth Reader* in 1844 had broken new ground and many believed changed the tone of the series. The style was that of William McGuffey, but the content was that of Alexander McGuffey. In the *Fifth Reader*, there was more of a focus on literature including poetry. The *Fifth Reader* was aimed at the pre-college or freshman level student, but Smith marketed it as a home Reader as well. Some note that Alexander was better qualified to "write" the *Fifth Reader*, but really the style and learning techniques that made the series successful belonged to William McGuffey. Smith had encouraged and made payments for Alexander to do the sales legwork.

The 1843-44 revisions were also a significant step in the history of the series. They had six years of feedback from thousands of teachers, which Winthrop Smith had encouraged to write back on problems. It was critical that they be addressed because Smith had made it a promise in his advertising. He had par-

---

1 Letter Catharine Beecher, Walnut Hills, Ohio to W.H. McGuffey, July 1, 1845, Miami University McGuffey Archives.

ticularly promised that revisions would be based on teachers not publishers. McGuffey added notes on reading, spelling, and speaking. The questions at the end of the various compositions were also improved. In many ways, the 1844 editions were the most teacher-friendly of the editions. Alexander's *Fifth Reader* was to have these revisions as well, and the brothers living together helped facilitate these revisions. So even with all the personal problems, McGuffey had a lot of work to take up his time. Much of the work done on the revisions set the tone for future editions and helped teachers better use the Readers. Daniel G. Mason, a Cincinnati teacher at Woodward, helped McGuffey in the revisions of the *First and Second Readers* in 1843.

Winthrop Smith hired an editor to handle revisions in 1843, Timothy Pinneo, a Yale graduate and a graduate of the Medical College in Cincinnati in 1834. Pinneo had gone to Maryland but returned to teach natural philosophy in Marietta College. He had several health problems and a strong abolitionist view. He also had demonstrated expertise in grammar and literature. Pinneo not only worked with William McGuffey but also worked with Alexander on the *Fifth Reader* and *Spelling Book*. Additionally, he added to the textbook line of Winthrop Smith with a *High School Reader, an Eclectic Speaker*, and a *Spelling Book*. One reason for bringing on an editor was the divide up the focus needed for a rapid selling series. It, specifically, gave Smith more time to focus on advertisements and innovations. One of those innovations was to add original engravings to the 1844 revisions.

The 1844 revision was to serve several purposes. First was to correct any spelling, punctuation, or grammar. This was critical to sales, since the teachers the texts served demanded accuracy and correctness. Another point was to respond to the feedback of teachers, which Smith had promised in his sales approach. Some stories were dropped and others added. Smith and McGuffey wanted the Readers clean of any denominational issues. Many in the "College of Teachers" were used to review and identify potential problems. The 1844 revisions, in particular, eliminated lines that were in any way offensive to Catholics and Germans. This non-denominational approach favored McGuffey's support of common schools and Smith's desire for national sales. Finally, Winthrop Smith's operation in Cincinnati put him on the gateway to the South, and he wanted to tap this growing market. Smith wanted to be politically correct to maximize his market. The 1844 revisions addressed references to slaves or slavery and eliminated the story of William Wilberforce, British anti-slavery icon. McGuffey technically had little recourse to any changes that Smith wanted, but Smith needed McGuffey because of his direct ties to the area teachers and the "College of Teachers." Smith had another problem; his marketing success had created the brand name of "McGuffey." Still, they seemed to have had the ability to compromise as well as common goals so that the relationship worked smoothly.

One of Pinneo's jobs was to address differences between the McGuffeys and Winthrop Smith. William McGuffey's focus remained teaching and methods, while Alexander was more interested in the literary selections. In particular, William worked on the rhetorical notes and exercises. Pinneo did make some literary changes, but none seem to have bothered McGuffey. The "rules" added to the readings were those of William McGuffey and were an improvement over the early Readers. The rules were short and gave the student tips on reading and speaking such as, "Speak each word distinctly and be careful to pronounce correctly." The "errors" section showed the student common mistakes such as "*mor-nin* for morn-ing; *con-sar-ned* for con-cern-ed; and *pre-haps* for per-haps." McGuffey also added a "spell and define" section to help highlight difficult words in the compositions. Again, we see McGuffey's interest in the teaching methods. Some of these teaching points would be removed in the 1879 revisions in which McGuffey had no direct input.

This approach to the details of teaching was a major selling point for the Readers. It helped Western teachers who often lacked experience. Remember that there were no Colleges of Education in the 1800s. College graduates had no lessons in how to be teachers. The McGuffey Readers helped fill that gap in trained teachers. The endless reviews and call for feedback by Winthrop Smith also helped hone the teaching value of the whole series. Smith, in turn, used positive feedback letters as part of his sales promotion. The approach quickly won over teachers in Ohio, Kentucky, and Indiana. Smith did as much to promote the fame of McGuffey. His advertisements hailed the credentials of William McGuffey and his experimental approach to the development of the Readers. In many ways, Smith turned McGuffey into an American legend with his marketing strategy. By 1870 the McGuffey name had become an important piece of property. Much has been made by some of McGuffey's lack of financial gain, but he was paid in the 1840s for his revisions and advice. The details of those payments are not fully known. The marketing and promotion of McGuffey and his Readers did play into McGuffey's vanity and love of intellectual status.

McGuffey probably never looked at Woodward College as a long-term position. One of the first new opportunities was an offer to become pastor of the First Presbyterian Church of Dayton. It's not clear how serious McGuffey was about the possibility of becoming a pastor, but he had the attributes to be an excellent one. His mother had always hoped that he would become a minister and pastor, and much of his early education had tended in that direction. While at Miami, he was a pastor at the small nearby church at Darrtown while he was also speaking often at the student Sunday services at Oxford. At Miami, his preaching had even outshined his teaching. The same was true in Athens. His manner and style of speaking favored the pulpit over the lecture podium. He had built a reputation of a theological expert in Presbyterian as well as Methodist circles. The position at

Dayton, the hometown of his wife Harriet, probably made the position a bit more attractive. What is doubtful is whether the position could satisfy his ego and desire for academic achievement.

The quick leave of Ohio University had also put a great strain on the family. Initially, the family boarded at the home of Mrs. John Herron at the corner of Fifth and Pike Streets. The quarters were extremely cramped for a family used to large campus homes. McGuffey also missed the ability to plant trees and shrubs. After a few months he moved in with his brother Alexander. His brother Alexander, being the brother-in-law of Daniel Drake, had experienced a quick build-up of his law practice. Alexander and his wife Elizabeth lived in a spacious house with four servants. William McGuffey also seemed to have created some short -term financial problems over his job loss. His Cincinnati friend Edward Mansfield and his brother covered some debts. The living arrangement did strengthen the friendship between William's wife, Harriet, and Alexander's wife, Elizabeth (Drake) McGuffey.

At the same time, friends and family such as Daniel Drake were proposing that he fill an opening at the University of Virginia. Daniel Drake had been professional associate, friend, and family since Drake's daughter was married to Alexander McGuffey. Drake had powerful friends at the University of Virginia including one of the founder's nephew's, Joseph Cabell. The University of Virginia was at the time the second largest university after Harvard. There is no doubt that McGuffey was qualified for the position of chair of Moral Philosophy, but there were some issues. The University of Virginia was not a welcome home for old school Presbyterians. At the time, the University of Virginia was religiously liberal. Virginia, of course, was a slave state and opposed any form of abolition. Much has been made about McGuffey as anti-slavery, but ultimately McGuffey saw it as a state-rights issue, and while an evil, it should be addressed morally. Such a view satisfied neither the abolitionist nor the Southern plantation owner. Overall, McGuffey probably considered it unlikely that a Southern university would bring in a northerner for a Moral Philosophy Chair.

In fact, the election of McGuffey by the Board at the University of Virginia was a difficult one. The Trustees had originally elected Thomas Cooper who would later become the President of the University of South Carolina. The election was nullified when it was discovered he was an atheist. McGuffey's name was put in nomination along with that of Thomas Dew of William and Mary College. McGuffey had strong opposition in one member of Virginia's founding families — Jefferson Randolph. The issue was that McGuffey was considered an "emancipationist." In addition, Randolph did not want a Presbyterian minister in the position, and McGuffey would become the first minister hired as a professor. The aristocratic, slave-holding Randolph was an old line Anglican. Thomas Dew was elected but turned down the position. The election of McGuffey remained close, but some trustees were convinced that an "emancipationist" was far enough away from an abolitionist to elect him. Jefferson Randolph remained an opponent of McGuffey for many years.

Chapter 11. University of Virginia Professor

On July 28, 1845, William McGuffey was appointed a "chair" and professor of Moral Philosophy at the University of Virginia, but the results of his two-year job campaign were just starting to surface. In accepting the job, he had to turn down the position of pastor at Dayton's First Presbyterian Church. Earlier in July a friend, S. P. Chase, had found the State University of Missouri interested in McGuffey as president.[1] The Missouri was a very lucrative job with an annual salary of two thousand dollars per year and a beautiful home. Even after he arrived at Virginia, he received an offer to be president of Washington College of Lexington, Virginia in 1848. This position paid one thousand dollars per year plus an additional four dollars per student per year.[2] McGuffey seemed inclined to listen to his good friend Daniel Drake about the prestige attached to the University of Virginia. The Chair of Moral Philosophy at the University of Virginia was the equivalent of most college president positions.

In a letter from a member of the Virginia Board to Daniel Drake, the proceedings of the University of Virginia Board were described: "At the meeting on the 1st of July, Professor Dew, the President of William and Mary College, a gentleman of very great popularity and reputation in our state, received the nomination of the Board, but having declined it, and the meeting was crowned yesterday, when the strong impression made by the various communications before the Board of the eminent attainments and qualifications of Dr. McGuffey led to his unanimous and cordial selection. To me, the event is one of unmixed satisfaction of the

---

1 Letter from S. P. Chase, Cincinnati, Ohio to W. H. McGuffey, University of Virginia, July 4, 1849, Miami University Archives
2 Letter from Washington College Board of Trustees, Lexington, Virginia to W. H. McGuffey, University of Virginia, October 2, 1848, Miami University Archives

highest nature, for, in addition to the lively sense I have of the superior talents and various recommendations of Dr. McGuffey for this important post, I look to his appointment as a means of multiplying and strengthening our ties with the Northwest and West, which I have long and most anxiously desired, as having, in my estimation, a vital bearing upon the destinies of Virginia." When McGuffey hesitated, Daniel Drake sent him fifty dollars and demanded he go visit Virginia.

The University of Virginia was a much different school than those of Ohio. The University of Virginia had been founded by Thomas Jefferson and incorporated in 1804. Jefferson had set up the university to not have central authority but a highly structured bureaucracy. There was, for example, no central president but shared leadership with a Rector and Board of Visitors. This setup gave McGuffey a lot of autonomy as head of Moral Philosophy. In ways, McGuffey's position was equivalent to most college presidents. This setup would particularly favor McGuffey teaching and administrative styles. Jefferson spent years in the design of the buildings, and the university opened its doors in 1819. McGuffey's lecture room was on the ground floor of the famous Rotunda. Professors' homes were adjacent to dormitories for each professor to supervise. These groupings were called pavilions, and McGuffey was in charge of "pavilion 9." The pavilion design had been that of Jefferson himself and included gardens and trees, which McGuffey was very fond of, between pavilions. As he had done at Miami and Ohio University, McGuffey planted his favorite trees on campus. One of the maples lived for over one hundred years and became known as the "McGuffey Tree." McGuffey did find happiness in the beautifully landscaped campus of the University of Virginia.

Interestingly, Jefferson had fought hard to kept "religion" out of the university, and most feared the Presbyterian bias. Jefferson favored the low-key nature of Unitarians versus religious fever of Episcopalians and Presbyterians. Still, the Virginia legislature had most control because it footed the bill, and the university reflected the strength of the Episcopal Church in the state of Virginia. The University of Virginia, however, was at the time considered one of America's finest. Its organization consisted of eight schools: ancient languages, modern languages, mathematics, natural philosophy, moral philosophy, chemistry, medicine, and law, with McGuffey as Chair of Moral Philosophy School. These schools functioned independently, and the chairs were truly equivalent to most American frontier colleges. It was every bit McGuffey's most prestigious job.

Still there is great irony in McGuffey going to Jefferson's University of Virginia. While McGuffey and Jefferson would have agreed on common schools, the details of each vision was much different. Jefferson opposed even the slightest use of Christianity in education, preferring a Deist approach. Jefferson opposed any political bias even more, particularly the Federalist point of view of central government often seen in McGuffey's Readers. Jefferson, for example, set the policy of textbooks for the University of Virginia's Board: "There is one branch in which we are the best judges, in which heresies may be taught, of so interesting a character to our own state, and to the United States, as to make it a duty in us to lay down the principles which are to be taught. It is that of government. . . . It is our duty to guard against the dissemination of such [Federalist] principles among our youth, and the diffusion of that poison, by a previous prescription of texts to be followed in their discourses." This of course would have ruled out the discourses of George Washington, Alexander Hamilton, Chief Justice Marshall, Daniel Webster, Henry Clay, and Abraham Lincoln, all so prevalent in the McGuffey Readers. McGuffey saw Federalism as patriotic, not political. The University of Virginia never enforced Jefferson's policy.

Charlottesville, Virginia is a few miles closer to McGuffey's birthplace in Western Pennsylvania than Cincinnati, but it was culturally a world apart from both Ohio and Western Pennsylvania. When William and Harriet McGuffey first came to Virginia, their daughters Mary (sixteen) and Henrietta were left at the Steubenville, Ohio boarding school of Dr. Beattie for a year. The Virginia move was a bit of a culture shock for William and Harriet. The beautiful neoclassical home-required a cook and a butler. Most professors fulfilled these needs with slaves, but McGuffey opposed the idea of owning slaves. He compromised by renting slaves, which old friends often criticized him for. Henrietta seemed to be more strained by the whole arrangement. In addition, the McGuffeys struggled with the heat, humidity, strange food, and red ants.

The student body of the University of Virginia was more consistent with McGuffey's view of college education. The student body at Virginia was aristocratic with long family pedigrees. The students were generally wealthy and represented the top politicians of the state. McGuffey had always been a bit of an elitist when it came to college, which was inconsistent with his common school approach. McGuffey, however, despised the free spirited and undisciplined behavior of some Western college students. For McGuffey, college was serious business, not a time of social and political experimentation. The University of Virginia, while not Presbyterian, did have the religious discipline that McGuffey also favored. The position of Chair also seemed to be the perfect match to balance McGuffey's ego, attributes, and skills.

Politically he was a Whig in a state controlled by the Democratic Party. This was difficult for McGuffey, who was a friend and supporter of Whig Party founder Henry Clay.[1] The Whig Party reflected the political, economic, and moral values of McGuffeyland. The Whig's core was Western Pennsylvania, the Western Reserve of Ohio, and the Transylvania area of Southern Ohio, Kentucky, and Indiana. The Whig Party also had a New England contingent led by McGuffey idol

---

1   Alice McGuffey Ruggles, *The Story of the McGuffeys* (New York: American Book Company, 1950), p. 115

Daniel Webster. The Whig Party had coalesced around the anti-Jacksonians, anti-Masons, anti-slavery proponents, and protective tariffs in the economic backdrop of the Panic of 1837. More importantly, the party caught the fire of the West, forging morals and economics into the basis for American capitalism. The "Iron Whigs" of the Western Reserve and Western Pennsylvania, in particular, started the building of an industrial heartland. Similarly, the "Intellectual Whigs" of the Transylvania area started the movement towards abolition, common schools, and a republican form of government.

The Whigs also led the Methodist re-awakening of the West. Predestination of the Presbyterians morphed into the McGuffey proverb of "where there is a will, there's away." The Whig Party did manage to win the presidency in 1840 and 1848 with William Henry Harrison and Zachary Taylor. In congress, Henry Clay of Kentucky and Daniel Webster of Massachusetts held Whig leadership. In the late 1840s, the Whigs also had the rising star of Abraham Lincoln. When McGuffey moved to Virginia, the Whig Party was being torn over slavery. Anti-slavery supporters were divided between abolition at all costs and the more moderate approaches. In the 1840s, a tough fugitive slave law had caused a storm in the North among antislavery forces. Henry Clay and Daniel Webster hammered out an unpopular compromise in 1850, allowing a type of balance between new states and territories on slavery. Moderates like William McGuffey, Alexander McGuffey, supported the compromise of 1850 and Daniel Drake but tore the Whig Party apart. In any case, life was uncomfortable in Virginia for a Whig.

Another early setback for McGuffey was his hope to spread the concept of common schools nationally. This had been a huge success for McGuffey and the "College of Teachers" in Ohio. He hoped to repeat it in Virginia. He teamed up with the University of Virginia's chaplain William H. Ruffner and professor John Minor to canvass the state. He used his vacation and weekends to visit Virginia cities and lecture, but Virginia was a tough audience. Virginia was a much different environment than the West of Ohio and Kentucky. While Thomas Jefferson first suggested common schools, Virginia had an aristocratic social structure and a large slave population. This structure favored education of the upper class. McGuffey found little support, but twenty years later his associate William Ruffner would succeed.

The biggest problem in McGuffey's early years at the University of Virginia was his wife Harriet. Harriet seemed to always have trouble with geographic changes that separated her from family and friends. In particular, she missed her sister-in-law Elizabeth who had become her closest friend. She had exhibited similar health problems with the move to Miami and Ohio University. This time things seemed much more difficult. A true measure of culture shock was involved. McGuffey would throw himself into his work, but Harriet was alone. He was not only working into the night grading and preparing, but he used vacation and weekends to lecture around the state. As he became more involved in his duties, Harriet was even more isolated. Much has been made of her inability to cope with the Southern life style, but it appears deeper than that. Always consumed by his teaching, McGuffey seemed to have crossed over to a workaholic with his new position, making Harriet's life all the more difficult. Descriptions of her staying in bed suggest at least the possibility of depression, but there was also more to it.

On the other hand, McGuffey seemed to strive at the University of Virginia. The well disciplined students and rigorous requirements suited his style. Offers to be President of Washington College at Lexington and State University of Missouri would be refused. But Harriet was not alone in finding the transition to the Southern culture difficult. McGuffey's sixteen-year-old daughter Mary was appalled by the practices of slavery. Mary hated the idea of owning another human being, and the practice of whipping a slave was particularly repulsive. Their black butler, William Given, was just slightly older than her and had been forced into servitude without any education. Mary began to teach him to read and write. Years later, William Given became a Presbyterian minister and the first black pastor in Washington, DC. Unfortunately, Harriet found no such diversion to help her cope with the Southern culture.

Harriet's condition seemed to worsen through the fall of 1849. She spent months in bed, avoiding running the household. At times she appeared to be improving, only to relapse again. The family doctor seemed to have believed it to have a psychosomatic component and suggested that she return to Ohio for a visit in the spring of 1850. Physically, she was unable to return by herself, and McGuffey was finishing up the school semester. McGuffey made arrangements for a Presbyterian minister who was traveling to Cincinnati to accompany her. Harriet arrived in Cincinnati to stay several days with Alexander and Elizabeth before going to Dayton to visit with family.

At the end of June, McGuffey received an urgent telegram informing him that Harriet was critically ill in Dayton. McGuffey quickly finished his grading duties and left by train for Dayton. He left the children in Virginia, as he wanted to travel quickly and unburdened. At the time railroads were considered fast but very unpleasant travel. He took the train to Huntington (West Virginia, today) and then the steamboat to Cincinnati. After his arrival in Dayton, Harriet seemed to be improving, and McGuffey sent a letter back to his children suggesting she would soon return. A few days later the bad news of her death arrived in a letter opened by his son Charley. This was according to the memoirs of his daughter Henrietta, who was sixteen and in Virginia.[1] It is in conflict with the memoirs of Alice McGuffey Ruggles (the granddaughter of Alexander and Elizabeth Drake

---

1 Henrietta McGuffey Hepburn, "Memoirs" (University of Miami archives, Walter Havighurst Special Collections)

McGuffey, born in 1879), whose story is third hand at best.[1] Ruggles reported that: "Harriet died before William could reach her. He arrived at the old farmhouse where they had been married, to find her already laid out in the coffin." The record supports the view of Harriet dying some days after William's arrival and the memoirs of daughter Henrietta.[2] The exact nature of the death is unknown. Biographer Dolores Sullivan suggested "'inflammation of the bowels as appendicitis"; however, the long nature of the illness might suggest something else.

The children remained in Virginia for the funeral and burial of their mother at Dayton's Woodlawn Cemetery. McGuffey returned somber and depressed, unable to give the three children any emotional support. The next year was extremely difficult for all of the family. McGuffey remained functional, performing the necessary duties but little else. He was said to teach, only to return home and go to his room. The children were left to take care of themselves. McGuffey was never an affectionate father, but, clearly depressed, he doomed his children to some very dark days. The children would run out to meet him coming home, only to find a cold greeting. Finally, they were asked not to run out. McGuffey remained in this depressed fog at least into the winter of 1851.

That winter McGuffey started to date Miss Laura Howard, the daughter of the Dean of the Medical College. Laura or "Lura" was 33 years of age while McGuffey was 51. Laura was a Southern Presbyterian but accepted the institution of slavery. The situation for the children hardly improved. Finally, in May, McGuffey announced to his children that he planned to marry Laura Howard. The reaction was "shock and surprise," as might be expected. The children had known only housework and little comfort after the death of their mother. They naturally cried when the announcement was made, feeling a type of betrayal. McGuffey's initial response was stern and selfish, but he had to address the feelings of his children. He proposed a trip with the three children, something the family badly needed.

First, McGuffey sent the children to Ohio to visit family. They visited Alexander and Elizabeth in Cincinnati who now had four children at their large home. After a few days, they went to see their mother's family in Dayton. At the time Mary Haines was twenty-one, Henrietta was twenty, and Charley was fifteen. Then McGuffey met up with them in Niagara Falls, America's top tourist attraction in the 1850s. After Niagara, they went to Quebec City and then on to Burlington, Vermont. McGuffey briefly visited the University of Vermont. That night in the hotel, Charley became sick with what was called a "violent case of cholera." A doctor was called, but Charley died before daybreak. Because it was summer and the death was ascribed to cholera, the body could not be taken to Dayton until cold weather returned. The situation required the family to struggle

---

1 Alice McGuffey Ruggles, p. 108
2 James Scully, p. 133

through a brief funeral and entombment while in Burlington. Some of the professors and students from the University of Vermont attended the ceremony to help the bereaved family so far from home. Certainly, the family had found no solace on the trip.

Much has been made of William McGuffey sending his offspring to Cincinnati just "two years after the great epidemic of 1849." All this is from the very biased biography of William McGuffey by the granddaughter of Alexander, Alice McGuffey Ruggles. The bias and weakness in this third- and fourth-hand biography will be discussed later. Alexander McGuffey had lost a daughter during the cholera epidemic in Cincinnati during 1849, which deeply hurt Alexander and Elizabeth and her grandfather the physician Daniel Drake. Alice McGuffey Ruggles noted: "William McGuffey dared to bring his children into the cholera belt at the most dangerous season." The suggestion that McGuffey was a poor and uncaring father should be balanced by the fact that cholera was a problem throughout the United States and in the Cincinnati area two years earlier. Mrs. Ruggles describes in detail the pioneering germ theory of Daniel Drake. Drake was McGuffey's brother-in-law and best friend and would have warned him if he thought the trip dangerous. The fact is, cholera was a common disease of an unknown origin in the 1850s, and McGuffey bears no responsibility for that. And there is no record whatsoever of McGuffey feeling responsible.

McGuffey went ahead with his plans to marry Miss Howard, and on September 21, 1851, they were wed. The death of his son had deepened his depression, but the marriage brought new hope. The two daughters never really warmed up to Laura, but they did appreciate the help around the house. Laura was skilled at the management of slaves and knew how to control the ant problem. Mary and Henrietta disagreed passionately with Laura's acceptance of slavery. For Laura's part, she quietly tolerated the children's interactions with the slave help. McGuffey, who was never an abolitionist, seemed to find more tolerance for slavery through his new wife. Death struck the family again when William's oldest sister, Jane, died on July 9, 1852. McGuffey had another setback in 1852 with the death of his friend and mentor Daniel Drake. On May 5 of 1853, Laura gave birth to a daughter. Named Anna, she seemed to be the light of McGuffey's new life. This newfound warmth must have been disturbing to Mary and Henrietta since they had only known a very stern and disciplinarian father.

The difficult and strained family relationships lasted only a few years. On June 15, 1853, Mary Haines married William Walker Stewart, a physician, in Dayton, Ohio. On May 3, 1857, tragedy struck once more when McGuffey's young daughter died of scarlet fever. This time McGuffey seemed almost to accept the tragedy, while Laura went into a depression. Still, the tragedy had once again forced McGuffey into his books and teaching. On July 10, 1857, Henrietta married Andrew Hepburn, a professor. In 1871, Andrew Hepburn became President of Miami University. McGuffey and Laura were finally alone, and they both seemed to settle into the routine of a Southern university. McGuffey was offered the presidency of Miami University in 1854, but he was now a Virginian.

McGuffey was very proud of his son-in-law Andrew Hepburn, as noted in this 1857 letter to his sister: "Henrietta expects to be married on the 10th of July (her birthday) to Rev. Andrew D. Hepburn — who has received a call to the Presbyterian church in Harrisonburg, Va., only a few hours run on the railroad from the University — Mr. Hepburn is a son of Judge Hepburn of Carlisle, Pa. — The judge is a Presbyterian elder, and an active, benevolent Christian . . . Henrietta's intended is one of the best scholars in the country — and will, it is thought, make an excellent pastor." Clearly, McGuffey saw a bit of himself in the young man. McGuffey stayed in close touch with both his daughters, but their moving out was probably the best for all involved.

As a professor, McGuffey seemed to age well, like wine. One of his former students at the University of Virginia, United States Senator from Mississippi John Sharp Williams, praised him: "I sat at the feet of Gamaliel, when he taught and lectured upon Moral and Mental Philosophy at the University of Virginia. I have had many teachers on this side and a few on the other side of the Atlantic. Dr. McGuffey possessed the ability to transplant ideas from his own mind to the minds of others and have them grow to a degree never possessed by any other man with whom I ever had contact as a teacher. He constantly dwelt upon the 'attention' and 'repetition' as the secrets of good 'memory.' His habit in the hour and half which he spent daily with us in the classroom was to consume one-half hour in examining the class on reading and lecture of the previous day, after prescribing the reading for the next day's recitation, then to straighten himself up (he had a slight stoop) with his hand on the desk and his back to the blackboard and have the class question him on any subject that had been gone into before."[1]

The sales of the *McGuffey Readers* continued at a fast pace throughout the 1840s and 1850s. During the 1850s, one Cincinnati salesman, Obed J. Wilson, became a sales phenomenon for the McGuffey series. Wilson had come to Cincinnati in 1846 from New England Puritan stock, an education based on the *New England Primer*. He had come to Cincinnati to join his brother in teaching. For five years he taught school and studied the law until his eyesight forced a career change. Wilson's pleasing personality and frontier Methodist and schoolteacher network made him a natural textbook salesman. Wilson was extremely aggressive in his sales efforts and was even accused of paying off teachers. Obed Wilson could play a key role in the major revision of the Readers in 1853. The editing of the Readers for the 1853 seemed to come at the perfect time to help McGuffey's depression from a string of deaths. The 1853 revision turned out to be a major review, and

---

1 Frank Davidson, "The Life and Moral Influence of William McGuffey," (Master Thesis: The Ohio State University, 1935), p. 47

McGuffey approved changes and made notes. The *Sixth Reader* would be released for the first time in 1857 and was assembled by Alexander McGuffey, who was the literary expert, but McGuffey signed off his approval.

The *Sixth Reader* was a major breakthrough for the Readers. Aimed at the high school and college level student, it was a true text of literature. It was this text that introduced students to the world of literature. It had one hundred eleven of the world's greatest authors including Milton, Bacon, Dryden, Irving, Hawthorne, Emerson, Longfellow, Holmes, Lowell, Addison and six selections of Shakespeare. It included the long remembered speeches of Patrick Henry, Daniel Webster, John Marshall, and Thomas Jefferson. The *Sixth Reader* found its way to the personal libraries of many. One historian called it "a veritable Thesaurus of Good English and American Literature. With it, McGuffey's fame and overall sales soared to new levels.

Chapter 12. The Civil War and Final Years

The rising war clouds were particularly disturbing to McGuffey. He had hoped that moral education could have resolved the slavery problem. The Compromise of 1850 had again raised his hopes, but the compromise proved but a Band-Aid. McGuffey had struggled personally over slavery with his abolitionist friends in the "College of Teachers" and his second wife who supported slavery. He struggled professionally as well. McGuffey had added the story of William Wilberforce, the British politician that ended slavery, in his original Reader, but the editor purged it in 1844. Editor Winthrop Smith wanted it out because he wanted to increase sales in the South. McGuffey's lessons on holding the union together did survive cuts. McGuffey's lesson, *"Duty of the American Orator,"* was also in the original *Fourth Reader* and survived until the 1879 revision. Thomas Smith Grimke of South Carolina, who had presented it to the "College of Teachers" in the 1830s, wrote the lesson. Grimke stated: "Be it then among the noblest offices of American Eloquence to cultivate, in the people of every state, a deep and fervent attachment to the union." For McGuffey, the union stood above all.

In 1855, his father died in Washington County, severing yet another tie to the North. There is no doubt that there was a shift in McGuffey as the Civil War approached. Through his wife and the University of Virginia, he became part of the Southern society. McGuffey had always been a believer in state rights, and those beliefs grew stronger as war grew closer. McGuffey never came to accept slavery, but he came to tolerate it as a states' rights issue. One of his brother's daughters, Anna McGuffey Morrill, remembered: "He (William McGuffey) became quite Southern in his sympathies after living in Charlottesville through the Civil War. My father (Alexander) was an ardent Unionist. I do not think that his Southern sympathies led to any family estrangement. I do know my father told him when he came North after the war to be careful what he said."[1] McGuffey was also known to have referred to Union soldiers as the enemy.

McGuffey, as well as the Readers, remained committed to holding the union together. An allegorical story of *"The Seven Sticks"* was added in the 1857 edition of the *Third Reader* to at least offer support for the union without offending the South. The story ends with the following: "But if the bond of union be broken, it will happen to you just as it has to these sticks, which lie here broken on the ground." Another lesson, *The "Necessity of Education"* by Lyman Beecher, had been in the original Readers, going back to 1837 (although it was moved up to the *Fifth Reader* in 1857) and had a plea for a strong nation. The plea reads: "May God hide from me the day when the dying agonies of my country shall begin! Oh thou beloved land, bound together by the use of brotherhood, and common interest, and perils, live forever — one and undivided." It should be noted that from the very first Readers, a number of lessons opposed war in general. McGuffey had always hoped to avoid civil war at all costs. His basic belief was a common vision of a nation that would lead to common schools and a common culture. McGuffey remained committed to holding the nation together even if that meant slavery in some states. He further believed that moral education would in the long run end the moral issue of slavery.

The 1857 revisions of the Readers were purged to be user friendly in the South. Winthrop Smith's publishing firm saw the South as a huge market and for years had been finding sales success in the border states, penetrating even into Mississippi. During the war, through local presses, Smith continued and expanded sales of the *McGuffey Readers*. From a marketing standpoint, the South represented a true growth market. Prior to the Civil War, almost all Southern textbooks were printed in the North. As the war started, Smith lined up with the Nashville publisher, the Methodist Book Concern, and they actually expanded market during the war. This Nashville publisher struggled to keep up with demand. As the Union troops occupied Southern areas, Smith had supplies of texts sent in quickly. McGuffey was not part of the sales effort, and while modified and muted, the Readers still supported that slavery was a moral evil. Many have judged McGuffey as coming over to support slavery, but that was not true. McGuffey had to be a Whig politically; and when the Whig Party morphed into the Republican Party, it was assumed McGuffey did, too. The record suggests the he did eventually become a Democrat, which at the time was the party of the Southern states and the party of anti-tariffs. McGuffey's position in the South made him once again an important asset to the publishers after the Civil War.

---

1   Anna McGuffey Morrill, "A Daughter of the McGuffeys," *Ohio Archaeological and Historical Quarterly*, Volume XLII, January, 1933, p. 261

That movement to the Democratic Party for McGuffey personally started as the Whig Party took more extreme views. Western Whigs moved to abolition and Eastern Whigs moved toward the anti-Catholic Know-Nothing Party. By 1850 New York had more Irish-born citizens than Dublin. The Irish worked at anything available and youths joined gangs to pass the time. Drinking seemed to be the major pastime of the Irish, which often upset the Puritan values of the east coast. In 1849 a secret group of nativists known as the Order of the Star-Spangled Banner formed in Boston to eliminate the growth of Irish Catholics. In New York, nativist politicians and Whigs formed an anti-Catholic party known as the "Know Nothing Party." The Irish immigration would, however, overwhelm the opposition. By 1854, the Know-Nothing had strong political support in New York and Boston. The Know-Nothings had evolved from gangs in the Five Points of New York, where they fought Irish gangs such as the "Plug-Uglies," "Dead Rabbits," and the "Roach Guards." The 1854 Congress included five senators and forty-three representatives with ties to the Know-Nothings. There were governors and state legislatures with Know-Nothing persuasion in seven states. The Know-Nothings opposed the Irish, German, Chinese, and all immigrants, rejecting the very heart of McGuffey's common vision. The Civil War would split the Know-Nothing party over slavery, with the core supporting slavery, and it disappeared in the North in the face of Irish victories on the battlefields.

McGuffey opposed any politics such as abolition that would lead to war, and the Republican Party with its abolitionist views and high tariff policy was leading the country to war. More than anything McGuffey wanted to see the union preserved. Prior to the Civil War, the *McGuffey Readers* had been consistent in their support of the union. Even as a Whig, McGuffey had been concerned by tariffs because he viewed them as a tax, and McGuffey opposed all forms of taxes. Tariffs had openly been a subject of debate in the "College of Teachers" early in McGuffey's career. McGuffey's friend, Thomas Smith of South Carolina, had warned McGuffey in the 1830s that tariffs could lead to war. The tariffs were favored in the North to protect the manufacturing industry. The South opposed the tariffs because it hurt their farming dependence. Tariffs, more than abolition, were initially driving the country towards war. Moving to the South only gave McGuffey yet another reason to oppose tariffs and the new Republican Party. McGuffey, however, was never active politically nor did he talk of politics.

Personally, while McGuffey supported states rights, he demonstrated tolerance and acceptance of blacks in Virginia. McGuffey was known to give financial support to help build a black church in Charlottesville. In his personal affairs, McGuffey treated his servants with respect and dignity. His daughters had been appalled at the South's attitude towards blacks and were happy to return north. He encouraged the education of blacks as he had all his life. Still, with his second wife, McGuffey learned to be more tolerant of Southern slaveholders, a change that perplexed his Northern family and friends. When McGuffey died, black Presbyterians of Charlottesville Church asked for permission to attend services at the University and were granted permission. The issue of slavery itself perplexed him at many levels. Even his very strict Covenanter background, which opposed dancing, drinking, and many accepted social norms, seemed to be tolerant of Presbyterian slaveholders. He had grown up in Presbyterian communities that, at times, were ambivalent towards slavery. During the war, McGuffey was said to have withheld his tongue with northern family members and friends. McGuffey's daughters and son-in-laws were all on the side of the union.

As the war years dragged on, Virginia and the University of Virginia experienced very dark days. Most of the students had enlisted in the Confederate army, and those remaining were forced to live under Spartan conditions. Attendance, however, dropped to under two hundred students from over four hundred prior to the war. Money, food, and supplies were collected weekly for the army. Virginia remained on the front lines throughout the war. Incomes of the professors were reduced, and McGuffey had to make major reductions in his standard of living. The fighting never came close till the end of the war, but there were often rumors of invading armies. In March 1865, Union General George Armstrong Custer marched raiding troops into Charlottesville, creating fear at the university. The faculty and community met with Custer to assure the safety of the university. Custer spared the university, but somewhat indigent, had his troops camped on the lawn around the Pavilions with fires for several days.

During the height of the war, McGuffey's brother's wife, Elizabeth and sister of his friend Daniel Drake, collapsed and died in her garden. Elizabeth had been close to McGuffey's first wife and his daughters. The war had put many strains on the McGuffey family as well as on his career. Alexander and Elizabeth had remained completely loyal to the union, while William McGuffey became a somewhat reluctant confederate. William's wife, of course, was completely devoted to the Confederacy, while his daughters were unionists. But as the war progressed, William became more understanding if not supportive of the Southern cause.

The end of the war brought even more new challenges for McGuffey and his publishers. For McGuffey, he was appalled at the collapse of infrastructure of the Southern States after the war. Conditions in Virginia were actually much worse after the war. In a letter to his wife's sister in 1865, McGuffey detailed the problems: "All over the country — the fences were burnt – barns and farming tools, mules, and oxen carried away or eaten up — and these people are without money! Now, with the best intentions in the world to help their late servants, they have but little in their power — and while many of the white race must perish this winter, a much larger proportion of the black must disappear before spring — no matter who is at fault, or whether anybody is to blame for this state of things — thousands will be in their graves before next Christmas! — no power can keep it — at least none on earth!" The collapse of the Confederacy, however, would be minor compared to the reconstruction period that was to follow.

McGuffey's publishers were experiencing a mini boom as textbook shortages in the South after the war had created demand. During the war, the firm of W. Smith was reorganized. A new firm of Sargent, Wilson, & Hinkle emerged on April 20, 1863 with Edward Sargent, Obed Wilson, and Anthony Hinkle as general partners, and W. Smith as a special partner. The firm made a major expansion into the Mississippi Valley because books could be shipped by river from Cincinnati. While sales had been good during the war, much of the accounts were uncollectible. The end of the war brought financial stability and new opportunities. The firm hired William McGuffey to take a trip through the Carolinas, Georgia, Alabama, and Mississippi of the Deep South to fully assess the situation. Information on the market was difficult to obtain, and it was hoped McGuffey with his educational ties could better access the conditions. McGuffey could also create a real sales boom. For McGuffey, it was an opportunity to establish stronger ties with the publishers.

McGuffey proved an intrepid reporter of Southern Reconstruction. He met with legislatures, governors, college presidents, and schoolteachers. The study required several months of travel. No written report was made but we read the written notes of Henry Vail, an editor at the firm, who reported: "For days he held his listeners spellbound . . . He repeated conversations with unquestioned accuracy and described with humor the gross ignorance and brutality of some of the Southern legislators, the looting of the capitol at the end of session, the indirect robbery . . . the reversal of all the conditions of life, and the growing unrest of the men who had heretofore been rulers. It was such a picture as at that time no Northern paper would have dared to print — it was the truth." McGuffey was deeply affected by the devastation and lack of moral behavior. He questioned whether the war had really helped humankind overall. Virginia fared much better than the Deep South, and by 1868, the University of Virginia was back over four hundred students.

In an 1865 letter to his sister, McGuffey described the problems of blacks at the end of the war: "Everything is much changed by the freeing of the negroes. White people will be benefited by the change, after a little — But it is very uncertain what will become of the blacks — They do not know what to do with themselves now that they are free — and very many of them will die for want of food and clothing and such, and medical attendance — Their former owners are for the most part trying to do for them all they can — but that is but little — out of every hundred negroes, old and young, not more than twenty were working men — and most of these twenty were taken away by the war — and have never returned. Most of them probably died or were killed — So now there is nobody to raise bread and meat for those too young or too old to work — The white inhabitants, all thro for — and this they can do only with great difficulty — The war swept away a great many of their able bodied men — and left thousands of widows and orphans, without money and without means."[1] McGuffey would come to hate the evils of Southern reconstruction.

McGuffey seemed always to complain about the poor salaries at the University of Virginia, which preferred to put the money into buildings. McGuffey seemed to have learned over the years the futility of fighting with the administration, and this constant complaining among professors helped reduce frustration. Amazingly, he had many friends on the faculty. It was probably more respect than his personality, and his adoption of the Southern viewpoint. In the late 1860s, McGuffey had become an icon on campus. Known as "Old Gruff," he was considered a demanding professor. He was a tough grader and often pushed poor performing students to drop his class. Students found his lectures clear and straightforward, and this was most prized by students. He also appeared genuinely concerned that students understood his lectures. While he lacked a sense of humor, his students were very fond of him. His dress was conservative and well prepared. He owned several coats of different weights and textures, which the students were said to gauge the weather by. McGuffey had become an important part of the history of the University of Virginia as well as that of Miami University.

University of Virginia historian Philip Bruce summarized McGuffey's impact: "The University of Virginia has always been a mirror which faithfully reflected the various influences that had given such a salient individual to the Southern people. And never was this fact more perceptible or impressive than after the end of the war when the South was in the first unsettled stage of an involuntary peace. With the exception of Schele, Boeck, and McGuffey — the last, one of the most stalwart and masterful figures in that entire company — the members of its faculty were Southerners or Englishmen by birth. But Mallet and Holmes as well as McGuffey and Schele were not to be distinguished in the smallest degree, either in sentiment or sympathy, from their colleagues of Southern nativity." McGuffey made his mark at Virginia as a professor more so than the originator of the Readers. Certainly, he achieved a great deal of personal satisfaction that had eluded him earlier in his career. His home became the University of Virginia.

During McGuffey's time at Virginia, the Readers went through some significant revisions and editions. There were a number of revisions during and just after the Civil War due to a rush of competition into the book market. The South, having no textbook publishers, had lived for years off used textbooks. Mrs. Obed J. Wilson did the 1863 revision of the *First Reader*, probably without the review of McGuffey. The war restricted the movement of people and mail. There were

---

1 Letter from W. H. McGuffey to Harriet, December 25, 1865, A 1406, Box 1, The Henry Ford- Benson Research Center

some minor revisions in 1866 and 1867 of the other Readers, which McGuffey probably did review. In the late 1860s, McGuffey started a four-volume project on "Mental Philosophy," which was to be his *magnum opus*. Amazingly, McGuffey had done little true writing throughout his career. The four volume series was never fully published, but a copy does exist at Miami University. It is really a summary of some of the basic beliefs behind the Readers. Minnich called it the theory of special creation and innate intelligence. This innate intelligence is built in by a creator and refutes Darwin's Theory of Evolution. For McGuffey, his creator drives man to higher levels of behavior. Interestingly, McGuffey's ideas of a higher order of virtues are similar to the work of Abe Maslow and his "Hierarchy of Needs" some seventy years later. He agrees with Maslow that things like the desire for esteem and friendship are basic human needs.

McGuffey's life improved as the horrors of reconstruction ended, and once again McGuffey found hope and solace in his teaching. While most biographers point to McGuffey's years at Miami as the pinnacle of his career, his later years at Virginia were his happiest. In all, he taught twenty-eight years at Virginia versus ten at Miami. Like Thomas Jefferson before, McGuffey had become the sage of the university. Students filled his classes and sought his advice. The publishers, once again, looked for his advice. He had successfully made the transition into Southern society. The University of Virginia offered him the freedom to teach, and the Southern discipline of the students best suited his style.

In 1870, a Miami graduate visited McGuffey and reported the following: "It was not, the Doctor of my portrait gallery that I saw, but an active man of robust health and elastic step. . . . It took but a few moments for us to become thoroughly enrapted with the Doctor, and the visit was throughout to us, one of unalloyed enjoyment and mental profit. . . At home he was a genial host. . . he discoursed on his experience and methods in grape growing. . . . Every morning at five o'clock, the doctor took a walk to the top of this hill and returned home by a different route."[1] Grape growing had been a hobby of McGuffey since the 1840s. In an 1872 letter to his son-in-law Andrew Hepburn, he described his routine: "I rise at five in the morning and Laura comes down at six. We have breakfast at seven thirty. After breakfast we sit on the back porch and read. We dine again at two o'clock. Supper is at six thirty and Laura and I often ride from seven to eight. In the evening we sit in the front portico. I walk three miles around the mountain almost every day."[2] Normally, McGuffey lectured at three o'clock after dinner.

Over the years, McGuffey had grown close to his son-in-law, Andrew Hepburn. Hepburn had become a professor at Miami University. McGuffey's popularity had been a boon for Miami University and hoped to have him back. In 1871, Miami University offered William McGuffey the presidency or chair of the Phi-

---

1 John Covington, *The Miami Journal*, Volume II
2 Letter from William McGuffey to Andrew Hepburn, August 1, 1872 (Miami University archives- McGuffey Papers)

losophy Department.[1] At age 71, McGuffey was no longer interested in taking on such new responsibilities, particularly since Miami was experiencing an enrollment decline and serious financial problems. McGuffey was also deeply committed to his Virginian wife. Still, he had to be deeply honored that Miami wanted him back. After McGuffey turned down the offer, his son-in-law Andrew Hepburn took the position. McGuffey helped broker the deal. His son-in-law had been struggling on his professor salary for years. McGuffey had earlier suffered a failed effort to get him a higher paying professorship at Princeton.

McGuffey took a short vacation with his wife in 1872. In late 1872, he was starting to anticipate the end, while a enjoying the peace in these twilight years. In a letter he noted: "Solomon says that a good wife is from the Lord and I have had two of the very best — better than I deserve."[2] He appeared to be healthy to the very end. In the spring of 1872, he was planning his summer vacation to be in Dayton when a cold overtook him in March. On March 15, 1872, a fever hit him after his three o'clock lecture. He took to bed, but the cold lingered for days. By early April, his two daughters, Henrietta Hepburn and Mary Stewart, were asked to come to Virginia as things turned for the worst. His daughters and son-in-law Andrew Hepburn arrived in several days. After a few days, there was some improvement, and Mary Stewart and Andrew Hepburn returned home. Henrietta Hepburn stayed on to help, but after several weeks there was further improvement to the point that there was talk of him going back to Ohio. In late May, Henrietta returned to Oxford, but no sooner had she returned after a two-day trip, she was telegraphed to return. She returned to Virginia to find him in a coma. McGuffey never regained consciousness and died on May 5, 1873.

Henrietta was making arrangements to have the body returned to Dayton to be buried beside his first wife. The faculty formally requested he be buried in Virginia: "The faculty of the university of Virginia, having heard with great concern, that it is in contemplation to convey the remains of Dr. McGuffey to another state for burial, would earnestly request the family of their lamented, revered colleague to suffer the field of his longest and most arduous labors to be his final resting place, and while they would not lightly thwart the wishes of those who stand in so near and so tender a relation to their departed friend, they would respectfully represent that a man of merit so exalted and reputation so extended belongs in death as in life to a wider circle that awaits him, wherever he may be laid, but it seems to be peculiarly fitting that he should sleep here, where his living presence was most felt, and his greatest work best understood, where his example will be a perpetual power, and his loss an unceasing sorrow, and the faculty hope that the institution, which he did so much to adorn and to advance, may be permitted to have the honor of guarding his remains as it will always cherish and revere

---

1 James Scully, p. 139
2 Letter from William McGuffey to T. Harris, October 4, 1872 (Miami University archives, McGuffey Papers)

his memory." Henrietta accepted the request, and the funeral took place at the University's Rotunda. The respect and love of the Virginia faculty showed that McGuffey had truly found home.

CHAPTER 13. THE ONE-ROOM SCHOOL HOUSE

"The next duty devolving upon parents, in relation to teachers, is to furnish them with suitable tools, with which to work. They must, we have seen, have comfortable shops — a school-house is the teacher's shop — but this will not avail, unless those shops be furnished."
— William McGuffey, 1834

To fully understand McGuffey and his Readers takes some knowledge of the one room school. The one room schoolhouse defined the McGuffey period throughout America. The one room schoolhouse is an animal that is foreign to most of the population today. It seems almost inconceivable that eight grades would be taught in one room. Add the problem of each student having a different text and numerous skill levels. Some students could spell, some could read, and some could do neither. Students were also at different math levels than their reading level. Often some did not even speak English. Attendance seemed at times optional, and discipline was the major part of the teacher's job. Teachers were basically temporary workers, often between jobs such as a young William McKinley. Teachers had no training other than their own schoolhouse experiences. The schoolhouses were dark and smoky. Students had to be segregated by sex, age, and skill. Different groups of students were reading aloud, writing exercises, doing math problems on the blackboard, and studying at the same time. Still, with all the problems, these schoolrooms were the gateway to American society and the middle class. The *McGuffey Reader* was designed for, and to some degree, by the one-school schoolhouse. Clearly, the *McGuffey Reader* helped give order to the chaotic one-room school.

In the 1600s and most of the 1700s, teaching and schools were connected to churches, except on the frontier where subscription schools were run out of houses or under trees. One-room schoolhouses started to come into being with churches in New England and with communities in Eastern Pennsylvania. The following is a description of a Pennsylvania schoolhouse in the 1700s: "The houses or cabins, used for school purposes, were of the simplest structure, being built of logs, or poles, and the space between them filled with chips of wood, and plastered with mortar made of clay. Heavy poles extending from one end to the other generally secured the boards on the roof. The chimney was built of sticks of wood plastered and almost large enough to occupy one side of a house. The furniture was also of the simplest kind. It consisted of benches, made of logs spilt in two and hewn down to the proper thickness, supported by four legs. The stools and tables were made of the same material in a similar manner."[1] Floors were often dirt, but in the bigger communities floors were made from puncheons (logs split in half with smooth side up). In the 1700s, schools east of the Alleghenies had glass panes, but glass could not be transported over the mountains to the west. The lack of glass required oiled paper to be used in long thin strips along the walls. Schooling was the responsibility of the community, and the building of the school was a community effort.

Most 1700s schools were simple rectangular log structures, with some eastern schools having clapboards because of the availability of lumber mills. Eastern schools were structurally superior. Even an octagonal design with glass windows on each wall became popular because of its better lighting and space. In Pennsylvania, many of these earlier schools focused on landscaping. Trees were needed for shade to cool the school in the summer. Trees of different species were planted to help students learn to identify them, and this practice may well be the linkage that McGuffey saw between trees and education. The operation of the 1700s schoolhouse required a lot of effort from both the families and teachers. Wood for the fireplace had to be supplied and cut by the families. Teachers arrived early to get the fire going, sharpen quill pens, and fill the oil lamps. Children had to walk to school from miles around with few roads. When a road to school was needed, it was a community project to prepare one.

Common schools brought improvements in the East and West. The one room schoolhouse made some improvements in the West from McGuffey's boyhood school to the 1850s when his Readers became dominant. Common schools meant more money for better construction. One change was the use of cast iron stoves for heating versus fireplaces. Stoves offered a more consistent and higher heat. Glass windows had started to appear in the 1850s, but these were limited to one or two because of the expense. Clapboard became more common because

1 Henry J. Kauffman, *The American One-Room Schoolhouse* (Morgantown: Masthof Press, 1997), p. 9

it better retained heat. Floors were improved also. Purchased desks replaced the homemade log benches. In 1840, a manufactured desk cost about 60 cents. School architecture started to be standardized to meet state codes and requirements.

McGuffey argued for major improvements to schools in his 1836 lecture to the "College of Teachers." He passionately argued: "Children cannot learn when uncomfortable . . . Time was, when the log school-house, with gable-end chimney, clap-board door, and long, narrow windows, papered and greased, was all that could be looked for, in a country that was still a wilderness. But that time is now past. And yet, even these cabin colleges were often more comfortable, and better conducted, than some of our public schools, at present day. It must make the heart of philanthropy bleed, to see the youth of our country so frequently collected, (when in school at all) in uncomfortable, and even filthy hovels, in which the farmers of the neighborhood would hardly consent to house their sheep; surrounded by every thing calculated to disgust them with learning, and to make them loathe even the sight of a slate or a book." McGuffey and the "College of Teachers" led the movement for state standards for school environment.

In the1840s, states appointed superintendents and boards to oversee local schools. States set rules and regulations. In Michigan in 1847 required the following items:

An evaporating pan for the stove

A thermometer for temperature checks

A clock

A shovel and tongs for stove

An ash pail

A well supplied wood house

A well for pure drinking water

Two separated privies

States started to require teachers to have the school heated an hour prior to school, and in some districts this was spelled out in the teacher's contract. Most states started to require the use of individual desks by 1850, eliminating the log bench. Wooden floors also became state requirements. Ventilation requirements were set to assure clean burning and no recycling of "burnt air" into the school. McGuffey had often remarked on the importance of good ventilation. Many of the states required a tube from the outside to the floor under the stove. The use of wood stoves and oil lamps could make the school like a coalmine on winter days. Some states specified where the stove was to be located or that a screen be around the stove to protect students.

William McGuffey had been one of the earliest to argue for the importance of a comfortable school. In his 1834 essay, McGuffey noted the importance: "In the first, we must provide suitable accommodations for our schools. Children cannot learn when uncomfortable. And they cannot be comfortable, either in cold weather, or in hot, unless the schoolhouse, or recitation room, be such as can be both warmed and ventilated, as occasion may require... Children are creatures of association and habit; and much depends upon the cheerfulness and taste of that which is connected with their early mental efforts, as to whether they shall become attached to study, and take a delight in thought; or shall contract a disgust for every thing like literature and science."

Schoolhouses were expensive operations for the rural areas they serviced. In the latter half of the nineteenth century, a schoolhouse cost from $400 to $800 with additional one hundred dollars for furniture. The building of privies might add another $150 to the overall cost. A well cost about twenty dollars. Fuel costs for wood or coal were fifteen to twenty dollars per year. In the 1890s, a school bell cost from seven to twenty-five dollars in the Montgomery Ward catalog. Most bells were on poles in the schoolyard until the 1890s, when most schools added a belfry to the roof of the structure. The belfry also eliminated the need for a separate flagpole. These costs made for long debates at the school board meetings for these thrifty farmers. In the 1870s, school districts started selling bonds to finance new schoolhouses. Farmers were also responsible for roads to the schoolhouse, which is why Alexander McGuffey built a road in Ohio for young William and his sister to get to school.

Besides the physical plant, states also audited and improved educational resources. In Ohio, Samuel Lewis of the "College of teachers" had pushed for school libraries in 1837. A state audit of 11,000 schools in New York in 1838 showed only a handful to have a library. The Governor of New York added $50,000 to an overall budget of $160,000 for school libraries. Neighboring Pennsylvania, however, had no such requirement for libraries until the late 19th century. On the other hand, a common school in Boston had a 170-book library. Interestingly, with state requirements for school libraries came state control. Often teachers could not purchase library books, but a state administrator was assigned to stock libraries. In rural areas school trustees might select the books, since the school library also functioned as a lending library for the locals. States started to request common texts as well. In the seventeenth century the texts consisted of the Bible, hornbook, and a primer. In New England, the *New England Primer* was the de facto state text. Ohio and the 'College of Teachers" became the first to push for more standardization of texts, reference maps, and the establishment of school libraries. McGuffey noted in 1836: "The next duty devolving upon parents, in relation to teachers, is to furnish them with suitable tools, with which to work. They must, we have seen, have comfortable shops — a school-house is the teacher's shop — but this will not avail, unless those shops be furnished."

The 1850s saw the evolution of the traditional blackboard. The simple blackboard was considered experimental in the first half of the nineteenth century. Woodward College in Cincinnati and the "College of Teachers" were true pioneers in the use of the blackboard. "Professional" teachers in various states start-ed to demand its inclusion. Early blackboards were "painted." Carpenters made the earliest efforts in the blackboards. Smooth, unknotted boards were jointed tightly, and then a dull black paint was used. One problem was the intense dry heat of the schoolroom, which caused the joints to open and warping. Another more permanent board used a plaster paint of lamp-black, plaster, and varnish on a smooth wood backing. Some recipes called for an all plaster sheet or type of artificial slate. By the late 1850s, slate blackboards cost about three dollars a board (about sixty dollars today). School boards and state administrators were slow to spend the money. While schools were slow to invest in the big boards, individual slates became a necessity for students in the 1850s. Chalk crayons had to be handmade out of Plaster of Paris and wheat flour. They were rolled wet and then dried on the stove.

Another improvement of the 1850s was the availability of manufactured desks and chairs. When McGuffey went to school in the 1810s, log benches were stan-dard. Usually these were split logs on short legs without backs. A long board on the sidewalls offered a surface for writing. The long board was mounted right below the wall length slit of an oilpaper window to maximize light. By the 1830s, long board desks were put in front of a bench with about ten students. The 1850 desk and chair were manufactured in units. The unit was made of wood and cast iron and had a shelf for books. The units were made in eight different sizes to better accommodate students.

The 1850s brought the use of steel pens as well. Prior to 1850, quills were used for writing; and they were messy, requiring re-sharpening or "re-cutting." The teacher had the responsibility of sharpening pens. Ink was generally manufac-tured at home using tree bark and the chemical copperas prior to 1850. In the 1850s, peddlers carried imported powdered ink. Pencils also came into use in the 1850s. Slates were the preferred writing tool because of the cost of paper and pen-cils. Even these small slates were very expensive, and care was preached to avoid the high cost of breakage. Small slates were bound with oak framing to prevent breakage. Generally, the slates were stored in the desk. Slates were not common to the 1850s because of the cost, but soon became a necessity to the schoolhouse.

As for the purchase of textbooks, this varied. The decision to supply text-books free to students was often decided at the annual school board meeting. Thrifty parents passed down texts in the family. Also there was resistance in the Midwest to pass on parental responsibilities to the community. The general trend in the 1800s was for the textbooks to be purchased by the students. The school often purchased the books to gain a discount and then resold them. The question of free textbooks was an important one, since as school classification systems progressed, some students could not attend unless they could purchase books. States became involved in the debate in the 1880s, but local school boards controlled the issue in the 1880s. One expert noted: "The recitation pedagogy of nineteenth and early twentieth-century rural schools were dependent on text-books. If children could not bring a schoolbook to class, they often simply did not attend. As a result, there was significant agitation for free textbook laws in all states of the Midwest. Rural districts in the older states of the Midwest such as Michigan, Illinois, and Wisconsin, resisted supplying free textbooks for all students until well into the twentieth century. Younger states such as Nebraska and the Dakotas, by contrast, led the way with such legislation much earlier." Wisconsin, for example, didn't enact a free textbook approach until 1909. McGuffey argued that books were the core of classification: "But this cannot be done without careful classification, which classification is impossible without a uniformity of class books." This had always been the belief of the "College of Teachers" in their effort for common schools, and the motivation behind McGuffey's Readers. McGuffey told the "College of Teachers": "We must furnish or compensate the teachers for furnishing uniform sets of suitable class books."

McGuffey had led the effort in the 1830s to have schools fully equipped even beyond free textbooks. In particular, McGuffey pointed out the necessity of a globe and a good set of maps for world geography. Many of the exotic animals discussed in the McGuffey Readers were from Africa and Australia, and the use of a globe helped the student better understand the world environment. McGuffey's lessons about oceans could also be illustrated. McGuffey often picked stories from countries such as Iceland to help illustrate world geography. McGuffey Readers and the first initiatives of the "College of Teachers" also stressed natural science and astronomy more than any other prior Readers. One important but expensive piece of equipment was the tellurian or season machine. The tellurian was a machine of brass balls representing the sun, the planets, and our moon that would rotate to illustrate seasons. It could help the student understand natural phenomena such as the long night in Iceland. Another ancillary piece of equipment was a set of solid geometric shapes such as cones and cylinders. Most teachers had an *omnium gatherum* or object box that had material samples such as brass, pewter, iron, silk, and cotton.

Here is a description of an 1880 one-room Pennsylvania schoolhouse: "The seats were plain pine board benches; the desks, of the same material, had plain tops, with backs raised about two inches above the top. Legs were two by four uprights, fastened to the floor. Two sat at each desk; a partition inside it was designed to keep books and materials of pupils separate. The floor was oak boards, split and rough hewn. Walls were partly wainscoting. The 'blackboard' was painted on the walls; slate, just coming into use, was opposed as a too expensive luxury. The rest of the walls and ceiling were plastered with a mixture of lime, sand and clay, and whitewashed about twice a year, at the beginning of the term in autumn and again at holidays. There were no blinds; but outside shutters, partly closed, kept out sun-glare; when entirely closed, to keep out cold and wind, the room was so dark, it was almost impossible to see to work, unless the oil lamps hanging on the wall were lit."[1]

The most obvious shortcoming of the one-room schoolhouse was the need to "grade" and classify students into various skill classes. From his experimental school, McGuffey had identified the need for good classification methodology. Furthermore, McGuffey early on realized the relationship between textbooks and classroom classification. McGuffey stated in 1836: "This cannot be done without careful classification, which classification is impossible without a uniformity of class books. As we value the improvement of the instructors whom we employ, to introduce as rigid a system of classification, and as great a uniformity of books, into the schools, as possible. But still more than books, and classifying is needed to furnish a school-room."

The progress of classifying students varied widely based on the unique distribution of students. Generally, the lowest class was the "ABC" class, which consisted of the beginners in reading. After 1850, the balance of the school body was generally divided by what Reader they were in. D. S. Domer, a teacher in the 1880s and 1890s, described some of the problem: "Classifying pupils was the next task that taxed my ingenuity. I had them write their names, if they could, and the Reader they were "in" at the previous school term. This showed me at once who were the writers. Some, who could not write, printed their names. The beginners were interviewed personally, to get their names. These would be the A B C class. Placing the others was more difficult. Some brought an advanced Reader, but could not read it at all, when put to the test. The promotions and demotions made some parents glad and others mad; mothers came and wanted their children changed [some things never change!]. I made enemies the first day. I was obdurate; I was running the school, and I would not change pupils unless I was convinced they could do the work that was assigned them. I handled some cases calling the pupils to read in the presence of their parents, who could then see and hear the child could not read, or do the other work of the class they had wanted to enter. The oldest pupils, whose records I could learn from the register left by my predecessor, I simply directed to the programme placed earlier on the blackboard."[2]

Classifying and grading students into groups created a management nightmare for the teacher and a distraction for the students. Students were often in different classes for arithmetic, reading, and writing. Teachers kept records of classes and individual progress in "classification registers." The popular *Welch's Teachers' Classification Register* (1884) included detailed instructions to help teach-

---

1 Thomas Woody, "Country Schoolmaster of Long Ago," *History of Education Journal*, Volume V, Winter, 1954.

2 Thomas Woody, "Country Schoolmaster of Long Ago," *History of Education Journal*, Volume V, Winter, 1954.

ers classify students. Recitations were by class while other students were try-ing to read or write other assignments. Recitation, copying, memorization, and reading were all going on simultaneously. The teacher had his or her hands full trying to moderate recitations and maintain some form of discipline. One student reminisced: "concentration was almost impossible, for there always seemed to be distractions." Besides the classifying of students based on reading ability, stu-dents were classified on arithmetic and spelling. Arithmetic consisted of students doing problems on the blackboard. It should be noted that by 1879, city schools were graded. The typical city school was a two-story brick or brownstone build-ing with four rooms on each floor.

By 1879, the school week was defined as Monday through Saturday from Oc-tober to May. The school day started in most schools at 8:00 A.M. with the ringing of the school bell. Most rural students had been up since 5:00 A.M., having break-fast and doing farm chores prior to leaving for school. Commonly, schools started with a Bible reading and the repeating of the Lord's Prayer. In some schools a song might be sung. School went to 4:00 P.M. with a morning and afternoon recess with a lunch period. Recesses were ten to fifteen minutes with a fifteen- to thirty-minute lunch. D. S. Domer recalled his 1880s Pennsylvania schoolhouse routine: "The programme went like this: I opened with Bible reading, repeating the Lord's Prayer, and singing a familiar song. Then came, first, the beginners; then arithmetic; reading classes; grammar, elementary and advanced; geography; history; physiology; and finally three or four spelling classes. The beginners re-cited three or four times a day; altogether thirty-three classes were heard in about 310 minutes, an average of less than ten minutes to each."[1]

The term "head of class" evolved during this time. Henry Kauffman described the process: "It was previously mentioned that the spelling class did not sit on the "recitation' bench. They lined up alphabetically at first (in the old times, along a crack in the floor) and the person at the head of the class was given a word to spell. If he was unable to spell the word correctly, it was given to the second person. If he spelled it correctly, he went to the head of the class. This procedure continued throughout the lesson, the smart ones eventually standing at the head of the class, the dull ones at the bottom. Though this was a standard procedure in all schools, our teacher was very careful not to humiliate children at the bottom of the class. They were encouraged and told to study harder so they would stand higher another time."[2] McGuffey supported the moving up to the head of the class. He stated in his *Fourth Reader*: "The plan of having the pupils go up toward the head of the class as they correct faults, thus stimulating attention in the listeners and care in the reader, will sometimes be found useful."

---

1 Woody, p. 48
2 Kauffman, pp. 4-5

One of the few activities, which the whole school participated in at the same time, was exercise in penmanship. Students were simply asked to copy letters or words in their copybook. The copybook also acted as a combination note-book, practice book, and diary. Students were often asked to copy "maxims" off the board into their copybook. Some schools used the *Spencerian Key to Practical Penmanship* (1866) as a copybook for writing. Platt Spencer of Geneva, Ohio developed this writing system. The Spencerian style was a beautiful script type of handwriting that was time consuming. While steel Gillott pens were available, Spencer developed his own pen. Students went directly to learning handwriting versus printing. It wasn't until 1894 that the more freeing style of A. N. Palmer was introduced.

The one-room schoolhouse teacher was far from a professional. It was looked on as a temporary job for people in transition from 1850 to 1890. Clark County, Illinois record from 1862 to 1879 illustrates the point: "During the seventeen-year period there were two terms each year; thus there were thirty-four teacher contracts signed. Of these, twenty were signed by males, fourteen by females. All fourteen female teachers taught summer terms. No females were hired to teach a winter term during this period. Twenty-one of the teachers taught one term and never returned to teach in the district. Four males and one female taught more than one term, but none of these teachers taught two terms in succession. Over the seventeen-year period, the average monthly salary for male teachers was thirty-three dollars. Female teachers, over the same years, averaged seventeen dollars per month. In this particular district there is no record of debate concerning the gender of the teacher to be hired. Records in other districts suggest that such debate was common."[1] In 1857, future President William McKinley took a job teaching in a one-room schoolhouse in Poland, Ohio for twenty-five dollars a month.

During the 1880s and 1890s, a schoolteacher made an average of five hundred dollars per year. That was a low average compared to other professions of the time.

Some occupation salaries for the Gilded Age were:

Skilled craftsmen	$800 per year
Department Store Buyer	$1200
Bookkeeper	$2000
Insurance Agent	$1200
Railroad Clerk	$800
Warehouse Clerk	$1100
Editor	$2500
Schoolteacher	$500

---

1 Paul Theobald, Country School Curriculum and Governance, *American Journal of Education*, Vol. 101, No. 2, February, 1993

The major qualification for a teacher was the ability and willingness to discipline. One teacher recalled his interview applying for the job: "I was asked upon applying for the job. At the school was whether I believed in "licking," and whether I was afraid of the boys in school. A negative answer to the first question, or an affirmative answer to the second, would have ended my career then and there." Male teachers were quick to use the "rod" because of the tendency of students to misbehave. Teachers commonly had a bundle of "hickories" beside the desk. One teacher noted the importance of demonstrating his strength to the students: "By such demonstrations I showed I would be physically able to punish boys as old and big as I was." As we have seen from McGuffey's belief in discipline, discipline was key to the functioning of a one-room schoolhouse. With so many simultaneous activities occurring, discipline was required to maintain order.

The strength needed to administer "discipline" was one factor that kept women out of teaching, but there was also a perception problem. In 1830, there were almost no women teachers (known as "schoolmarms"). New England did have "dame" schools, schools initially operated out of women's homes, but in the 1830s progressed to the schoolhouse. Catharine Beecher had brought this New England view to the "College of Teachers" of Ohio in the 1830s. Beecher and McGuffey had promoted the use of women as superior to men as teachers. Actually, the movement to women teachers grew in the 1800s because they came at half the price of men, which appealed to thrifty school boards. By 1880, women accounted for fifty percent of the teachers, and by 1900 the percentage was seventy.

The one-room schoolhouse proved to be a powerful means of early education in America. One of its weaknesses was the "class" system of mixed skills and ages limited the ability to discuss and even answer the questions in the Readers. This weakness became more problematic in the higher grades (users of the *Fifth* and *Sixth Readers*). In the 1830s, McGuffey and the "College of Teachers" had become advocates of "secondary" or "high school" education. Woodward College had pioneered the idea of a high school education in 1831. By the end of the 1830s, there were private high schools in Dayton, Akron, and Springfield. In 1838 Samuel Lewis proposed to the state of Ohio a system of secondary schools to serve the townships: "There are some townships that have the means and the desire of establishing central township schools or academies, and in most of our townships, the youth over twelve years of age could with convenience attend such a school. The number of townships now prepared for this measure is small, but will be increasing." The first public (tax based) high school in Ohio opened in Cleveland in 1848; Boston and Philadelphia had opened public high schools a few years earlier. By 1851, there were sixty high schools in the United States, in 1870 there were 800, in 1880 there were 1,200, and by 1890 there were 2,526 high schools. Most of these high schools used McGuffey's *Fifth and Sixth Readers*.

Chapter 14. The McGuffey Reader

> "McGuffey, a Scots-Irish Presbyterian minister, living on the Midwestern frontier during the first half of the nineteenth century, merely transferred his own strict moral code into lessons he either wrote or selected for the first Readers."
> — Dolores P. Sullivan, McGuffey biographer

The *McGuffey Readers* were truly not revolutionary, but evolutionary. McGuffey borrowed as much as he innovated, but the result was a superior product. *McGuffey's Readers* have been hailed as pioneering in the development of textbooks, but the roots of the Readers can be seen in the *New England Primer* and Webster's *Blue Back Speller*. McGuffey secularized the *New England Primer* and evangelized the *Blue Back Speller* to Christian moral based text. McGuffey built his stories from Webster's moral catechism, illustrating morals in the story versus the question and answer catechism approach of Webster. Webster built in a non-denominational approach versus the strongly Congregational framework of the *New England Primer*. While still strongly Christian in today's terms, *McGuffey Readers* were acceptable for public schools of the time because it avoided Christian dogma differences. The *McGuffey Reader* could be used in all parts of Ohio's Western Reserve with the mix of Christian dogma from New England Congregationalists, Presbyterians, Methodists, Quakers, German sects, and Baptists. McGuffey Readers were a major improvement in style and methodology. Furthermore, McGuffey improved on the woodcut illustrations of both the *New England Primer* and the *Blue Back Speller*. Finally, he added questions to the stories to help the teachers use the text more effectively. The combination of stories and improved illustrations added a fascination to the young student. The Readers were able to reach the average student such as a young Henry Ford, not just the future scholars.

The area where the *McGuffey Readers* broke new ground and were clearly revolutionary was the "point of view" of the Readers. Compared to early readers such as the *New England Primer* and even the Bible as a teaching text, McGuffey was the Walt Disney of the period, a text that children could relate to. McGuffeyland was full of great memories which remained a lifetime, as shown by Henry Ford's love of the Readers. There were lessons on exotic African animals, great travel adventures, and lessons on the natural world around them. McGuffey researcher James Scully noted: "With all the innovations made by McGuffey in his Readers, his major contribution was in the type of selection he made for his books. Here for the first time on a large scale were stories and articles and poems that appealed to children as children and not as infantile adults, laboring under the threat of hell-fire and damnation. Child life began to come into its own, or at least a part of its own, in story and song. Here were children playing, at least at times, for work was always at hand in the frontier society. At any rate, little attention was paid to the joys of living. To us now this element of joy of living may seem indeed small, but we must remember how unusual it was in the shadow of the *New England Primer*."

In the 1700s, the *New England Primer* and the Bible were the beginning texts for American children. Benjamin Harris first published the *New England Primer* in 1690. It was extremely popular in New England in the 1880s. It was a Calvinistic Puritan text and was also a catechism. One of its most memorable prayers remains: "Now I lay me down to my sleep; I pray the Lord my soul to keep; if I should die before I wake; I pray the Lord my soul to take." The *New England Primer* also gave us folksy Puritan proverbs such as "An idle mind is the Devil's workshop." The *New England Primer* was never popular with the Lutheran based Pennsylvania Quakers and Germans. Its Calvinistic views ruled out Anglicans as well. Still, the *New England Primer* sold about three million, and dominated the New England coast. William McGuffey did use the *New England Primer* as a child and while teaching in Paris, Kentucky. He was able to evaluate its strengths and weaknesses from both perspectives.

The "hornbook" was used with the *New England Primer* because the Primer lacked a strong methodology and routine. The hornbook offered the oldest approach to learning, going back to the 1600s in England; and its popularity continued into the late 1800s. The hornbook looked like a wooden paddle. It consisted of an eight inches by three inches rectangle with a handle. At the end of the handle was a hole with a leather thong so the hornbook could be hung on the neck. On the paddle, a piece of paper or parchment was covered by a thin transparent piece of horn. Brass screws attached the horn sheet. Hornbooks were used for phonetic learning. A similar paddle made out of stiff paper was called a battledore. The beginner's hornbook would have the alphabet in upper and lower cases, the vowels, consonants, and the combinations "abs" such as ab, eb and ib. The hornbook was a great lead-in for the *New England Primer* as well as the McGuffey Series.

The *New England Primer* had two faults which limited its use in American common schools. First, it was a religious text that not only used religious imagery to teach but also taught Calvinist dogma, including a Westminster Catechism. Besides pure biblical readings, it included Puritan hagiography such as the martyrdom of John Rogers. The Puritan approach was acceptable to Congregationalists and most Presbyterians but would be problematic for Lutherans and Methodists, let alone Catholics. Early Pennsylvania Germans refused to use it. Even in New England the new liberal Desist Unitarian movement found the New England Primer totally unacceptable. At least McGuffey made his Readers acceptable for most Protestant Christians. Catholics in the 1800s were usually taught in their own schools, using Catholic texts such as the *Orbis Pictus*. The other problem of the *New England Primer* was that it lacked a standardized alphabet. A recent critic noted: "the alphabet of the *New England Primer* includes '&' as its final character, contains the long s (ſ), and many editions present ligatures as though they are extra characters. The alphabet varies between twenty-four and twenty-six letters, sometimes within the same edition."[1] The Primer also varied fonts and types as well as upper and lower cases. This alphabet and phraseology was like a foreign language to the frontier West.

Webster's Blue Back Speller, while not a "reader," was an extremely popular introductory grammar book. The *Blue Back Speller's* sales are estimated at one hundred million, making it a best seller more than any single McGuffey book. McGuffey himself had started with the *Blue Back Speller*. It is said that the *Blue Back Speller* dominated in the 1780s to 1830s. Commonly, families purchased the *Blue Back Speller* as a starting home text. The Webster Speller replaced the highly religious approach of the *New England Primer* with a moral approach. Many of the Democratic Jeffersonian frontier communities found the *Blue Back Speller* too steeped in Whig ideology. The moral approach of Webster made it acceptable to all Protestant denominations as well as to Catholics. Webster's moral catechism praised property and industry. The Speller clearly promoted the early roots of capitalism in America.

Readers were for older students who had advanced beyond spelling and word recognition. The *New England Primer* was not really a Reader. The first American Reader was Noah Webster's *An American Selection of Lessons in Reading and Speaking* in 1785. Webster put together some other Readers but not as a graded series. Webster's Readers never had the sales of his *Speller*. Prior to 1800, Readers lacked organization and standardization. They were merely collections of stories and compositions that lacked direction. McGuffey and his publisher had made an extensive study of all textbooks, and the lack of direction was obvious. Readers

---

1   Patricia Crain, *The Story of A* (Stanford: Stanford University Press, 2000), 42

included material form third grade to college without being organized in order of difficulty. The graded system was non-existent in the 1830s; such issues were left to the teacher and class. The *McGuffey Readers* offered the first coordinated and integrated Readers.

The limitations of the *New England Primer* in Pennsylvania and West created a need for another text. To fill that gap, Lindley Murray published the *English Reader* in 1795. *Murray's Reader* is considered by some people to be the first Reader in America. Murray actually published a series of lower level Readers. Lindley Murray was an American Quaker, who returned to England to develop his Reader. The War of 1812 slowed the wide usage of the Murray Reader, but its popularity grew and peaked in the 1830s. Murray sold the rights to printers across the country, and they were published in every major United States city. The Murray Reader was never used in New England but did find support in Pennsylvania and Ohio. They had established a market in the Western Reserve of Ohio by 1830 and started to win over some schools in the Transylvania area by 1833 prior to the release of the *McGuffey Readers*. The Murray Reader pioneered the use of rhetorical exercises, which McGuffey later incorporated. Murray started publishing his books with an American printer in 1823 in Boston. Cincinnati printers started producing it in 1833.

McGuffey was not the first to look at a more standardized and universally accepted text. The *Franklin Reader* tried to broaden the audience to the Quakers and Germans of Pennsylvanian in 1802. The *Franklin Reader* was still extremely religious in nature, but it did expand into moral stories and improved illustrations. The *Worchester Reader* never generated a lot of sales, but its copyright lawsuit plagued *McGuffey Readers* in the first year. The *Worchester Reader* was an effort from Eastern publishers to crack the lucrative market. In reality most of the Readers, including those of McGuffey, were more evolutionary than revolutionary. McGuffey's superiority rested in his accumulation of the best approaches in one text.

Goodrich School Readers were another effort of Eastern publishers to win the Western market. The *Goodrich Reader* was modeled after Murray. Goodrich was from Connecticut and had never been west of Pittsburgh. Samuel S. Goodrich modeled his Readers and Spellers after those of Lindley Murray. The *Goodrich Reader* was published in Louisville to suggest a Western connection, but the style clearly favored the New England student. Samuel Griswold Goodrich was himself a storyteller and an essayist. McGuffey actually used two stories of Goodrich in his *Third Reader* to illustrate the danger of rashness. McGuffey used over fifty percent American based material, while Goodrich and Murray used British stories and heroes. Goodrich, however, did start to develop American heroes, which McGuffey would follow. The other key attribute of the *McGuffey Reader* was its Western twist. McGuffey truly understood the Western mind and child. He focused on American heroes such as George Washington, Thomas Jefferson, and Daniel Webster. McGuffey selected Western American writers for many of his compositions, many from the "College of Teachers."

The evolutionary history of Readers must include Lyman Cobb and Samuel Worcester. Both of these men made important contributions, which McGuffey built on. Lyman Cobb wrote the *Juvenile Reader*, which was published in 1830. The *Juvenile Reader* was published in Ithaca, New York, and clearly had an eastern bent. Still, Cobb broke ground by writing the first graded series. Cobb built up the series from one to two to many syllable words. Samuel Worcester's Reader in 1826 used teaching notes, a method which McGuffey would adopt. Both of these men borrowed from *the New England Primer*. However, while innovative, neither the *Worcester* nor the *Juvenile Reader* became big sellers. Both were very good textbooks, but neither could match the marketing genius of Winthrop Smith. In 1832, Albert Pickett of the "College of Teachers" introduced a Western style-advanced Reader. Another early model was that of James Hall's 1833 *Western Reader*. The *Western Reader* was published in Cincinnati and addressed the Western mind, but it was never a popular seller. It had lacked the coordination of a series, which had become the real need of growing common schools. McGuffey's series would address the basics and the needs of grade school through high school. Interestingly, Albert Pickett and James Hall were active in the "College of Teachers" promotion of the *McGuffey Readers*.

The appearance of McGuffey's *Eclectic Readers* did not eliminate the use of Webster's *Blue Back Speller* but actually increased sales. In fact, many of the Ohio schools required finishing the *Speller* prior to moving to the *McGuffey Readers*. McGuffey adopted Webster's methodology, pronunciation, and spelling, making the *Blue Back Speller* a companion text for home and school. McGuffey advanced texts and education with this adoption by standardizing the language as well as the culture. In particular, McGuffey supported Webster's style over the more formal old English of the eastern texts.

The biggest contribution of McGuffey was the blending of America's Western culture into one. Like the Western Reserve and the Cincinnati Enlightenment, the *McGuffey Readers* were a mixing bowl. A McGuffey critic and Ohio State professor James Rodabaugh summarized the mixture: "McGuffey's books are an evidence of the influence of the West, New England Puritans and Virginia Cavaliers, Scotch-Irish democrats and thrifty Germans, all formed the new society of the West. It was a conglomeration of nationalities and cultures. Harmony depended upon compromises between the cultural groups, and in producing this harmonious relationship, McGuffey's Readers played an important part . . . there was enough of the Puritan in them to satisfy the New Englanders who had migrated to the Northwest; there was enough of the Cavalier to attract the aristoc-racy of Virginia and the Carolinas; there was enough individualism to interest the Scots, and enough of a code of thrift to meet the demands of both the Scots and Germans. McGuffey was influenced by the breakdown of cultures in the West, and in turn, his Readers served to unite the various culture groups and mold them into one."[1]

One issue that remains a problem to this day is the complexity of the author-ship of the *McGuffey Readers*. Alexander's role has been challenged over the years. The center of the controversy stems from a 1900 Pittsburgh article interviewing Alexander. Alexander stated: "My brother was very busy and as I had abundance of time on my hands he agreed to undertake the work with the understanding that the burden of it was to come upon me, I working under his supervision. The readers were to be published under his name in order to give them prestige. The firm agreed to this arrangement, so they brought over a great load of old school readers from which, as from other and higher sources, I was to make the selec-tions. The work took all of my spare time during the winter of 1836 and half of the 1837.[2] Biographer Dolores Sullivan quoted another 1918 newspaper article "riddled with erroneous information" that also makes the case for a major role by Alexander. The nature of the article suggests its source was the earlier article. Hugh Fullerton suggested in 1927 that McGuffey had most of the Readers pre-pared prior to being offered the contract[3], and his work with the experimental school certainly supports that.

Alice McGuffey Ruggles (related on Alexander's side), who was often critical of William's fame, noted: "To William belongs the initiative and the first four Readers. The Fifth and Sixth, the two most often quoted, most dearly loved, are Alexander's. Both men lived and died quite unconscious of their real contribu-tions to posterity." This seems consistent with the actual record. Ruggles had also noted that the publisher reduced Alexander's name and initials to small print on the Fifth and Sixth Reader to fool the public, which is also consistent with the re-cord. Pro-William biographer Harvey Minnich stated: "He [Alexander] assisted McGuffey in the completion of the series." The record supports that Alexander was an important assistant as was Catharine Beecher. There is no question that the idea and concept was William McGuffey's. The selections of the first four Readers are very close to the topics discussed in the "College of Teachers," which William was active in. More so than any other influence, the "College of Teachers" is seen in all the Readers, many of which contained articles from the members of the "College of Teachers."

1 James Rodabaugh, *Ohio Archaeological and Historical Quarterly, Volume 46*, 1936, pp. 294-299.
2 Dolores Sullivan, p. 105
3 Hugh Fullerton, "Who Was That Guy McGuffey," *Saturday Evening Post*, November, 1927.

Besides authorship, critics often focus on the Christian bias. *McGuffey's Readers*, while strongly Christian in nature, were non-sectarian. In story lesson twenty of his *First Reader*, he states: "All who take care of you and help you were sent you by God. He sent His Son to show you his will, and to die for you." McGuffey was clear about his Christian bias: "The Christian religion is the religion of our country. From it are derived our notions on character of God, on the great moral Governor of the universe. On its doctrines are founded the peculiarities of our free institutions. From no source has the author drawn more conspicuously than from the scared Scriptures. From all these extracts from the Bible I make no apology." This religious nature of the texts was actually a market demand of Western parents. Parents wanted religion and Christian principles taught, what they didn't want was dogma and denominational views. The Bible, Ten Commandments, and Golden Rule found common agreement. It had been the "College of Teachers" that impressed the guiding principle on William McGuffey, who was often tied up in dogma battles of his own church. The "College of Teachers" and McGuffey came to the conclusion that morals were common to all religions and could be the basis of a common school textbook.

The McGuffey approach stood out because it was a coordinated effort to blend reading and moral education. McGuffey's blended approach was not new, but it was better in execution than previous efforts. W. Cameron used the following analogy for the *First Reader*: "Take McGuffey's *First Reader*-what do we see behind his one syllable words? We see the child as a little barbarian, little savage. He puts a cat and a hen together in a box and sits on the lid while a terrific eruption ensues... This small First Reader takes the infant barbarian mind and plants the seed of another point of view, even if it be but the hen's point of view; it plants the thought of responsibility, and leads one to look at oneself objectively as part of the whole."[1] McGuffey's lessons always had a moral point but he never had to restate it at the end. He took the reader there without hitting the reader over the head. Cameron further states: "The *Second Reader* enlists the forces of moral intelligence to lay the foundations of manly integrity, it remains for the *Third Reader* to continue the upward progress, and in its pages emerges a social being."

The 1841 revisions corrected errors and mistakes in editing, not lesson selection. The 1843 revisions, in particular, addressed the issue of assuring non-denominational nature of the series by addressing lesson selection. The preface noted that the contents were reviewed by "highly intelligent clergymen and teachers of various Protestant and Catholic denominations." The lesson, "The Character of Martin Luther," was also removed from the *Third Reader*. Interestingly, McGuffey's Halloween story, "Never Do Mischief," was removed in the 1843 revision. The story had two boys playing a ghost and driving a playmate

---

1 W. J. Cameron, "The Mind of McGuffey" A talk delivered at Miami University, July, 1937, Benson Research Center Archives

into mental derangement, or as the story says "a perfect idiot." Most stories like "Harry and the Guidepost" in the *Third Reader* focused on debunking the idea of ghosts. Actually, the *McGuffey Readers* had been anti-ghost and Halloween, which was true to the Presbyterian view of such things being the legacy of Irish Catholic immigrants. Never before had customer feedback been used so extensively in the development of school texts.

Another goal of the 1843 revisions was to eliminate references to slavery and moderate regional tensions. The lesson "Character of Wilberforce" that hailed the elimination of slavery in Britain was dropped in 1843. Phrases and lines from other stories such as "The Miseries of Imprisonment" were eliminated and the line, "the millions of my fellow creatures born to no inheritance but slavery." This is one area where McGuffey and the publisher broke from the consensus of the "College of Teachers." The "College of Teachers" had always been a hotbed of abolitionists. The publisher, in particular, wanted a text that was acceptable in all states, and politics like religious issues had to be neutral and moral based. This type of revision was needed because *McGuffey Readers* served mainly Northern and Southern Border States. Every effort in 1843 was taken to assure neutrality. This neutrality served the company well in the future. The final role of this revision was to fully purge the series of errors, which teachers had noted in use. Winthrop Smith was extremely sensitive to parents and educators, who feared revisions were simply a money making scheme.

The *McGuffey Rhetorical Guide* was released in 1839 and had been compiled by Alexander McGuffey. Its revision came with the review of Winthrop Smith and Alexander McGuffey in 1843. It would be released in revised form in 1844 as the *Fifth Reader* of the Eclectic Series, which was also developed fully by Alexander McGuffey. The *Fifth Reader* added sixty pages of the principles of elocution. The *Fifth Reader* was to be for high schools and some academies. It contained the world's greatest literature. In particular, students were introduced to American writers such as James Fennimore Cooper and Washington Irving, which was Alexander's expertise. The *Fifth Reader* became a huge sales success, finding its way into many home libraries.

The year 1846 represented a review of the overall series by editor Timothy Pinneo. Pinneo had a background in the development of *Pinneo's Grammar*, which replaced the popular *Harvey's English Grammar*. He was interested in revising the *McGuffey Progressive Speller*, which had not been able to take market share from *Webster's Blue Back Speller*. The Speller had been work of Alexander McGuffey in 1838, but it held to the McGuffey theory of reading first. The revision approached the old style of *Webster's Blue Back Speller*. Pinneo's work moved the series to a fully integrated series, which greatly improved overall sales. In addition, Pinneo and Winthrop wanted to add a women's Reader to the Eclectic series. In the 1840s, the education of women had remained a separate entity. Even in the "College of

Teachers," the views were divided, but the marketplace continued to separate girls into their own schools, thus developing a demand for special women Readers. William McGuffey believed that common education should be inclusive, and texts would be able to address a common vision for all. Pinneo decided to target the higher-level women seminaries for a new Reader, while promoting the other Readers for all sexes.

The development of this Reader for women was to be the counterpart of the *Fifth Reader*. The heart of the Reader was to be "distinctly feminine" poems and readings. William McGuffey had never been extremely fond of poetry, but Alexander had added more to the *Fifth Reader*. Alexander was better suited to author these literature based Readers. Alexander would work with Pinneo on selections for what would become known as the *Hemans Young Ladies Reader*. The title honored Felicia Dorothea Hemans, and the Reader contained twenty-four of her poems. The addition of the *Heman's Reader* strengthened the overall series but sold, to some degree, as a separate entity. Because most Western girls had first experienced the *McGuffey Reader*; it was a logical next step to move to the *Heman's Reader*. The "College of Teachers," led by William McGuffey and Catharine Beecher, continued to preach educating girls and boys together with common texts.

The real secret to the longevity of the McGuffey Readers was their flexibility. That flexibility was based in review and revision. Winthrop Smith had made review by teachers central to his business plan, but Smith also had a marketing plan. He had studied the competition and adjusted, as we have seen. Furthermore he adjusted to population trends. As German immigrants poured in the 1850s, a German edition was published. Stories were added and subtracted, errors corrected, and questions changed every few years; but 1857 and 1879, major revisions were driven by market shifts. *McGuffey Readers* owned the market from 1840 to 1870 in the states of Ohio, Indiana, Kentucky, Pennsylvania, Michigan, and Illinois. The 1853 revisions added articulation exercises as well as some minor alterations to assure Southern sales. In the *First Reader*, hyphens were used between syllables in the lessons. All five Readers were issued as "Newly Revised." This practice was extended to the *Second* and *Third Reader* before the experiment was discontinued in 1865. Teachers and students found the hyphens as distracting, and Smith always listened closely to the teachers that used the books.

The 1857 editions and revisions addressed another shift in the market. Prior to the 1850s, the *McGuffey Reader* covered a board range of subjects. Particularly, lessons on animals such as elephants, whales, tigers, lions, giraffes, and others appeared throughout the series. In the 1850s, geography and other specialized texts appeared, reducing the need for McGuffey to cover board categories. Lessons such as "Whale Catching" in the *Second Reader* were eliminated. The Speller was again upgraded as a new edition of the *Blue Back Speller* and was also released in 1857. The 1857 revision also reflected a shift by the editors to more realism.

Hagiographic characters and stories such as "The Rich Boy" and "The Poor Boy" were removed in 1857. Some minor revisions were made to the Readers prior and during the Civil War to assure Southern acceptability. Between 1860 and 1870, they controlled a large segment of the South as well. Most competitors followed the lead of the *McGuffey Readers*. In 1863, the *High School Reader* was added to the series. The *High School Reader* offered an advanced book of new material for the emerging secondary education system in Ohio.

The *Sixth Reader* came into being with the 1857 editions, being the work of Alexander McGuffey, Thomas Pinneo, Obed Wilson, and Mrs. Obed Wilson; but it mainly consisted of upgraded material from the *Fourth* and *Fifth Readers*. It was considered a "Thesaurus of Good Literature." It contained works from 111 authors including Shakespeare, Milton, Bacon, Dryden, Addison, Browning, and Tennyson. American authors included Hawthorne, Longfellow, Emerson, and Irving. Mrs. Wilson did add some new prose and poetry. She was the former Amanda Landrum, who had been a Cincinnati teacher and member of the "College of Teachers." Alexander and the Wilsons would become close friends. The *Sixth Reader* and the *High School Reader* was another effort to target emerging markets and trends in education. The term "high school" was used in the 1850s as major cities started to add these advanced and specialized schooling. The advanced nature and board curriculum required a more specialized Reader.

Winthrop B. Smith & Co. adjusted their prices for the 1857 edition. The prices reflected a new sales strategy to discount price if purchased by the dozen. This discount pricing was meant to entice schools to start purchasing books for students. Thrifty farm school boards had resisted free texts, but per dozen pricing appealed to these thrifty farmers and school boards started purchasing books to realize quantity discounts. The price for books (based on a purchase of a dozen) were:

Pictorial Reader	$. 07
Eclectic Spelling Book	$. 07
First Reader	$. 07
Second Reader	$.15
Third Reader	$.21
Fourth Reader	$.24
Fifth Reader	$.42
Sixth Reader	$.54
High School Reader	$.70
Herman's Reader	$.54
Ray's First Arithmetic	$.08

The competition did not roll over; Sanders introduced his *Union Readers* in 1861. Sanders Union Readers dramatically increased the use of pictures and added pages on principles of elocution, explanatory notes, and rhetorical notes. Sanders gained some sales in the East, but *McGuffey Readers* remained dominant in the Midwest and South. However, all said, Sanders managed to sell over thirteen million books. McGuffey Readers, during their hundred-year span, never successfully controlled market share in New England, which preferred the Calvinistic religious bias.

The 1866 revision or special editions were printed to address the Civil War. The 1866 editions were particularly aimed at the Northern States, while the 1857 editions were pushed in the South. Four lessons were added to the *Sixth Reader* that addressed the Civil War: "Calling the Roll," "The Dying Soldier," "The Picket," and "The Brave at Home." The soldiers were pictured universally, and the themes were consistent with the anti-war theme of earlier Readers. McGuffey had been hired after the Civil War to survey the South, and his opinions were critical to changes in the series up to the *Fifth Reader*. McGuffey had been appalled at the carpetbaggers and their poor treatment of the old Southern aristocrats. Southern schools were resistant and fearful of "Northern ideas." The *Sixth Reader* had been originally assembled by a collaboration of Alexander McGuffey, Obed J. Wilson, and Thomas Pinneo, and it is doubtful that William McGuffey had little but a weak vote of final approval. Alexander McGuffey did review most of the revisions in the 1860s. Still, William McGuffey's report on the war-torn South made an impact on the publishers. The lesson "Picket," while using a universal soldier, was clearly from the North. This lesson was eliminated in the 1879 major revision, which hoped to eliminate any hint of bias.

During the war, Winthrop Smith sold his share in the publishing firm and a new firm, Sargent, Wilson, and Hinkle, emerged. With the addition of Lewis Antwerp in 1866 and the retirement of Edward Sargent, the firm became Wilson, Hinkle, and Company. While sales had been outstanding throughout the war and after, profitability had fallen. Part of this was due to the opening of the South which created a boom market, and then new competition came into being. Harper Brothers out of New York mounted a true market campaign with its *Willson Readers*. Harper Brothers used agents with sales incentives to sell to schools and descended to Ohio and Indiana like the carpetbaggers on the South. Agents worked on commission for the initial sales, but nothing for continuance of sales. *Willson Readers* took significant share from the *McGuffey Readers*. The sales pitch was that the *Willson Readers* offered to combine science and literature. *Willson Readers* focused on the use of animals and natural science to teach reading. Wilson, Hinkle, and Company reacted to regain market share with some post-war revisions, but most of the effort was in new marketing.

The market in the 1870s was changing. Many public schools started to purchase books, which initially had been the responsibility of the parents. Schools caught in the recessionary times following the Civil War tended to use the books for many years, requiring the publisher to look for novel ideas to sell books. This change brought a new partner, Robert Quincy Beer, into the firm of Wilson, Hinkle, and Company. Beer took over the marketing of the books and made some key changes. Beer established a three-tier price strategy in 1869. There was the retail price ranging from twenty cents for the *First Reader*, forty cents for the *Second Reader*, fifty-five cents for the *Third Reader*, sixty-five cents for the *Fourth Reader*, $1.05 for the *Fifth Reader*, and $1.25 for the *Sixth Reader*. An introductory price was established at two-thirds the retail price as an incentive to try the Readers. There was also an exchange price of one-half the retail price if the old books were turned in. A special introductory price was established if a school purchased the books and turned in competing Readers. In this case, the school qualified for the exchange price. Beer increased salesmen in the Midwest and South to implement this new sales strategy. This price strategy created huge growth and quickly brought the firm to high profitability. Beer died in 1871, and a new partner, Caleb Bragg, came in to implement the new marketing strategy. Caleb's strategy also addressed the change in the marketplace, where school districts started to supply books to students in some of the more Western states such as Wisconsin and Illinois.

In 1877, the firm would become Van Antwerp, Bragg, and Company. The competition turned to an improved product to overcome the new marketing strategy, but *McGuffey Readers* had established themselves as a consistent product. Sales once again boomed, *Willson Readers* lost ground and Southern sales exploded. Part of this was a sales failure of the *Willson Readers* to deliver in the classroom and market. In 1875, Thomas Harvey released a new five Reader series, but *McGuffey Readers* held the market. Things changed again in 1877 with the introduction of the *Appleton Readers*. The *Appleton Readers* were the brain child of Andrew Rickoff, superintendent of Cleveland schools; William Harris, superintendent of the St. Louis schools; and Professor Mark Bailey of Yale University. These Readers were a graded series that addressed the concerns of West and East. They broke new ground with their excellent illustrations and new stories. The lessons were better prepared for a post Civil War nation. The *Appleton Readers* had a strong sales force as well, and sales of McGuffey were dropping in the Midwest. Editor Henry Vail of Van Antwerp, Bragg & Co., who now owned the series, planned a massive revision. Henry Vial had liked the Harvey series, and he asked Thomas Harvey to join his revision team, which included Robert Stevenson of Ohio, Edwin Hewett of Illinois, and Amanda Funnelle of Indiana. This team would generate the famous 1879 revision after McGuffey's death.

The major focus of the team was the illustration of the competition, which had hurt McGuffey sales in the Midwest. The *McGuffey Readers* had pioneered the massive use of illustrations, but they had not kept up in artistic techniques and technology. Since the Civil War, magazines like *Harpers* had produced beautiful illustrations using better technology and artists. Two of America's best illustrators got their start with the *McGuffey Readers*. One of the first things the new team did was to hire Howard Pyle (1853–1911), one of America's best illustrators. Howard Pyle would illustrate the 1883 classic *The Mercy Adventures of Robin Hood*, which remains in print today. Pyle is considered the father of modern illustration. The initials of the artists can be seen in *McGuffey Readers* of 1879 and later. Tom Moran (1837–1926) was another famous illustrator hired for the 1879 revision. Even more important is that illustrations were coordinated with the actual stories. In addition, the team added pre-notes to lessons that gave biographical information on authors. The addition of biographical notes had given the *Appleton Readers* popularity among teachers. Many teachers wanted help to better prepare lessons and had called for this. A few "remarks" and footnotes were added as well. New stories were added that followed the Horatio Alger rages-to-riches paradigm, adding stories such as *"Henry, The Boot-Black."* These stories would become the touchstone of the Gilded Age Readers.

The 1879 revision adapted to a post-Civil War America without sacrificing the original direction of McGuffey. The 1879 revision moderated its religious backbone, but it still remained Christian. The revision reflected the shift in the general population to a less evangelical temperament. The "Lord's Prayer" survived the cut, but moved from the original *Second Reader* to the *Third Reader*. The "Sermon on the Mount" also survived the cut. But all mention of God except one was eliminated from the *First Reader*. Biographer Dolores Sullivan noted that the mention of God was "two lessons in the *Second Reader*, in four lessons in the *Third Reader*, and only ten lessons in the *Fourth Reader*." The lesson "The Cool Shade" was cut from the *Second Reader*, and this story had been foundation to argue that nature was evidence of the existence of a Creator. "The Cool Shade" story caused a significant backlash in the market. Powerful Christian lessons in the *Third Reader* such "The Bible," "More about the Bible," "Character of Jesus Christ," "Solomon's Wise Choice," "The Goodness of God," "Character of Martin Luther," and "Gospel Invitation" that appeared in the original did not appear in the 1879 revision. The *Fourth Reader* actually increased in its use of God. There was, however, an overall effort to tone down the Christian bent for the changing population. Not that the population was any less Christian, but it was more Catholic, and Catholics were concerned about the Protestant tone.

The more interesting thing is that while the 1879 edition reduced the religious content, is actually increased the moral, which would have been consistent with McGuffey's approach. John Nietz noted the trend: "Nearly, thirty percent of the selections of the 1844 Fourth Reader was religious in nature. However, this percentage gradually decreased in the later editions until it was only three percent in the 1901 edition. On the other hand, the emphasis on morals increased until it reached forty percent in the 1879"[1] The original McGuffey revolution had been based on a more moralistic tone versus a religious one. New issues were surfacing in society that was questioning the relationship between religion and science. As they had in the past, the publishers adapted to the changes.

Personally, McGuffey had stood strong in the nineteenth century debate against Darwinism, but the Readers adapted to discoveries in science. The 1879 revision dropped the popular lesson of the *Second Reader* "How the World was Made." The story used Irish Bishop Ussher's famous calculation that the earth was created in 4,004 B.C. Bishop Ussher proposed this back in the 1600s, and it was widely accepted until the 1860s. Mathematics books often had the question: "How many minutes have passed since the creation of the world." Stanley Lindberg noted that after the *Origin of Species* was published in 1859, the 1865 revision dropped the reference to "six thousand years ago" and replaced it with "many years ago." While McGuffey might have disagreed with the theology, he would have agreed with keeping religious controversy out of the Readers. He had long ago realized that the real enemy to common school was religious or political controversies.

The 1879 revisions included improved illustrations and new learning tips. The best American artists were hired to improve illustrations and better coordinate the pictures with the story. The lessons were also more "Americanized," with many British stories replaced for American ones. With the use of slates in the 1860s, "slate work" exercises were added to the lessons. Another important task of the 1879 revision was an extensive review of reading difficulty, resulting in stories being modified or moved up in the series. The 1879 revision addressed the necessary healing of the United States after the Civil War. While McGuffey died 1873, his study of the condition of the South after the war had made a powerful impact on the editors. Editorially, it was in the best interest of the McGuffey Readers to promote rapid national healing, since South and North sales were critical for profitability. One story "The Dying Soldiers" was actually added to the 1866 edition of the *Fourth Reader* to make heroes out of soldiers on both sides. Many again felt the Readers overdid it, but making heroes out of both sides was an important contribution of the McGuffey Readers, which was the only text initially covering Northern and Southern school houses.

While the 1879 revision followed the spirit of McGuffey, it was the first major revision in which McGuffey had no say, and over half the material was replaced in the 1879 revision. The 1879 edition had to address a post-war America that was

---

1 John Nietz, "Why the Longevity of the McGuffey Readers," *History of Education Quarterly*, Vol.4, No. 2, June, 1964.

much changed. German archaists had led strikes and riots in the streets of major American cities, the world's largest steel plant had been built in 1875, attracting thousands of Southern and eastern European immigrants, and strict Puritanical values were eroding. Catholic immigrants were most of the new wave. Railroads, while few in the 1850s, dominated transportation in America. Industries such as glass, iron, steel, railroads, and coal employed millions. The public school system was well established in the nation. Additional liberal founding father essays such as those of Thomas Jefferson were added. McGuffey would have never approved. Ironically, the Jefferson selection was from his inaugural address and titled "Political Toleration." The religious base was toned down as well in the 1879 edition (something Jefferson would have approved). The 1879 revision of the *Fifth* and *Sixth Reader* had a major addition of poetry including some that would become American classics such as "The Raven" and "The Village Blacksmith."

Industrialization led to massive immigration, and massive changes in American culture. It would be the railroads and the industries they created that caused the second wave of immigration. The railroad expansion started in the 1840s but would increase six-fold between 1860 and 1900. There were 30,626 miles of track in 1860, by 1870 there were 52,299 miles, in 1880 there were 93,262 miles of track, in 1890 it increased to 166,703 miles, and in 1900 there were 193,346 miles of track. This exponential growth fueled the steel industry of Andrew Carnegie and the coalfields of Pennsylvania and Illinois. It also created great factories such as Baldwin Locomotive in Philadelphia and Westinghouse Air Brake in Pittsburgh. Railroad related manufacturers became the megaliths of industry. The Bath Iron Works of Maine, which was a major supplier to the railroads, was the largest manufacturing facility at the beginning of the Civil War with 4,500 employees. Manufacturing coarsened discrimination and vulgarity, but the *McGuffey Readers* stood for fairness. *McGuffey Readers* withstood the great upheaval of American society, only to redirect society back to its early values. Richard Mosier noted that "The McGuffey readers fought a continuing battle for tolerance to all sects and churches and the brotherhood to all men." It was a blessing that many of these American "Captains of Industry" had been raised on *McGuffey Readers*.

The Irish and Germans continued to immigrate through the 1870s. The German's dispersed to the Plains, but the Irish clogged the cities and the schools. The Irish faced competition for jobs and discrimination. Cities segregated the Irish into sections such as "Shanty Towns." Cleveland had "Whiskey Island," "The Triangle," and "Vinegar Hill." The Irish that clustered in cities such as New York often shared the ghetto with Jews, Germans, and other non-Anglo-Americans. The Irish corned beef and cabbage dish was unknown in Ireland and was borrowed by the Irish from the Jews, who found a use for a poor cut of beef. The Jews replaced the upward moving Irish in the New York slums. The main Jewish immigration came in the period from 1880 to 1910 and was estimated at over one million for the period. Seventy-one percent of these were from Russia, nineteen percent from Austria–Hungary, and five percent were from Romania. The Russian Jews made up most of the New York ghettos of the period. The Jews worked in garment and shoemaking sweatshops. The railroads, however, did offer a better life for the Irish. The 1879 revision was made to address these cultural and ethnic changes. William McGuffey's spirit of tolerance had set the correct tone for these new immigrants. In addition, the shift from a rural America to an urban America had accelerated in the 1870s.

Not everyone was pleased with the 1879 revisions. The loss of the religious content and rages-to-riches stories such as "The Chimney Sweep" in the *Second Reader* forced a reprint of the 1865 *Second Reader*. "The Chimney Sweep" is often believed to have been a possible model for later Horatio Alger rags-to-riches stories. This rare edition was sold along with 1879 revision of the *Second Reader*. "Henry the Boot-Black," the story added to the 1879 revision to replace "The Chimney Sweep," reached a similar level of popularity. These rags-to-riches stories were particularly popular with the new wave of immigration, and many believed were at the root of the popular support for capitalism over European socialism.

CHAPTER 15. AN AMERICAN VIEW OF EDUCATION

> "The care of Souls cannot belong to the Civil Magistrate because his Power consists only in outward force; but true and saving religion consists in the inward persuasion of the mind, without which nothing can be acceptable to God."
>
> — John Locke, 1689

Americans viewed education as a right and a necessity. Education was the entrance to the middle class and wealth. It was the means to break away from the class system of Europe, and from Scotland came the idea that education for all was a function of government. In 1848, Massachusetts Congressman and educator Horace Mann defined it this way: "Education, then, beyond all other devices of human origin is the great equalizer of the conditions of men — the balance wheel of the social machinery." The American view of education separated America from the world. Its love of education equaled its love of freedom. As the nineteenth century progressed, it was education that held capitalism against the Marxist movement of Europe as an equalizer. It was education that allowed an immigrant laborer's family to progress to the middle class in less than two generations. It was two spirits that guided this American view — that of the American West and that of the hills of Scotland. American education proved to be a continuation of the American Revolution. It proved Karl Marx wrong in that the power was not in the workplace but in the classroom.

McGuffey reformed American education, applying the principles of the Scottish Enlightenment. The idea of common education for all was born in Scotland and implemented by the Presbyterian Church. It is no accident that Scottish freedom philosophers such as Adam Smith and John Locke were also advocates of education. These men understood that freedom depended on the education of the common man. Without educated citizens, a nation was easy prey for demagogues. In the 1830s, McGuffey looked at Andrew Jackson as a demagogue preying on the masses, and it motivated him to bring education to all. Education of the masses was the very heart of freedom in McGuffey's view. You didn't need to try to win political points, but only educate the populace, and they would make the correct political choice. This was the difference between propaganda and education. It was Scotland and its immigrants that changed American education.

The Scottish belief in education was an old one. It was the Scottish Enlightenment that brought about the Scottish independence movement as well. The great Scottish warrior and national hero of the late 1200s, William Wallace (*Braveheart*), was a warrior/scholar versed in Latin and the world's literature. William Wallace remained a hero to young Scotch immigrants such as Andrew Carnegie. The Scottish Enlightenment is the taproot of American education. Its common approach to education took the Scotch literary rate to seventy-five percent by 1750. At the time England could claim only fifty-five percent. Even more amazing was that 1795 had 20,000 Scots in publishing and writing and 10,500 teachers out of a population of 1.5 million.[1] Most Scottish towns in 1750 had their own lending library. In addition, the high literary rate created a demand for home libraries. We saw that the school laws of Scotland had created an extensive common school system by 1700. The Scottish Enlightenment allowed the poor Scots to obtain an education equal to that of English gentlemen. It was this heritage that Scottish immigrants like the McGuffeys brought to America with the same amazing results. The American literacy rate soon surpassed that of England in the late 1700s.

Their greatest gift was their schools and educational system. Far from the frontier hillbillies they are often pictured as, the Scotch-Irish believed in book learning. Like their whiskey stills, their log cabin schools dominated the frontier. Many of America's colleges such as Princeton, University of Pennsylvania, University of Pittsburgh, Washington and Jefferson, Geneva College, and Westminster College, owe their creation to Scotch-Irish log cabins. The mixed and pragmatic college curriculum was a result of the Scottish educational system. Andrew Carnegie would say: "The United States was Scotland realized beyond the seas." Often the Scotch-Irish system intermixed with the frontier Germans, as did the McGuffey family. This Scottish based frontier system built liberal arts across the curriculum into an integrated approach such as "writing across the curriculum."

This Scottish scholarship gave us the love of liberty and freedom. The very root of Jefferson's line of the "pursuit of happiness" goes back to the Scottish enlightenment. The Scots-Irish independence, thrift, belief in education, and indus-

---

1　Arthur Herman, *How the Scots Invented the Modern World* (New York: Three Rivers Press, 2001), p. 25

trialism built our nation. Fifteen American presidents have claimed Scotch-Irish ancestry, including three of pure Ulster Presbyterian lineage: Andrew Jackson, James Buchanan, and Chester Arthur. Philosophers and leaders included Alexander Hamilton, William McKinley, Patrick Henry, James Madison, John Calhoun, Daniel Boone, Sam Houston, and twenty-one signers of the Declaration of Independence. More importantly, the frontier Scotch-Irish changed the American West (today's Midwest) with the idea of education as a birthright. The Northwest Ordinance of 1787 stated: "Religion, morality, and knowledge, being necessary to good government, and the happiness of mankind, schools, and the means of education shall forever be preserved." Only Scotland and the American West had put education on the level of human rights and property rights.

The Ordinances of 1785 and 1787 set up the tax base and land base for schools, and these ordinances brought American democracy to the frontier. A three man elected board was set up for the administration of these country schools. Many farmers, such as McGuffey's father, had become elected officials and school administrators. It was in the election of the school board and the school board meetings that gave Americans their first real taste of democracy in action. A school board member functioned as part principal, part superintendent, part purchasing clerk, and part maintenance man. It was at the school board meeting that heated debates led to teachers' salaries and money allotted for repairs or building a new school. It was in dealing with these frontier school boards that McGuffey found a true sense of American education.

Certainly McGuffey's philosophy of education was based on three British scholars — Adam Smith, John Locke, and David Hume. John Locke was a big part of that Scottish enlightenment, and many believe to be one of McGuffey's primary sources. In 1693, John Locke published his *Thoughts on Education*, which argued for a new approach. Locke believed that virtue and wisdom should be empathized over basic principles. Locke foresaw education as necessary for a society to be free. Education was the core of civil behavior. This approach certainly had the foundation of McGuffey's moralistic approach. Although, Locke and McGuffey arrived there from different religious perspectives, they came to the same principle. In 1834, McGuffey concluded, "No thought is more true, and no truth were important, than that general intelligence is the only palladium of our free institutions."

Another striking similarity between Locke and McGuffey was the belief that while religion was the basis of virtuous or moral religion, religion should not be part of education. Locke had seen the differences in religion tear at the foundations of schools in Britain. Locke argued for a non-sectarian approach, as did McGuffey. Both believed that common schools required a non-sectarian approach. McGuffey noted in his speech to the "College of Teachers": "Let us then, fellow-teachers, avoid, on the one hand, the inculcation of all sectarian peculiarities in religion." Locke realized that for Scotland to have common schools required one to find common ground among Presbyterian sects, Episcopalians, and even Catholics. Neither Locke nor McGuffey had a problem in the basic Christian bias of education in the1800s. Locke further believed in a graded system and the use of "interesting" texts. A great deal of credit must be given to William McGuffey, personally a strict "Old School" Presbyterian, to keep his personal views out of his Readers. He even included the best writings of some American Transcendentalists and Unitarians, who opposed the use of any Christian principles in education.

William Channing (1780–1842) was one of those Transcendentalists and one of the founders of the Unitarian creed. Channing opposed much of Christianity, but still believed that religion in general was the basis for society. *McGuffey's Third Reader* of 1837 included Channing's lesson on "Religion, The Only Basis of Society." Channing and McGuffey agreed on the point that morals were the real issue, and the only source of morals was religion. Most "Old School" Presbyterians were appalled by the inclusion of an "anti-Christ" such as Channing in the Reader, but McGuffey never lost sight of his non-sectarian goal in education. McGuffey also greatly respected the Transcendentalist view of self-reliance and the "elevation of the laboring class."

William Channing was a supporter of the New England version of Cincinnati's "College of Teachers." The leader of this Transcendentalist educational subgroup was Channing's friend Amos Bronson Alcott (1799–1888), who was a New England schoolteacher. Alcott might well be considered the "McGuffey of the East." In the late 1820s, Alcott started a campaign for common schools. He came to the same conclusion of McGuffey that common schools needed to be non-sectarian. Alcott as a Unitarian opposed the overbearing Calvinism in New England schools. Alcott also broke ground by breaking the rote nature of New England education. Alcott, like McGuffey, focused on directed conversations, storytelling, and nature walks. Alcott would open a number of pioneering schools, which would be discussed in the meetings of the "College of Teachers." Alcott would, however, be drawn into dogma battles on religion, which would erode his support and popularity.

Another of the philosophers that touched McGuffey was Scot David Hume. Like Adam Smith and Locke, he was at best a marginal Christian. David Hume was even considered an atheist and was persecuted by the Scottish Kirk, but it is not in religion we find a similarity to McGuffey. Hume more than anyone believed that education was the only prevention against totalitarianism. Like Smith, Hume argued morality was an innate virtue that required education to perfect. While the differences in religion were often great, common to all of these men was the absolute necessity of education to a society. Still, we should not make too much of the similarities of philosophy. McGuffey was not a philosopher, but a practitioner. McGuffey was closer to the philosophy of American Benjamin Rush, who said, "Knowledge is of little use, when confined to mere speculation."

The pragmatic application of McGuffey's views came from several great American educators. One of those was Benjamin Rush (1746–1813). Benjamin Rush was a signer of the Declaration of Independence, a congressman, and a famous physician. Born in Philadelphia, Rush graduated first from Princeton (then the College of New Jersey). He had graduated from the Medical College of the University of Edinburgh in 1768. While Benjamin Rush was at Edinburgh, he came to believe in the Scottish educational systems. After a successful career as a scientist and a physician, he turned his energy to education. In 1788 Benjamin Rush defined the American educational potential to John Adams: "America has ever appeared to me to be the theater on which human nature will reach its greatest civic, literary, and religious honours. Now is the time to sow the seeds of each of them." Rush pushed in the 1700s for common schools and called for more basic education. Rush reorganized the College of Philadelphia's medical school to conform to the "Edinburgh model." Rush was so committed to a nondenominational approach to education that he founded Dickinson College in Western Pennsylvania. He developed a new type of curriculum there to include science and mechanics. Benjamin Rush was highly influential on American education as well as William McGuffey.

Daniel Drake had experienced the "Edinburgh model" when he attended the College of Philadelphia in the early 1800s. Drake would bring Rush's model and ideas to his Cincinnati College in which he combined a science and arts curriculum. Rush's ideas on common schools, curriculum, and nondenominational teaching would become the heart of Cincinnati's "College of Teachers." The idea of nondenominational education was clearly revolutionary at the time. Prior to that, American colleges and schools were related to various churches. Rush correctly realized that our nation needed a common base of education or we would remain divided. Rush realized that American culture needed common schools, and the vehicle for unity would be Christian morals, not dogma. More than anyone, William McGuffey borrowed and incorporated Rush's vision. Rush and Drake influenced McGuffey's selections as well. Early Readers included a great deal of natural science and geography.

Another icon of McGuffey and the "College of Teachers" was John Witherspoon, who became President of Princeton in 1768. Witherspoon was happy to leave the rigid rule of the Scottish Kirk. He revolutionized the system of Princeton. He added literature to the curriculum of the Moral Philosophy department, which McGuffey would emulate at Miami. Witherspoon took the emphasis off the assembly line production of ministers at Princeton to educate the average man and turned to a moralistic approach. He created two student clubs for intellectual discussion. James Madison and Aaron Burr were early members. Debates were organized every Friday night at Nassau Hall, which would also be emulated decades later at Miami with the formation of McGuffey's Erodelphians. Interestingly, like Miami, the students' political debates often ran over into the streets. Rhetoric became the cornerstone of Witherspoon's approach so that students: "may learn, by early habit, presence of mind and proper pronunciation and gesture in public speaking."

The 'College of Teachers" greatest supporter of common schools and a national approach to education was that of Lyman Beecher. McGuffey included an essay on education by Lyman Beecher in his *Fourth Reader*. Beecher argued: "The great experiment is now making, and from its extent and rapid filling up, is making in the west, whether the perpetuity of our republican institutions can be reconciled with universal suffrage. Without the education of the head and heart of the nation, they cannot be. The question to be decided is, can the nation, or the vast balance power of it be so imbued with intelligence and virtue as to bring out, in laws and their administration, a perpetual self-preserving energy? We know the work is a vast one, and of great difficulty and yet we believe it can be done."

The spirit of national education was the heart of the "College of Teachers." Calvin Stowe, son-in-law of Lyman Beecher and member of the "College of Teachers," defined that core vision in 1836: "To sustain an extended republic like our own, there must be a national feeling, a national assimilation; and nothing could be more fatal to our prospects of future national prosperity, than to have our population become a congeries of clans, congregating without coalescing, and condemned to contiguity without sympathy. The graphic imagery, which the genius of oriental prophecy applied to the unwieldy and loose jointed Roman empire, would in this case be still more fatally applicable to our own widely spread republic." Lyman Beecher and McGuffey saw education as the healing glue that would hold a divided nation together. The Civil War ended that hope, but education would be the healing balm for the nation after the war. Both men feared that the war would the beginning of the "dying agonies" of their country. McGuffey was blessed to see his nation come together after the war and return to a path of common education.

Another of the early fathers of American education was Noah Webster. Webster was the first to call for national and common schools. Webster's own textbook was the first to move from religion to a moral base for education. Webster, in 1787, talked about the development of a "national memory." Webster said: "As soon as he opens his lips, he should rehearse the history of his own country; he should lisp the praise of liberty and of those illustrious heroes and statesmen who have wrought a revolution in her favor." Webster argued that American education had to get beyond Christianity as a common factor and develop American heritage as a common factor. But before that could happen the nation needed a common language.

Samuel Johnson said that language is the "pedigree of a nation," which was something that William McGuffey well understood. The Scotch-Irish and Germans in Western Pennsylvania had twisted and added new words to the Western vocabulary.

Western Pennsylvania today remains the best linguist legacy of the Scots-Irish with strong accent of the population and the unique vocabulary as discussed earlier, with terms such as hollows, burghs, and runs. McGuffey not only had to teach the American tongue, but he had to address the "errors" so common in the Western dialect. America could have slipped into a nation of extreme dialects. McGuffey saw language as a dividing factor that would only strain the political and regional divisions.

Noah Webster had begun the process of unifying the nation's language, but there were actually competitors. In New England "Old English" with its 24 letters was the preferred base. Germans felt that German should be used exclusively in their communities. *Webster's Blue Back Speller* was the first step at a common alphabetical base for the words of America. Webster sought to use language as a means to spread Calvinist virtues. Webster more than anyone else understood the power of language in promoting ideas. It was McGuffey and his Readers that made the West, Websterian. McGuffey realized that language could be the basis of discrimination against the poor and those from the frontier. He had seen such discrimination used against even the well-educated Scotch-Irish who often spoke differently than the elites of New England and Virginia. This led to an emphasis on elocution. McGuffey's *Fourth Reader* makes the point in Lesson XV: "It is, indeed, a most intellectual accomplishments. So is music, too, in its perfection. We do by no means under value this noble and most delightful art, to which Socrates applied himself even in old age. But one recommendation of the art of reading is that it requires a constant exercise of mind. It demands continual and close reflection and thought and the finest discrimination of thought. It involves, in its perfection, the whole art of criticism on language." In McGuffey's America, these linguistic errors were becoming local dialects. This was particularly true in Western Pennsylvania, Northern Kentucky, Tennessee, and Ohio.

In the original *Fourth Reader*, McGuffey and the editors addressed the issue of "errors" in the preface: "The errors marked in pronunciation are such as more frequently occur in reading and in common conversation; and are sometimes heard even in literary society, and in addresses to the public from literary men. A variety of mispronunciation is sometimes given on the same word; because such variety prevails in the community. But what has been done in this, as in everything else, must be taken as incipient attempt at correcting the errors, and supplying the defects that exist, and prevail, to the detriment not only of elegance, but of accuracy in our oral and literary communication with our fellow citizens."

At the end of the lessons of the *Third* and *Fourth Reader*, McGuffey addressed errors. Many of these errors were the mispronunciation and misspellings common among the Scotch-Irish, for example, in the Fourth Reader, the common problem of terminating words with an "in'" instead of "ing." McGuffey points out *"mor-nin," "o-ver-flown-in," "light-nin," and "shout-in."* Another problem was the shortening of words based on sound such as *"'bout"* for about, *"perty"* for pretty, and *"spr-it-id"* for spirited. And, of course, that Western Pennsylvania favorite to this day, *"Wash-in-ton"* for Washington. McGuffey, like Noah Webster, believed the problem had to be addressed as early as possible, and parents could only teach correctly if they were educated correctly.

McGuffey included an essay on *"Elocution and Reading"* in his *Fourth Reader*. The essay states: "The business of training our youth in elocution must be commenced in childhood. The first school is the nursery. There, at least, may be formed a distant articulation, which is the first requisite for good speaking. How rarely is it found in perfection among our orators. . . . It involves, in its perfection, the whole art of criticism on language. A man may possess a fine genius without being a perfect reader, but he cannot be a perfect reader without genius." Many today overlook McGuffey's long-term commitment to the American language. Without McGuffey, the country could have easily become one of disparate dialects. Of course, such regional dialects would have slowed commerce, but national unity and even common schools would have been difficult.

Another national leader in education, Horace Mann, saw language as the cornerstone to a common school curriculum. Lastly, the ideal of an American education as a birthright and the universal belief in common schools was influenced much by Horace Mann. Horace Mann had become Secretary of the Massachusetts State Board of Education in 1837. From this position he became a national leader in education and the common school movement. Mann's ideas were consistent with Ohio's "College of Teachers." From 1838 to the 1850, Mann's annual reports became classics in education, covering all topics from philosophy, curriculum, and schoolhouses. Mann was a strong supporter of the common school that was non-sectarian, although in practice like McGuffey, liberal Protestantism would be the base. Mann feared that private or religious based schools would limit the spread of tax-based common schools.

Calvin Stowe saw language in 1836 as the core of the nation: "It is altogether essential to our national strength and peace, if not even our national existence, that foreigners who settle on our soil, should cease to be Europeans and become Americans; and as our national language is English, and our literature, our manners, and our institutions are of English origin, and the whole foundation of our society English, it is necessary that they become substantially Anglo-Americans.

Let them be like grafts which become branches of the parent stock; improve its fruit, and add to its beauty and its vigor; and not like the parasitical mistletoe, which never incorporates itself with the trunk from which it derives its nourishment, but exhausts its sap, withers its foliage, despoils it of its strength, and sooner or later by destroying its support, involves itself in ruin."[1] Drake and the "College of Teachers" in Cincinnati were decades ahead of the nation as non-English speaking Germans poured into the city. There is little question that the "College of Teachers" and the Executive Committee to which McGuffey belonged, fully reflected William McGuffey's view.

Another member of the Executive Committee, Daniel Drake, stated the mission of common schools as "social amalgamation." Daniel Drake was proposing a social revolution on the level of that of Karl Marx, only it was not to take place in the streets but in the schools. Drake stated it clearly in 1836: "Let us then persevere, and we may hope to shape the rising generation to our own model, and give such activity to the work of social amalgamation, as will, at last, secure uniformity of character; and may raise that which left to itself would be a foreign and inferior mass, into an element of social strength and beauty — in harmony with the other elements of Western Society." In the 1830s, enlightened citizens were starting to understand that the American Revolution had to be continued in the schools as waves of immigrants came to America. A young Abraham Lincoln made it central to his first political campaign in 1832: "Upon the subject of education, not presuming to dictate any plan or system respecting it, I can only say that I view it as the most important subject which we as people can be engaged in. That every man may receive at least a moderate education, and thereby be enabled to read the histories of his own and other countries, by which he may duly appreciate the value of our free institutions, appears to be an object of vital importance." Lincoln, like the "College of Teachers," believed the problems of the 1800s was related to lack of or poor education. This belief was particularly strong in the Western states of the period. In the end, the McGuffey Readers created or at least extended the American Revolution.

For McGuffey and leaders like Daniel Drake, Daniel Webster, Henry Clay, Edward Everett, and Horace Mann, there was a political reason for common schools. The 1830s was experiencing a counter-revolution against the Jacksonians. This counter-revolution would coagulate into the Whig Party. Cincinnati was at the center and the Transylvania Enlightenment was the seed for the Whig Party crystallization. The Whigs opposed slavery but also opposed the radical views of abolitionists. The Whigs had consistently supported the slavery compromises of their leader Henry Clay. For the Whig, slavery was a moral issue that had to be addressed, not a political one. For these nova Whigs, Jackson was a demagogue

---

1 Calvin Stowe, *Transactions of the Fifth Annual Meeting of the Western Literary Institute and College of Professional Teachers* (Cincinnati: Executive Committee, 1836)

who had played on the uneducated masses. Senator Daniel Webster summarized the Whig view of education in 1831: "We do not, indeed, expect all men to be philosophers or statesmen, but we confidently trust, and our expectation of the duration of our system of government rests on that trust, that, by the diffusion of general knowledge and good and virtuous sentiments, the political fabric may be secure, as well against open violence and overthrow, as against the slow, but sure, undermining of licentiousness." McGuffey and these leaders took a most unusual approach to their political concerns. Instead of taking the political stand against a party or President, McGuffey saw the issue as a lack of understanding and morals. Such an approach required a deep belief that they were morally right. Education is also a slow revolution, which is measured in generations, not election cycles. The real strength of this belief and approach is that it kept the "politics" out of education.

Chapter 16. Pedagogy and Methodology

> Its popularity doomed the Primer to the dustbin in nearly every city and town where it showed up. McGuffey's Eclectic Readers would take their place in the pantheon of American brands such as Coca-Cola and Ford.
> — Ron Powers, author of *Mark Twain: A Life*

McGuffey Readers gained market superiority because they addressed the needs of a growing nation. There were many competing Readers on the market by 1840s, but McGuffey's rose to the top. His Readers offered techniques and teaching aids that were lacking in the competing Readers. The *McGuffey Readers* went further than any competitor in addressing the concerns of teachers. He had honed his Readers and his methods in his experimental backyard school at Miami University. After the 1838 editions, he worked with the feedback from a panel of educators and teachers. In addition, feedback was solicited from teachers. The real brilliance of William McGuffey was his ability to teach both moral philosophy and the basics of intellectual development. Prior to McGuffey, no one had ever tried to do both, with the possible exception of Noah Webster. Noah Webster included both in his *Blue Back Speller*, but only McGuffey combined them in the lessons. This was the task that many early pioneer mothers had tried to do with the Bible. It was McGuffey who found the key to teaching fundamentals and morality.

Too much is made of the influence of Swiss educational reformer Johann Heinrich Pestalozzi on the work of William McGuffey. Pestalozzi's idea of teaching was published in his book, *"How Gertrude teaches her Children,"* in 1801. The link seems to be in Pestalozzi's use of the term "eclectic." Biographer Harvey Minnich further supported the linkage by quoting Boswell Smith: "It is the companions of his (Pestalozzi) labors, most of whom resided in Germany or Switzerland, that we owe the formation of another school which has been styled the Productive School, and which now predominated in Germany and Switzerland. It might, perhaps with equal propriety, be termed the Eclectic School; for it aims at embodying all the valuable principles of previous systems, without adhering slavishly to the dictates of any master, or the views of any party." There were similarities in that both believed in sequential lessons and teaching from the viewpoint of the child. McGuffey probably was aware of Pestalozzi's ideas, but McGuffey's techniques clearly evolved from his own experiences in education. McGuffey rarely talked of theory, but focused on experience. McGuffey did possibly have some local contact with Pestalozzi methods at Locke's Female Academy. Dr. John Locke was promoting the Pestalozzi approach, and Locke was a friend of Daniel Drake and member of the "College of Teachers."

Some of the attachment to Pestalozzi appears to be intellectual revisionism to defend McGuffey's pragmatic, moralistic, and patriotic approach. H. G. Good, in his *History of American Education*, noted: "as Horace Mann said many shared Pestalozzi's views and applied his principles who had never heard his name. Many also must have independently developed views and practices similar to his. It is by no means safe to square similarity to a source with derivation from it." The roots of the McGuffey approach can better be found in the log cabin schools of Western Pennsylvania and the Western Reserve of Ohio. Some interest in Pestalozzi was inspired by the Calvin Stowe trip to Europe and report to the "College of Teachers." Furthermore, Pestalozzi's approach was clearly inconsistent with that of McGuffey in several aspects.[1] Pestalozzi hated the subject of history and its use in curriculum and abhorred men such as Napoleon. Pestalozzi was said to have called history "a tissue of lies." McGuffey created a cult of heroism that included Napoleon, Alexander the Great, George Washington, Daniel Webster, Benjamin Franklin, and Alexander Hamilton. The Pestalozzi methodology was in vogue in the 1830s. The point is that Pestalozzi is long forgotten, while McGuffey remains a well-recognized figure.

McGuffey made a revolutionary change pedagogy and methodology. Prior to McGuffey, students learned to spell before they learned to read. This is why the *Original Blue Back Speller* was so popular in the early 1800s. As much as two years was invested in spelling prior to the start of reading. In 1828, Samuel Worcester proposed that reading could come before spelling. Even more revolutionary was Worcester's proposal of a French technique that learned words without knowing the letters. Most teachers never accepted Worcester's suggestion. McGuffey, on the other hand, proposed going from letters to reading without spelling first. McGuffey saw that the *New England Primer* had used pictures to help students

---

1 Harry Good and James D. Teller, *A History of American Education* (New York: The Macmillan Company, 1973), p. 180

learn the alphabet. McGuffey used words in sentences and tied them to pictures. This technique started with the *Eclectic Primer*, which in lesson one combined full page pictures with the following words: boy, man, hen, top, hat, rat, cat, and pot. Finally, in the *Primer* the words were then combined into short little stories. McGuffey started with one-syllable words, which made up the *Primer*. Furthermore, McGuffey kept sentences to ten words or less and did not use paragraphs. The *Eclectic McGuffey Readers* represented the first well-coordinated grade school series. One did not need to jump from the *Blue Back Speller* into a number of different texts. The other feature of the *McGuffey Readers* was that they not only addressed the student but the teacher as well. For years, the "College of Teachers" had detailed the lack of teacher qualifications. Texts had to come teacher-friendly, leading the teacher and student through the learning process.

Before the *McGuffey's Readers*, spelling was the first step for a student. Learning your ABC's took anywhere from eighteen months to two years. In the West, using Webster's *Blue Back Speller*, the student learned the alphabet by jumping in without the use of pictures. It was a tough task for the brightest of students. The student moved to a long list of syllables and then on to endless pages of words for spelling. Ten years before *McGuffey's Readers*, the *Worchester Reader* did try the process of combining spelling and reading, which clearly impacted McGuffey's thinking, although McGuffey had laid out his general approach to teaching reading in his 1833 London paper. While the Worchester Reader integrated the use of pictures in these early lessons, they were poorly coordinated. The *McGuffey Primer* used two times the number of pictures and used animals and people versus the inanimate objects of the *Worchester Reader*. McGuffey borrowed the best of the *New England Primer* and the *Worchester Reader*. The *McGuffey Primer* was released a year after his first two Readers. This 1838 Primer never sold well, and schoolteachers held to the regime of using the *Blue Back Speller* prior to moving to the *McGuffey First Reader*.

The McGuffey Eclectic Series was one of the earliest to address the major problem facing frontier schoolmaster. That was the lack of a standardized graded system of promotion. The McGuffey editors realized that the development of the overall series offered huge sales potential. Every term the teacher faced classifying students as to their level of spelling and reading. Students in different reading series were problematic. Teachers wanted and needed a standardized series. Still, markets make up their own "minds," and publishers tended to specialize in Primers, Readers, and Spellers versus the consistency of a series. Credit must be given to Winthrop Smith whose vision kept the effort going for years, often facing failures and setups. It was a hard sell to get teachers to change methods that had existed for years.

In 1849, the Primer was totally revisited to address the teaching problems. The Primer was split into two books, the *Eclectic Primer* and the *Pictorial Primer*.

The editors hoped that this would make the translation to reading smoothly and take away the marketing edge of the *Blue Back Speller*. Most publishers of Readers in the West had given up on competing with the *Blue Back Speller* that seemed to be in every Midwest home. Smith was committed to the McGuffey approach of tackling reading and spelling at the same time. The *Pictorial Eclectic Primer* of 1857 was to be the first step, or as the preface put it, "introduction to the *McGuffey First Reader*." It was a visual masterpiece, offering real ease of learning of early Spellers. It had a total of 172 engraved illustrations, covering a wide range of scenes, animals, and children playing that were coordinated with the text. Smith empathized with three attributes of the *Pictorial Primer*: simplicity, progression, and spelling.

Teachers started with the student memorizing the alphabet, which remains the time honored start to education. While the McGuffey approach didn't demand it, most teachers in the nineteenth century followed with the learning of the vowels and consonants and the "abs," the "abs" being the combining all the vowels with twenty consonants such as ab, eb, ib, and so on. This was a remnant of the *Webster's Blue Back Speller* and the tried and true methods of eighteenth-century mothers. To some degree, this was due to the continued use of the *Blue Back Speller* in conjunction with the McGuffey series in the nineteenth century. The true McGuffey method went from learning the alphabet to reading, using simple words and pictures.

The *Pictorial Primer's* approach to spelling meant the true combined reading and spelling objective. The 1838 *Electric Progressive Speller* was never competitive with the *Blue Back Speller* because it basically was an improved copy. The Progressive Speller by Alexander McGuffey was a concession to some teacher resistance in going directly from the alphabet to reading. The Progressive Speller added vowels, consonants, and the "abs" combinations. The long lists of words were retained, however, and the *Pictorial Primer* broke new ground. The *Pictorial Primer* was a pleasure to read in comparison. It started with simple words and sentences then moved to short little stories. The only words of more than one syllable were Mary and Lucy. Unlike the competing Primers, the *Pictorial Primer* had no paragraphs and the longest sentence was ten words. From the student's perspective, the *Pictorial Primer* was user-friendly. The stories were basic without much moral issue. It clearly set the groundwork for a student to move seamlessly into the *First Reader*. The series and its progression was reviewed by McGuffey's associates in the College of Teachers." This review by the College of Teachers was published in the back of the 1838 *Third Reader*.

The Primers addressed the equivalent of today's kindergarten and first graders. The *First Reader* would, by today's standards, address late second grade or early third grade. The *First Reader* was designed to address three difficulties identified by review of Cincinnati teachers. These three difficulties were delineated by the

College of Teachers were: "the difficulty of forming words from letters, of forming sentences from words, and of gathering the meaning of words from the sound alone, without material assistance, as to this particular, from the sight." These basic learning stories were mostly written by McGuffey and had been honed in his experimental school. Interestingly, this review suggests that "pictures are employed to excite curiosity, and lessons fashioned to illustrate the pictures connected with them." Clearly, these early educators realized the importance of visual learning. The Primers also set up a progression for both the student and teacher for the next Reader.

The *First Reader* had received the most scrutiny by teachers and the publishers so that it would serve as the cornerstone of the series. The *First Reader* was revised in 1849 to make this a smooth transition. The editor stated: "a careful progression has been preserved, thus leading the little learner forward, step by step, by an easy gradation, which, while it pleases, will at the same time instruct him in the use and meaning of language." A 1945 study of McGuffey Readers concluded: "Without doubt, McGuffey graded his readers merely a 'feeling' for the growth of the children in reading step by step, or perhaps year by year. If so, he certainly hit upon a real progression."[1] This sequenced progression would always be the strongest selling point of the Readers.

The *Second Reader* had the following review by the College of Teachers: "In this work, longer words, and longer sentences are gradually introduced. Having by this time acquired the ability of reading, it is proper that the pupils should use it for purposes of instruction. We observe that, in the *Second Reader*, much important information is interwoven with the texture of sprightly stories, which a child can hardly fail to remember. To facilitate this effect, questions are appended as *hints* to the teacher, when he examines his scholars concerning the meaning of what they had read." The *Second Reader* has distinct increasing levels of difficulty, covering today what would be third to fifth grade. Moral lessons are more fully developed by the end of the *Second Reader*.

When the student started the *Third Reader*, it was assumed that a mastery of reading had been obtained. The focus in both the *Third* and *Fourth Reader* was to expand the vocabulary and definitions of words, but it also moved the student into the world of literature. For many McGuffey alumni, the *Third Reader* was the favorite. Questions now were pointed at the meaning of various words. The *Fourth Reader* took the student to a full appreciation of literature. The College of Teacher's review for the *Fourth Reader* stated the goal as: "practice in the various styles of prose and verse; to introduce the pupils to the highest kinds of composition; and to exercise them in the principles of intonation." The *Fourth Reader* developed a market of its own, a type of frontier *Readers' Digest*. The other feature was a review and updates.

---

1 E. W. Dolch, "How Hard Were The McGuffey Readers?" *The Elementary School Journal*, 1945

One thing for sure was that Winthrop Smith got it right with the revisions in 1849. The progressive series made inroads in common schools throughout the nation. New teachers, in particular, were drawn to the series, which allowed for grading and consistency. In Pittsburgh, Lucius Osgood noted the success of the McGuffey progressive series. In 1855, Osgood released a progressive series of his own. Osgood did make a good transition from Primer to First Reader but lacked the market of the *McGuffey Readers*. Smith had the market before the Civil War and had to wait for progressive series competition until the 1870s. Still, the market for McGuffey's Primers remained the slower sellers. Teachers preferred, based on their own early experience, to teach spelling first, and then stuck with the *Blue Back Speller* in many cases. McGuffey's strong belief in his method came from his own experience in learning and teaching other languages such as Greek, Hebrew, and Latin. Furthermore, McGuffey tested this approach in his Miami grammar experimental school.

As noted, McGuffey found some teaching market resistance to his direct approach. William McGuffey described his approach to reading and spelling in the original *Third Reader* preface: "The plan of teaching the pupil to spell, in conjunction with the exercises in reading, will, it is believed, be found eminently beneficial in fixing in the memory the orthographical form of the words, not only as they appear in the columns of a spelling-book, or dictionary, but in all the variety of their different members, oblique cases, degrees of comparison, moods, tenses, while the exercise of defining produces a similar effect in regard to the meaning of the terms employed; since the learner is required to find out the meaning of each term defined, from the connection, without having recourse to an expositor. It is the connection alone, that can convey to the mind the true meaning of the words. No two words in any language are exactly alike in signification. How then can definition, merely, be made to convey their import?" The longevity of the Eclectic Series, eventually, won teachers over to the McGuffey method of reading.

One innovation of the McGuffey Reader was the use of illustrations although his first editions lacked quantity and quality. In 1837, the small firm of Truman & Smith lacked the resources for original engravings. The first engravings were British, which was not uncommon for publishers of the period. Textbooks used standardized English engravings with discernable characteristics such as cottages, scoop bonnets, and knee breeches. After the release of the 1844 revisions, some original engravings were added. Winthrop Smith tried hard to improve the quality of these engravings in 1853. Smith had received much feedback on the importance of illustrations. Wood engraving, however, was expensive and there were few wood engravers on the market. The process required a tedious reproduction of each of the artist's pencil lines using a brush to highlight tints of light and shade. This brushing was done on a whitened wood block. The engraver then craved in the full die impression. The *McGuffey Readers* were one of the first to apply the new technology of photo-engraving with the 1878 revisions. Photo-engraving allowed the artist to produce a larger picture in greater detail and then have them reduced by photography. You can see the signatures of the artists in many of the pictures in the 1878 edition.

McGuffey had originally been a proponent of illustrations. Their use in the alphabet of the *New England Primer* had always impressed him. McGuffey's western focus also created a need for original American textbooks illustrations. Particularly, McGuffey's focus on animals required new engravings. McGuffey's own experience as a primary school teacher had shown him the importance of illustrations in learning. Visual learning was a major part of the young mind's learning. McGuffey knew this first hand with the early use of visuals to learn the alphabet going back to the 1500s with Catholic primers. The same powerful tool could be used to the advantage of a teacher with stories.

Interestingly, some teachers saw illustrations as a problem. These educational Luddites felt pictures short-circuited the learning process of reading, even fearing that pictures would make the reader dependent on them. As part of an 1838 advertisement, President of Woodward College and member of the "College of Teachers" Dr. B. P. Aydelott noted in defense: "I differ from some respected friends on the subject of pictures in school books. It appears to me that a very important use may be made of them in the early stages of education. In this view you seem to accord with me, as you have liberally used this means of interesting and instructing, in the First and Second Readers, but more sparingly in the Third, and I hope will entirely omit it in the volume to come."

In 1863, E. J. Whitney came to the firm as an engraver, and a Mr. Herrick was hired as an artist. This occurred with the promotion of Obed J. Wilson to editor. Wilson brought a new vision for the series, but the Civil War restricted sweeping changes. This new team looked to take on a major improvement of illustrations throughout the series. A new management system was implemented. E. J. Whitney and Herrick prepared their drawings to precisely fit the space requirements of the editor. In addition, as an editor, Wilson helped to make suggestions as to the nature of the drawings needed to fit the composition. Prior to this, art was added from stock drawings. Mr. Herrick would then rough the drawings on boxwood blocks that were first sent to the editor for approval. After approval, the wood engravings were produced. Finally, the blocks were used to produce electrotype for printing.

From a teaching perspective, McGuffey did a lot of work in the 1844 editions. These editions included lessons in enunciation and rules for reading. The 1844 edition of the McGuffey *Fourth Reader* had twenty-six pages dealing with tones, articulation, inflections, and emphasis. The *Fifth Reader* published in 1844 addressed the principles of elocution to assist the students in effective oral reading. The 1844 edition also addressed difficult words to spell and pronounce. This approach proved extremely popular with teachers, and the 1844 revisions seemed to assure successes. The *Fourth* and *Fifth Reader*, McGuffey added notes (rules) on reading. The first one in the *Fourth Reader* stated: "Be careful to pronounce every syllable distinctly, and not to join the words together. Nothing is more important to good reading than attention to this rule, and yet most young readers violate." Reading pace, articulation, and even tone were stressed. McGuffey suggested that students who read too fast or ignored stops be put in a special class. Alexander McGuffey's *Fifth* and *Sixth Readers* went even further in the art of elocution with a sixty-page guide. This guide on elocution included the novel use of diagrams to help the student with raising and fall inflection. Besides emphasis, Alexander introduced the idea of pitch. Alexander had been a student of the great debating societies of Miami University. Alexander added a real textbook inside the Reader.

The work of Alexander McGuffey in defining principles of articulation was further refined and strengthened in the 1879 revisions. These revisions focused further on elementary sounds. The 1879 revisions took articulation to a science far from the art that William McGuffey stated back in 1837. The 1879 moved to a more phonic approach that McGuffey had steered away from. The 1879 *Third Reader* starts out with a lesson on vocals, which are sounds of pure tone only. The ideas of a "diphthong," which modern learners of Hebrew are familiar with, were taught, a "diphthong" being a "union of two vocals commencing with one and ending with the other." In the *Fourth Reader* things like subvocals were explained, which are sounds where "vocalized breath is more or less obstructed," and aspirates that are "breath only, modified by vocal organs." Emphasis is taught in the *Third Reader* and then followed up with rising and falling inflection lessons in the *Fourth Reader*. These were amazing improvements but were difficult to teach in the primary grades.

Another evolutionary improvement of McGuffey was the use of rhetorical exercises. Murray's Reader had successfully used rhetorical exercises in the early 1830s, and McGuffey had been experimenting with the techniques at his test school at Miami. Public speaking was the passion of educators at the college level and was the distinguishing skill of a nineteenth-century scholar. The method was common at the college level of the times, but grammar schools tended to avoid it. However, in the smaller Scotch-Irish learning circles used by teacher/ministers, rhetoric was an often-used technique. Murray added a rhetorical guide in his Introduction, which Alexander McGuffey emulated in his *Fifth Reader*. William McGuffey had earlier added "Rules" to all his *Third* and *Fourth Readers*. Here is an example from the *Third Reader*: "RULE — In reading, avoid a formal manner and let your method be as much like conversation as possible. *Read* as you would *speak* the same words if you had no book before you."

Early in his career, McGuffey published a paper on the use of students' questioning in 1839.[1] This type of questioning was popular at the college level, and McGuffey found it just as useful at his experimental grammar school. McGuffey further made his case direct to teachers in his *Fourth Reader*. "On the subject of Questions appended to the lessons, there is, and can be, but one opinion amongst the intelligent in community. Where answers are furnished to every question the memory alone will be cultivated. But no teacher can give instruction without asking questions. The compiler will rejoice to know, that those who use his books, ask more intelligent questions, and in much greater numbers, than are to be found in the pages before them. This is the very design of that part of his labors. His wish is, to incite the teacher to the interrogative method orally, and then he cares not whether he asks a single question that is printed in the book. Still, he believes that some teachers may be found, who are not too wise to be assisted in this manner, and who may not only need but feel that they need such suggestions as are furnished in the questions." Unfortunately, the one-room schoolhouse did not lend itself to this interrogative method.

Many of McGuffey's views and methods were galvanized in his work with the "College of Teachers." Many of these were forged into principles for the teaching profession, and they include the diverse ideas of the "College of Teachers." First of these principles was the concept of the "professional teacher." McGuffey called teaching "the most respectable of all professions." Prior to McGuffey's success, teachers were mainly ministers earning money on the side or men using it as a temporary job. McGuffey addressed this in an 1835 paper before the "College of Teachers" titled the "The Relative Duties of Parents and Teachers." Biographer Dolores Sullivan summarized the point: "The ranks of teachers must be filled and the public compelled by the force of truth and experiment to award the faithful and competent instructors of youth, the honor and maintenance which are due." McGuffey felt the real weakness of the schools was the lack of professional teachers. Teaching was often considered a transitional job for men. Professional teachers were needed for the success of common schools and common textbooks. McGuffey further noted: "The other professions are full. We have doctors enough; we have lawyers enough; we have politicians more than enough; and if we have not preachers enough, we have certainly more than are wanted, or well paid! The last fact is evidence of the first. But in the business of instruction, where is the professional teacher, much less an adequate supply of professional teachers, to be found? This field of enterprise, if not new, is certainly almost unoccupied. No where else can talents, and learning, and worth find such certain and profitable investment."

---

1   William McGuffey, "Conversation in a Classroom," *Monthly Chronicle of Interesting and Useful Information*, March, 1939

McGuffey demanded much of the teacher, student, and parent. He addressed some of the responsibilities of all in his preface to the first edition of the Eclectic Fourth Reader in 1837. McGuffey urged teachers in the preface: "It is no disgrace to be ignorant; but, to be content to remain so, is a disgrace. Let the teacher have recourse to those sources of information, from which it may most readily be obtained; and his credit will not suffer by the fact being known. No one is fit to teach, who is too proud, too old, too indolent, or too wise to learn." McGuffey espoused the need not only for the education of the teacher, but a type of apprentice or "in-service" training period for teachers.

In this 1835 paper, McGuffey fully specified the responsibilities of being a teacher. As always, McGuffey saw these responsibilities in black and white. His demanding requirements for a teacher would lay the groundwork for future colleges of education. James Scully paraphrased the heart of McGuffey's paper: "The intellectual habits of pupils will be of teachers who form them. The pupil's mode of thought and even his character will be the results of methods used. Therefore, no man is fit to teach who does not have an understanding of human nature. An empirical knowledge of the mind will not be sufficient. Theory without practice is useless, and practice without theory would be aimless."[1] McGuffey talked of recognizing individual differences in students, being ready to help the slow learner and move the fast learner forward. This was one area where the one-room schoolhouse caused significant problems. McGuffey called on teachers to be examples of moral behavior. In this paper, McGuffey told teachers to: "Avoid on the one hand the inculcation of all sectarian peculiarities in religion and on the other hand beware of teaching the crude notions of modern infidelity."

The responsibilities that McGuffey put on the students are sometimes overlooked. As part of the "College of Teachers" Executive Committee, McGuffey put together a report on student exams. The report, "Most Efficient Methods of Conducting Exams in Common School High Schools and Academies," was published in 1836. The committee asserted that "The object of education in all schools, is twofold: -first, to develop the faculties; and second, to impart knowledge. Examinations are intended to ascertain how far these ends are attained. The best methods, then, of conducting examinations, will be those which will give the greatest assurance of arriving at correct conclusions, in regard to the fidelity of teachers, and the sound proficiency of pupils. Examinations should be so conducted as to serve, as a stimulus to all concerned in their results; and to this end, should be fair, rigid, protracted, and thoroughly accurate. In a word, as education aims at making a man what he ought to be, and furnishing him with an acquaintance with all that he ought to know; examinations should be so conducted, as to exhibit all the

---

1 James Scully, "A Biography of William Holmes McGuffey," (Dissertation: University of Cincinnati, 1967), p. 158

effects of discipline, instruction, and education — the formation of habits — the acquisition of knowledge, and the building up of character."

McGuffey was just as hard on the parents, feeling that it was their responsibility to guide and encourage students. McGuffey proved to be far ahead of his time in developing grade school methods. McGuffey pioneered the idea of parents visiting the school and being present at examinations. McGuffey believed that teachers should be brutally honest with parents about the abilities of the student. He stated: "Teachers should not flatter their patrons by allowing them to think that their children are capable of professions for which nature never intended them." More importantly, McGuffey lectured parents on their obligations about financing education. Parents were to supply the best schools and supplies. He also warns parents that the development of moral character is the responsibility of both the parent and teacher. He clearly put discipline on the shoulders of parents: "Parents must recognize that schools are not houses of correction. They are intended to educate, not to reform young people." He also noted that parents were better judges of "what is to be taught." McGuffey saw teachers as "servants of the public." McGuffey was farsighted in his views of shared responsibilities. Still, McGuffey saw the teacher as a professional on the level of a lawyer or doctor.

McGuffey's concept of a professional teacher was a bar for teachers. He demanded that they be highly educated and enthusiastic, but also to be satisfied with their lower compensation. Interestingly, McGuffey had always been personally focused on his own compensation as a professor. His real argument to teachers was not to let low pay interfere with their professionalism. McGuffey's view was true to his belief that hard work would eventually be rewarded. As biographer James Scully noted: "McGuffey was convinced that the more an appreciation for education could be instilled in the general population, the more teachers would be recognized for their true value in promoting the general welfare of all." McGuffey realized that teachers in the 1830s were fully underpaid, but he also realized many teachers were not qualified to teach. The problem in his view was that parents were ambivalent towards the education of their children. He believed in old Scotch-Irish principles of the parents paying for the best education possible. Scotch-Irish communities and parents would sacrifice, as did McGuffey's own parents, to assure the highest standard of education. His own parents had helped build schools and roads to schools. Part of McGuffey's strategy was to enhance the public image of education and promoting the fact that education was the key to the "right to rise."

One farsighted concept was the ergonomic design of the classroom and schoolhouse. In 1835, McGuffey foresaw the change with: "The time has passed when a log cabin will suffice as a school." McGuffey advocated that schools should be comfortable and cheerful to promote learning. He campaigned for the use of large glass windows to replace the oiled paper. Oiled paper gave a diffused light and the use of candles or oil lamps created a smoky environment. Dirt and soot was overwhelming in the 1830s schoolhouse. Glass windows would be expensive, but this was the responsibility of the parent. He argued for a "uniform set of class books, maps, globes, and other apparatus." Later in his career, he promoted the use of blackboards.

Another campaign of the "College of Teachers" was to bring women into the profession. Women could help to professionalize teaching. McGuffey's friend and personal editor Catharine Beecher was truly a pioneer in the preparation of women to become full time teachers. In fairness, Catharine Beecher and her sister Harriet Beecher Stowe were far from feminists; both Catharine and Harriet, while believing women had moral superiority, saw specific gender roles for women. When McGuffey's *First Reader* came out in 1837, there were few women teachers. By 1879 when McGuffey's major revision was released, about sixty percent of the teachers were women; and by 1900 that percentage reached seventy-five percent. McGuffey had supported women in teaching, at least at the grade school and high school level. Catharine had supported the use of the McGuffey Readers for women over gender-oriented Readers that tried to segment the gender market in the 1850s. One of these women-oriented books was the *Young Ladies Reader*, which a frontier women teacher from Ohio notes: "omitted the speeches of Daniel Webster and Patrick Henry, scenes from Shakespeare's plays, and extracts from Milton, Grey, Cowper, and others substituting liberally poems from Mrs. Hemans, Eliza Cook, and other prettiness of the kind, and various pale prose articles, probably from *Ladies Annuals*.[1]

---

1 Louis Filler, ed., *An Ohio Schoolmistress: The Memoirs of Irene Hardy* (Kent: Kent State University, 1980), p. 133

CHAPTER 17. A COMMON VISION

"In free countries, where the safety of government depends very much upon the
favorable judgment which the people may form of its conduct."
— Adam Smith

McGuffey's Readers were the result of the American crucible, and its blend of
many nationalities and cultures. William McGuffey helped shaped the American
view of what it meant to be an American. McGuffey was able to fuse culture, political, social, and religious variants into a workable definition. McGuffey's mentor put it this way: "Measures should be taken to mould a uniform system of manners and customs, out of the diversified elements which are scattered over the
West." This uniformity of culture had been the vision of the 'College of Teachers."
These Western intellectuals believed common schools required a common society, and a common society required common schools. The *McGuffey Readers* did
more than any other written instrument to create a uniform American culture.
McGuffey was able to break the exclusiveness of the Germans, while fusing their
thrift and social values in the American culture. McGuffey moderated the predestination of the Scotch-Irish Presbyterians and New England Congregationalists
into the Western right of self-improvement. McGuffey took diverse dogma of
Methodists, Baptists, Congregationalists, Anglicans, and Presbyterians to create
a Christian common base. He urged tolerance for Catholics, blacks, and Jews in
a socially segmented world. He fused and united where possible, found common
ground, and where necessary, forged compromise.

McGuffey's biographer Harvey Minnich detailed such a compromise in
McGuffey's Reader: "It comprised a course of instruction which successfully conducted its way between the rugged and sometimes violent abolitionist of the

North and the cavalier slaveholder of the South, between Protestant and catholic, between the ever-increasing immigrant and native born, between the radical sectarian and the liberal Jeffersonian." It was clearly a very polarized society in a constant state of flux with the immigrant mix significantly changing every decade. Almost every decade a new generation of Americans were physically created through immigration. The ability to re-generate a new generation of Americans from immigrants was the real contribution of *McGuffey's Readers*. Astonishingly, *McGuffey Readers* achieved this with a limited amount of strong bias between the groups. The *Readers* found acceptance from the many diverse groups. McGuffey's moralistic approach allowed him to focus on the roots of differences in causes such as slavery without supporting any definite political solution.

Part of the common vision of McGuffey's approach was distinctly "Western." The West of the period was primarily Ohio, Kentucky, Indiana, Illinois, Michigan, and Tennessee. This Western focus had been the mission of the "College of Teachers" since the 1830s. McGuffey and his associates had always argued that the West represented a different culture and society than the East Coast and South. Cities of the East such as the Puritan Boston and Quaker-dominated Philadelphia were far different than Cincinnati, Louisville, Lexington, Chicago, and St. Louis. These Western cities had mixtures of religions such as Catholicism, Lutheranism, Presbyterianism, Methodists, and Baptists. Many of the cities were bilingual (English and German). Nationalities such as Germans, Scots-Irish, Irish, English, Scotch, and French were thrown into a mixing bowl. In the border cities such as Lexington and Cincinnati, there were large free black populations. The evolving culture, language, and national view was different in the West.

Daniel Drake's essay on Western education was even included in *McGuffey's Fourth Reader*. Drake noted: "Measures should be taken to mould a unified system of manners out of the diversified elements which are scattered over the West. We should foster western genius, encourage western writers, patronize western publishers, augment the number of western readers, and create a western heart." Certainly, Drake's comments reflected the position of McGuffey as well. Biographer Harvey Minnich put it this way: "It was to be enough Puritan to fit into the religious mental mode of the descendents of the Ohio Land Company; enough Cavalier to fit into the moral and mental mode of the blue blood Kentucky, Virginia, and North Carolina; enough economic to fit into the thrifty mental mode of the Germans and Scots.

Like the Readers, the common school was a furnace for refining and alloying students into a uniform American culture. Children applied their own form of Americanization of the immigrant or ethnic student. While peer ridicule could be tough, it often proved the strongest form of Americanization. The playground helped motivate the immigrant to learn language quickly, but it could have many drawbacks. It could be cruel at times, but in the long run it reinforced American customs. David Tyack described the process as: "The Chinese boy's pigtail, Mexican girl's tortilla, the Italian child's baroque accent — these disappeared as a result of belittling comments or schoolyard scuffles." It was tough medicine far from the diversity of today, but like today, the playground often is where the immigrant is initiated into American culture. McGuffey's stories often addressed the need to apply more kindness in this natural juvenile process. It is a true tribute to McGuffey that his Readers stressed acceptance of diversity without promoting it as an ideal. For McGuffey, education meant the development of an American citizen.

Daniel Drake was the biggest proponent of Western education as an American standard. Drake, like many others, believed the West was unique, requiring a different approach than the pupils of eastern cities. Drake made the point: "A native of the West may be confided in as his country's hope. Compare him with the native of a great maritime city, on the verge of a nation, his birthplace the fourth story of a house, hemmed in surrounding edifices, his playground a pavement, the scene of his juvenile rambles an arcade of shops, his young eyes feasted on the flags of a hundred alien government, the streets in which he wanders crowded with foreigners, and the ocean, common to all nations, forever expanding to his view." The *McGuffey Readers* not only promoted Western values, but made those values, American values. Teddy Roosevelt was one of those young Eastern minds that was converted to Western values. In many aspects, the American West became the common vision. This "West" of McGuffeyland was described by Daniel Drake as "bounded by nature and connected by a series of rivers — the Mississippi, the Cumberland, the Missouri, the Illinois, and the Ohio."

Western Americans were far from political freedom seekers. They were self-interested people with economic factors intertwined with political and religious factors. While deeply religious, Americans put economics on an equal level. For them freedom met economic freedom. They were closer to the theories of Adam Smith than that of John Locke. The early Scots-Irish, English, Welsh, French, and German came primarily to seek economic freedom and self-interest. The Scot Adam Smith put it best in his *Wealth of Nations:* "The natural effort of every individual to better his own condition . . . is so powerful a principle, that it is alone, and without any assistance, not only capable of carrying on the society to wealth and prosperity, but of surmounting a hundred impertinent obstructions with which the folly of human laws too often encumbers its operations." European problems always had an economic root. Failed crops sent more immigrants to America than any political philosophy. Pure religious colonies had often failed in America. The successful ones such as the Pilgrims and German Separatists learned to tie in economic factors. Even today Americans are known to "vote their wallet" over religious or cultural factors. Economic success even became a religious virtue. The concept of economic self-interest came from the great traders of Scotland who controlled the international flow of tobacco and furs. Their Western relatives came to avoid government taxes, own a piece of land, and make their fortunes.

Just as importantly, these frontier Americans believed in equality and fairness. The class distribution and levels of Europe had been the bigness problems. The Scots-Irish and Irish, in particular, knew the cruel use of economic suppression by government. Even the Germans knew that in Europe, being born into a poor family was economic predestination. The Irish, Scots-Irish, and Germans wanted the chance to rise in society. Since taxes were often a tool of government suppression, they had a deep hatred of taxes in any form and a distrust of government. The Whiskey Rebellion in the 1790s showed the sensitivity to Federal and State taxes. The formation of an American democracy did not change those fears and sensitivity. Church taxes in any form were just as suspect to their scorn. Even the Presbyterians, who loved education, proved thrifty on taxation.

Language was a major problem in the 1850s after the first large wave of immigration after the Irish canal builders that started in the 1840s. The Germans wanted to retain their language and for that reason opposed common schools in Ohio. McGuffey's publisher made a concession to the German population in 1854 with German versions of the Readers. However, McGuffey and the country believed in a single language and its importance as noted in this McGuffey lesson: "Edward is very happy on New Year's Day, because he has just been given two dollars to spend as he pleases. While he is thinking of the pleasure the money will give him, he sees a poor German family, cold and hungry who cannot even speak the language. Edward is so sorry for them that he gives them his two dollars for food and shelter."[1]

In his first edition of the *Fourth Reader* in 1838, McGuffey included a famous composition of Henry Brougham (1778–1868), who helped defeat income taxes in Britain. The composition was actually an address for Parliament of the outrageous taxes of Britain entitled *"Ludicrous Account of English Taxes."* Brougham's rage remains popular to this day. Henry Brougham boldly stated: "Taxes-upon every article which enters into the mouth, or covers the back, or is placed under foot — taxes upon everything which it is pleasant to see, hear, feel, smell, or taste — taxes upon warmth, light, and locomotion — taxes on everything on earth, and in the waters under the earth on everything that comes from abroad, or is grown at home — taxes on the raw material — taxes on every fresh value that is added to it by the industry of man — taxes on the sauce which pampers man's appetite, and the drug which restores him to health — on the ermine which decorates the judge, and the rope which hangs the criminal — on the poor man's salt, and the rich man's spice — on the brass nails of the coffin, and the ribbons of the bribe — at bed or board, couchant or levant, we must pay." It may seem a bit political

---

1 William McGuffey, *Third Eclectic Reader*, 1879 edition.

today, but in McGuffey's day, it was frontier common sense to minimize taxes. The thrifty immigrants of Scotland, England, Ireland, and Germany well remembered the taxes of Europe, which kept them in economic chains. It had been part of the American Revolution and the Whiskey Rebellion of the 1790s. McGuffey always held true to his Scots-Irish Covenanter roots that politics should be kept out of our schools and churches.

Education became a strange exception because of the frontier belief in equality. Education in Europe had been reserved for the wealthy, and the American frontier would not tolerate such inequality. One of the few things that McGuffey might have found agreement on with Thomas Jefferson was the need for widespread education in a democracy. Thomas Jefferson's land plan for education was adopted in the Land Ordnances of 1785 and 1787. Those ordnances applied to the Northwest Territory of Ohio, Indiana, Wisconsin, Illinois and Michigan. In these states the Federal Government allotted one section of 36 sections in a township for a school, and this distribution became the definition of a school district, each section being one square mile. The Scotch-Irish and the Germans had started their own schools from Pennsylvania to Indiana, but buildings and schools were hard to come by. Where Jefferson would have disagreed with McGuffey would be in the control of schools by government or church. Where McGuffey saw the success of demagogues in the uneducated, Jefferson feared their creation in a government controlled school system.

Fathers of the West had set up community schools in the Northwest Ordnance in the 1790s, but states lacked the resources to fully implement common schools. McGuffey and the "College of Teachers" had worked with state legislatures to establish common public schools throughout the 1830s. The Germans presented a problem, however. The early German settlers had slowly formed community with or around the Scotch-Irish in Pennsylvania and the Western Reserve of Ohio, but German immigrants of the 1840s and 1850s started to segregate back to all German communities. This German segregation strengthened in the Ohio River cities such as Cincinnati and the rural farm areas in the West. They were determined to maintain the German language and culture. They opposed common schools that taught in English only. By the 1850s, some schools and texts like the McGuffey Readers started to use German and English. German Catholics, however, started their schools because of the Protestant theme in most common schools. *McGuffey Readers* continually evolved to avoid Protestant dogma.

Many modern critics attack the Christian or at least religious view of the *McGuffey Readers*, but they miss the point. The inclusion of religion and Christianity was not an issue in the 1880s, but was actually expected. The Northwest Ordinance of 1787 stated: "religion, morality, and knowledge are necessary to good government and the happiness of mankind." McGuffey actually pioneered tolerance and acceptance of many religious views. McGuffey was a strict "old school" Presbyterian and Covenanter personally, but his original Readers included an array of writers including the very liberal Unitarians. These were at the opposite end of McGuffey's beliefs. One example is Unitarian William Channing who wrote the lesson *"Religion the only Basis of Society"* in the original 1837 *Fourth Reader*. Channing's overall views were never popular in the West but had popularity with the New England transcendentists, yet McGuffey used one of his mainstream essays. This lesson was consistent with McGuffey's common view: "Religion is a social concern; for it operates powerfully on society, contributing in various ways to its stability and prosperity. Religion is not merely a private affair; the community is deeply interested in its diffusion; for it is the best support for the virtues and principles, on which the social order rests. Pure and undefiled religion is, to do good; and it follows, very plainly, that if God be the Author and Friend of society, then, the recognition of him must enforce all social duty, and enlightened piety must give its whole strength to public order."

While McGuffey personally was a strict Presbyterian, he softened the approach of common school education to religion. By taking out Christian dogma, he shifted the hard line religious approach of education to the Church versus the school. W. Cameron noted in his 1929 talk on "The Mind of McGuffey": "The moral intention and objective and the common sense that we note and approve in the McGuffey Readers were at once the result of his profound religious nature and a certain measure of classical revolt against the method and much of the extraneous amplification of what was taught as religion to children in his day." Viewing the McGuffey Readers, through the prism of the twenty-first century, would miss this type of analysis. McGuffey moderated the highly Calvinistic dogma of earlier readers, giving America at least one Christian ecumenical reader.

There was a type of low-grade struggle with "atheism" in the 1800s, but it was more deists, anti-clerics, skeptics, humanitarian and Unitarians versus the traditional Protestant theology. The battle had started with Thomas Jefferson who had many issues with traditional Christianity. Jefferson, like Jackson, was known for his anticlericalism, while most "College" associates saw Jefferson as a dangerous start to anti religion. Even the liberal Christian Lyman Beecher took on Jefferson publicly in 1815. The election of Andrew Jackson similarly caused McGuffey concern as Jackson brought his religion on Sunday attitude to Washington. With his conservative Covenanter background, McGuffey wanted a strong Christian tie with government, which led him personally to the Whig Party and later the Republican Party of the 1850s. Probably, the bigger divide nationally was between Catholics and Protestants.

To McGuffey's credit, even his first efforts worked against the anti-Catholic sentiment in the general population. Some Catholics, like the Irish canal diggers, had no choice but to send their children to common schools. McGuffey's success was not so much in his attracting Catholics to common schools, but in helping educate against the evils of discrimination. Schools throughout the 1800s were Protestant, at least in the minds of Catholics. The use of the King James Bible alone was problematic for most Catholics. Like McGuffey's moral approach to slavery, his moral approach to Catholic discrimination killed it at the root. Many McGuffey "graduates" showed a new acceptance of Catholics, at least in the work place. Since the American workforce would be predominately Catholic from 1880 to 1930, moderating the anti-Catholic views was important. McGuffey's teaching on charity included all Blacks and Catholics. It was the same for Jews, although much has been made of Henry Ford's anti-Semitism as coming from McGuffey. The link cannot be found as McGuffey's charity, love, and respect were not limited, but included all. This does not mean he accepted Catholicism, but he opposed religious discrimination for any group. His Readers aimed at moral education based on Christian principles not dogma.

McGuffey envisioned and hoped to bring Catholics into the common school system. In the preface of the 1843 edition, he stated: "NO SECTARIAN matter has been admitted into this work. It has been submitted to the inspection of highly intelligent clergymen and teachers of the various Protestant and Catholic denominations, and nothing has been inserted except with their united approbation. While the instruction imparted through works of this kind should be decidedly moral and religious in its tendency, it is believed that nothing of a denominational character should be introduced." There were a few minor slips about "papists" and substituting good men for Benedictine monks. McGuffey remained sensitive to Cincinnati Bishop Purcell review, and the 1843 revisions eliminated some offensive material. The original story, "*Character of Martin Luther,*" which was an extremely fair lesson noting many of Luther personal issues did contain one problematic phrase: "The account of his death filled the Roman Catholic party with excessive as well as indecent joy." The story was cut completely in 1843.

McGuffey and Winthrop Smith tried to achieve the same balance with the Jews. It was to their credit because the Jews represented a very small portion compared to the Catholic population. There was almost no sales value to purging anti-Semitic phrases. Even initially they adjusted Shakespeare's "*Merchant of Venice*" to take out Antonio's requirement that Shylock convert to Christianity.[1] In an original 1837 edition of the *Third Reader*, the lesson on "The Bible" includes the line that the Jews are: "the bitterest enemies of the Christian name." The lesson was purged by 1844. Any fair analysis of *McGuffey's Readers* must conclude that there is no anti-Jew sentiment. This approach is fully consistent with the core beliefs of McGuffey.

---

1   Stanley W. Lindberg, *The Annotated McGuffey* (New York: Van Nostrand Reinhold Company, 1976), p. 237

Even in the case of the American Indians, McGuffey took the moral high road. The original Readers did reflect some references to massacres, but later revisions not only eliminated these references but also added the truth of their mishandling. The original story of "Prospects of the Cherokees" did portray some of the problems confronted by the Indians. In 1844, the lesson "North American Indians" was added. These newer lessons highlighted the poor and immoral treatment of the American Indians. Again *McGuffey Readers* preached tolerance and acceptance against the popular bigotry of the time. In the 1853 Fourth Reader, a lesson on William Penn includes: "How can I, who call myself a Christian, do what I should abhor even in the heathen? No. I will buy the right of the proper owners, even of the Indians themselves." These facts are much different from modern critics that blame American education (and McGuffey by association) on justifying the taking of the Indian lands. *McGuffey Readers* had a true consistency in their application of Christian principles and that part of moralistic education and the McGuffey legacy.

Probably the best summary of the religious character of the Readers was by Richard Mosier: "it is clear that the morality and religion found in the *McGuffey Readers* were those of the overwhelming majority of Americans in the nineteenth century, and that in exerting their influence in matters of the religion and morality the McGuffey readers called many back to that stricter piety and sharper morality known only to the older generations, in the cause of religious toleration, as we saw in the case of the Catholic question, the readers performed nobly, speaking with liberality on the subject of toleration and decency. With respect to matters of religious and racial tolerance, with respect to simple piety and healthy morals, the McGuffey readers were and are supreme. That this strong emphasis on religious conviction and moral enthusiasm ultimately played into the hands of conservatism and reaction in politics and ultimately strengthened the influence of conservative arguments was hardly the fault of the readers but was rather inevitable in an age that found the pattern of ideas in the McGuffey readers so widely accepted in the system of values of nineteenth century America."

Clearly, McGuffey reflected the views of the nineteenth century, but he also reformed them and highlighted the best of them. He used his moral approach to argue the use of Christianity as valid. Morals were common ground to all of nineteenth century society. Where some disagreed was that religion was necessary to the foundation of moralistic education. Yet McGuffey's approach would calm the concerns of Jeffersonians, Jacksonians and Unitarians. Author Elliott Gorn summarized the purpose of the McGuffey Readers concisely: "Even in their golden age, the McGuffey Readers were never simply a snapshot of nineteenth-century America. A better metaphor is to think of them as a map for building a national culture, one drawn by bourgeois Protestants who were white, largely descended from English and Western European stock, and who expected the country to be just like them. The Readers' mantra of piety, conscience, and sober self-control helped socialized children into the ways of this Protestant middle class. Students who learned their lessons well and embraced the life offered them expected to enjoy the rewards promised."

Harvey Minnich of Miami University in 1936 summarized the success of the McGuffey Readers, noting five factors:

> 1. The method of teaching the beginner to read. Clearly, McGuffey was revolutionary in going directly from the alphabet to reading without teaching spelling first.

> 2. "The second item of supremacy was McGuffey's drills upon the syllable as a unit in word mastery; enunciation as a first essential in the spoken language, so necessary among foreigners struggling into a new language; short and simple sentences; a sequence of ideas that held the attention of the young learner; painstaking and continuous correcting of faulty pronunciation."

> 3. The simple methodology and arrangement of materials.

> 4. Uniqueness of the word "eclectic" and the iconic nature of the word "McGuffey."

> 5. The fifth and what Minnich considered the most important was the moral base and tone of the Readers.

Minnich clearly focused on the product, but Alice McGuffey Ruggles argued the success was really market driven. Ruggles noted: "Three elements went into the success of the McGuffey Readers: first, the intellectual hunger of the New West; second, the vision of the two gifted men [William and Alexander] who understood their need; and third, the salesmanship that brought the goods to the market."

Proof of McGuffey's success in a common American vision often came in strange circumstances. One of these comes from the history of the Civil War prison at Andersonville by John McElroy. It was stated of the Union prisoners: "The boys from Ohio, Indiana, Illinois, Iowa, and Kansas all seemed cut off of the same piece. To all intents and purposes they might have come from the same county. They spoke the same dialect, read the same newspapers, had studied McGuffey's Readers, Mitchell's Geography, and Ray's Arithmetic at school, admired the same great men, held generally the same opinions on any subject. It was never difficult to get them to act in unison."[1] Since the generation of the original McGuffey alumni is long gone, anecdotal evidence will have to stand in for research.

---

1 "Presentation of McGuffey Readers, February,15, 1929, *Ohio History*, Volume 36

CHAPTER 18. McGUFFEYLAND CAPITALISM

"There are minds in every community that are best employed both for themselves
and the public on easy tasks at low wages."
— William McGuffey

Much has been written about McGuffey and capitalism because of Henry
Ford's love affair with *McGuffey Readers*. It must not be lost in any discussion that
McGuffey was an educator, not a philosopher. Maybe more revealing was the
description of the education of Henry Clay Frick, the father of American capitalism. Frick biographer George Harvey described it as: "The curriculum comprised
the familiar three R's, slightly amplified, the books allotted being McGuffey's
Reader, Pinneo's grammar, Mitchell's geography and Ray's arithmetic." Other
McGuffey capitalist alumni include John Rockefeller, Andrew Carnegie, Charles
Schwab, Charles Goodyear, Thomas Edison, Andrew Mellon, George Westinghouse, H. J. Heinz, and many others. He did not mold roots of American society
but often merely spoke for them. More so than Max Weber's "Protestant Work
Ethic," McGuffey's rationalization for class structure and elevation of industry to
a virtue formed the basis of American capitalism. McGuffey took on Marxism before Marx had defined it as a political system. The fundamental support of capitalism came from McGuffey's unwavering support for individual property rights.
Likewise, his basic support of capitalistic concepts came before Capitalism was
defined as an economic approach. He saw the existence of poverty and wealth
as both in God's providence. Neither was intrinsically evil. McGuffey personally
feared Andrew Jackson in his day as promoting redistribution of wealth. Poverty
was to be addressed by the wealthy, not solved by political schemes to redistrib-

ute wealth. McGuffey actually accepted a bit of the other extreme of Alexander Hamilton's democratic aristocracy.

McGuffey could tolerate inequality, if everyone had the equal opportunity to improve. Free education to McGuffey assured that the playing field was level. Some of this probably evolved out of Calvinistic predestination modified by Presbyterian pragmatism. His logical defense of capitalism made more sense than his aristocratic approach to democracy. McGuffey, like many Americans, struggled with Democracy versus a Republic. McGuffey would tolerate a large class difference, which would not be popular today. McGuffey, however, was not designing a system or philosophy like Karl Marx, but trying to standardize common values that existed in society. McGuffey had biases like all of us, but he was not a radical, a revolutionary, or a reactionary. With all his biases and many critics on his belief in capitalism, it is universally accepted that he tried to promote the best of capitalism. His view was that moral responsibilities were an obligation of the wealthy, and morals must be first in the search for profits.

In McGuffeyland you were taught the importance of winning, but the winning counted only if rules were followed. Cheating and winning produced the most hollow type of victory, producing a trophy that would deteriorate in time. Many McGuffey alumni often talked of the hollow success of cheating. In McGuffeyland, similarly, earned wealth had more value than unearned. Wealth earned by hard work had more value than that earned by genius. Many great McGuffey alumni and industrialists said that the real trophy was in earning the money, not in its monetary value. They would rather fight hard to earn a thousand dollars than be made rich from an inheritance. They hated the thought of being in an old aristocracy. They feared that money passed down through the family destroyed character. Money was only the measure of their hard work. In the *Fourth Reader's* lesson on labor, it is summarized: "The education, moral, and intellectual, of every individual, must be chiefly, his own work. Reply upon it, that the ancients were right-both in morals and intellect — we give their final shape to our characters, and thus become, emphatically, the architects of our own future."

There is no doubt that the regions of America where the *McGuffey Readers* and common schools were strongest became the bastions of capitalism. These regions included Western Pennsylvania, Eastern Ohio, Indiana, Southern Michigan, and Chicago, Illinois. The common dominator of the great capitalists of the Gilded Age was the *McGuffey Readers*. Even more so, the common school and one-room schoolhouse was the breeding ground for capitalism. For example, the Connellsville area of Western Pennsylvania became the center of industrial America. This Scotch-Irish district had an extensive common school system using *McGuffey Readers* from the 1850 on. It was here that America's greatest capitalist Henry Clay Frick grew up, but he was far from alone. Connellsville birthed the coke industry for the steel furnaces of the country, and by 1900 had more millionaires per capita than any town in the world. The story was similar in the Scotch-Irish area of Eastern Ohio, Southern Ohio, and Pittsburgh, which made up the heart of McGuffeyland. It is this center of McGuffeyland that educated most of the 19th century presidents and elected them.

Some care should be noted in that McGuffey was not a propagandist for capitalism. Someone once said the capitalism was a stool with three legs, and those legs were economic freedom, property ownership, and moral responsibility. McGuffey's contribution was to craft the leg of moral responsibility. He was a propagandist for the virtues of hard work, industry, charity, and the ability to rise to the highest level of one's effort. In fact, the term does not exist in his original Readers. McGuffey always approached education from a moral viewpoint, so what he supported was the right of property ownership and what Lincoln called the "right to rise." The virtue of "industry" was defined in *Webster's Blue Back Speller* as "diligent attention to business . . . Our Creator has kindly united our duty, our interest, and happiness; for the same labor which makes us healthy and cheerful, gives us wealth." McGuffey exhorted the simple laborer, middle class storeowner and the wealthy manufacturer to work hard and save. The wealthy, having been so blessed, were required to give to the less fortunate. While McGuffey's stories praised competition, it was not the "survival of the fitness" popular with Gilded Age atheists, but the virtue of industry at the root. Critics rightfully point to McGuffey's idealism, but McGuffeyland was the moral ideal.

The nearest thing to a capitalist quote in the original 1837 series comes in the *Third Reader:* 'The road to wealth, to honor, to usefulness, and happiness, is open to all, and all who will may enter upon it with the almost certain prospect of success. In this free community, there are no privileged orders. Every man finds his level. If he has talents, he will be known and estimated, and rise in the respect and confidence of society." Note that McGuffey sees the capitalist call of man in the tradition of the American Scotch-Irish versus the Calvinist view of the Presbyterian dogma. Even as a strict "Old School" Presbyterian, McGuffey downplayed Calvin's predestination, as did the American frontier of his day. McGuffey called for acceptance of the existence of the poor but held out hope that through industry and persistence, one could rise to any level. This had been the belief that stirred the Methodist movement across Middle America. This was the concept behind America's embrace of capitalism.

The *McGuffey Readers* lack any direct praise of industrialization. In fact, Carol Billman in the *Journal of Popular Culture* even goes further to state: "His readers were most widely used in the South and West, and there is a decidedly anti-industrial strain in them. No cities, no large factories or big-time corporations — for him what was worth teaching about Americans and America lay outside industrialization and often before the later nineteenth century." This may have been true of the first editions in the 1830s, but the compositions included industry and invention as time went on. It is also consistent with McGuffey's approach to use moral building blocks to create a work ethic. McGuffey simply made "industry" and hard work virtues. McGuffey's simple country values played into the hard work ethic needed in the industrialization of America.

He even went further in tying industry to the virtue of Christianity, building the roots for the Protestant Work Ethic. For McGuffey, he often proposed the reverse that idleness was a sin in Christianity. This is laid out in many stories and lessons but the lesson "*The Consequence of Idleness*" in the 1837 *Third Reader* is typical: "This story of George Jones, which is a true one, shows how sinful and ruinous it is to be idle. Every child who would be a Christian, and have a home in heaven, must guard against this sin. As I have given you one story which shows the sad effect of indolence, I will now present you with another, more pleasing, which shows the rewards of industry." McGuffey did make a bit of a concession to Calvinism in that it was God who rewarded hard work, industry, and honesty. McGuffey's Honest George Elliot was one lesson that combined honesty and hard work into riches, but like grace, riches were from God. One critic described it: "Providential payola came to those who practiced thrift, industry, and perseverance." The same critic went on to describe the progression of God from the *New England Primer* to the *McGuffey Reader* as: "God became less the fearsome Judge than the Divine Underwriter who insured that the virtues of hard work, truthfulness, obedience, sobriety, and kindness would pay off here and in the hereafter." Of course, McGuffey saw it as a reward for the virtue.

McGuffey's personal struggle with the distribution of wealth, rich and poor, and Calvinistic predestination was shared by the nation as a whole. It is at the heart of the debate between Jacksonian Democracy and Hamiltonian Republicanism; socialism and capitalism; McKinley Republicanism versus 1930's Democracy; and Johnson's Great Society versus Reagan rugged individualism. The divide of wealth split Christians and sects such as the Presbyterians and Congregationalists in early America. Christians have been ambiguous about the reason but have made helping the poor a fundamental principle. Scotch-Irish struggled with free will of the individual against the predestination of God as well. It is an old problem, the world has always had poor, and it remains even an issue to this day. The struggle and the role of government and the role of the individual define American history. Economists, philosophers, religious leaders, and politicians have created endless approaches in wrestling with the problem. For the socialists, the divide between rich and poor is unfair and evil. The capitalist is forced to at least look at it and come to terms with the divide or rationalize it. The fact is Big Government has failed to redistribute the wealth as much as Big Business. McGuffey had no interest in political systems per sec, nor where they of much interest to Americans in the first half of the nineteenth century. McGuffey's plan was that the wealthy would redistribute the wealth to those in need. This of course required moral education. The answer was therefore not political or economic, but moral.

McGuffey personally was a pure Hamiltonian but with the heart of a Jacksonian. McGuffey's "solution" as always was value and moral oriented. It was a solution based on the philosophical mix of Americans forged on the anvil of Ohio's Western Reserve. McGuffey found the rationalization of the existence of wealth in the morphed Calvinistic idea that the elect became rich to benefit others. Out of the divine right to accumulate property then came the responsibility of stewardship for the poor. The overwhelming theme of his Readers was care of the poor. The capitalist or the socialist would be hard pressed to refute the basic premise of helping the poor. The beauty of *McGuffey's Readers* is that they require political interpretation. Social analyst Richard Mosier said: "It cannot be said, therefore, that the McGuffey Readers consciously supported any political cause; but all the basic ideas of the great conservative and religious synthesis were there." This is why we saw both Democrats and Republicans praise the moral approach of the Readers. The many separatist German communities in Ohio and Kentucky, which practiced a type of socialism and communism in the 1830s, found the same work ethic of McGuffey acceptable in their schools.

McGuffey's early lessons preached a type of acceptance of one's lot in life. McGuffey found a type of happiness in hard work, which in the later years of the 1800s would be questioned by many. In his *Second Reader*, his story "The Good Boy Whose Parents are Poor" states: "I have often been told, and I have read, that it is God who makes some poor, and others rich-that the rich have many troubles which we know nothing about and that the poor, if they are but good, may be very happy. Indeed, I think that when I am good, nobody can be happier than I." While such statements were consistent with American thought in the 1830s, critics in the 1890s would see it as a means to exploit the worker. McGuffey's statement that "religion was the consolation of the poor," would take on a different meaning in the 1880s, and augur Karl Marx's view of religion as the "opium of the masses." Actually, McGuffey's lesson *"Consolation of Religion to the Poor"* was a poem to the strength of religion in one's life. It also reinforced the theme that one must accept life on life's terms. McGuffey's call for acceptance and industry were not so much based in religion as in his Scotch-Irish upbringing. Industry was a prized virtue of the Scotch-Irish.

McGuffey's views on labor and religion were consistent with many divergent groups of the 1800s. The Transcendentalists and the Unitarians, who rejected basic Christian principles, believed that elevation of the "soul" of the working-man more important than his material condition. William Channing, a founder of both Transcendentalism and Unitarianism, voiced similar feelings in various lessons and editions of the McGuffey Reader. Channing argued the elevation of the laborer: "is not release from laborer. It is not struggling for another rank. It is not political power. I understand something deeper. I know but one elevation of a human being, and that is the elevation of the soul." This type of thought is still consistent with atheist sociologist Abe Maslow. What they all could agree on is that the laborer was not predestined or restricted to a certain class. While they preached acceptance, they also preached that one would rise above his birth class with hard work.

McGuffey, however, did not use acceptance in a negative sense or Calvinist predestination, but only as part of God's plan. The real capitalistic theme in McGuffeyland was the promise that hard work would bring success. This central theme can be found in his lesson "Value of Time and Knowledge" in his *Third Reader*: "But if you have minds which are capable of endless progression in knowledge, of endless approximation to the supreme intelligence; if in the midst of unremitting success, objects of new interest will be forever opening before you; Oh, what prospects are presented to the view of man!" Story after story linked that hard work could lead to success. McGuffey expounded that hard work could overcome disadvantages of poor birth, environment, and intelligence. In the *Fourth Reader* 1837 story "No Excellence without Labor," a poor wretch raises above a rich genius. The question is then asked: "Now, whose work is this? Manifestly their own. They are the architects of their respective fortunes. The best seminary of learning that can open its portals to you can do no more than to afford you the opportunity of instruction. It must depend, at last on yourselves, whether you will be instructed or not, or to what point you will push your instruction. Of this be assured — I speak from observation. THERE IS NO EXCELLENCE WITHOUT GREAT LABOR." This type of moralistic encouragement surely inspired many a student in the 1800s.

McGuffey promoted a trade and crafts education, realizing that not everyone was to be a scholar. This was not, as some claim, a type of predestation, but the idea that everyone has a unique vocation. The idea that everyone had a unique vocation was consistent with Martin Luther, but Calvin advanced it to mean predestination. Vocational education and training had been an early principle of the "College of Teachers" and visionaries such as Daniel Drake. It was expressed in a number of McGuffey lessons but best in the first edition of the *Sixth Reader*. In a lesson by Horace Greeley (1811–1872), the principle is defined: "To the ample and constant employment of the whole community one prerequisite is indispensable, that a variety of pursuits shall have been created or naturalized therein. A people who have a single source of profit are uniformly poor, not because that vocation is necessarily ill-chosen, but because no single calling can employ and reward the varied capacities of male and female, old and young, robust and feeble." Furthermore, McGuffey did not see vocational training as training hands for labor, but the training of the "intelligent artisan." This approach was part of the Lyceum System movement of the 1830s, and the concepts of Woodward College in the

1830s. The "College of Teachers" had successfully pushed to have these lyceums and "vocational schools" chartered in Ohio.

McGuffey was far from alone in his praise of industry as a virtue. Noah Webster said this in his 1824 *Blue Back Speller* in his "moral catechism" on the effects of industry: "One effect is to procure an estate. Our Creator, has kindly united our duty, our interest, and happiness; for the same labor which makes us healthy and cheerful, and gives wealth. Another effect of industry is, to keep men from vice." Work was viewed this way throughout America in the first half of the nineteenth century. It was the heart of the "Protestant Work Ethic," often cited as the root of American success in the nineteenth and twentieth centuries. The virtue of industry is developed progressively in the Readers. In the *First Reader*, we have the story of "John Jones," who was too poor to go to school but worked hard before play. In the *Second Reader*, the evils of idleness are attacked in "The Little Idle Boy" and "The Idle Boy Reformed." In the *Third Reader*, we find the lesson "The Consequences of Idleness." Max Weber was a strong anti-Catholic and racist. McGuffey's belief in hard work was just as acceptable to the immigrant Catholics as it was to the original Puritans of New England. Actually, McGuffey's view was more consistent with Pope Leo XIII of the industrial world than that of Max Weber.

McGuffey never railed against religions, systems or individuals but looked at the basic morals, which could make any political system effective. He lived by his ancestral Covenanter roots to kept politics out of religion and education. His personal philosophy was in capitalism, but he realized that capitalism had an Achilles Heel if not managed by men of morals and virtue. His best overall statement on wealth is reflected in the 1879 edition of the *McGuffey Fourth Reader*: "Wealth, rightly got and rightly used, rational enjoyment, power, fame, these are all worthy objects of ambition; but they are not the highest objects, and you may acquire them all without achieving true success. But if, whatever you seek, you put good-will into all your actions, you are sure of the best success at last; for whatever else you gain or miss, you are building up a noble and beautiful character, which is not only the best of possessions in this world, but also is about all you can expect to take with you into the next."[1] This view is consistent with a recent quote of Joe the Plumber: "Capitalism is a marvelous thing, but it needs a moral compass."

This approach certainly reflected the mind of America and was acceptable to most Christians. It addressed the fundamental right of Americans to pursue happiness. Many have viewed it as pro-capitalism, and McGuffey was capitalist, but fundamental principles were more important to McGuffey than economic systems. Still, this view honors a higher goal than wealth alone, while not seeing wealth as intrinsically evil. If you search the *McGuffey Readers* for direct support of capitalism, you will be disappointed. McGuffey only addressed moral and reli-

---

1 *Fourth Reader Eclectic Series* (Cincinnati: 1888), p. 153-154

gious issues in such a head-on approach. Furthermore, terms such as capitalism and socialism were not in common use through most of McGuffey's lifetime. The issue in those days was more like the rights of the individual versus the rights of the government for the common good. McGuffey was always a true to his Covenanter roots, staying clear of political activism and looking to moralistic education as the better alternative.

McGuffey was well aware that any system could be corrupted, and his goal was always to educate on morals, rights, and virtues believing the rest would fall in place. Capitalism offered a "right" that was fundamental to his beliefs. One his followers Abraham Lincoln called it "the right to rise." No one promoted this right more than McGuffey and his *Readers*. In Europe, the aristocracy, inheritance laws, taxes, the church, and politicians had taken this right away. It was the motivation behind the great Scotch-Irish immigration. McGuffey's stories often empathized the rags-to-riches. He threw off any ties to Calvinistic predestination. As one biographer put it: "he clearly believed that human beings exercised control over their fates and the Lord had not irrevocably made those decisions eons ago."[1] The immigrants of McGuffey's era were not so much political refugees as economic. Like most Scotch-Irish, McGuffey could live with class and wage inequality as long as the right to rise and the right of property existed. Slavery, of course, violated this fundamental principle of McGuffey as did socialism. It was not that he opposed the equality of Jacksonian Democracy or socialism, but both could threaten the right of property. Men were created equal, but their destinies were not all equal. Neither did he see capitalism as inherently Christian. He realized that greed could corrupt capitalism, but again he relied on basic virtues to keep capitalism in line. It would be a mistake to see McGuffey as an evangelist for capitalism. It was more that capitalism had a natural affinity for such rights as the right to rise and virtues such as hard work.

McGuffey realized the importance of the "right to rise" to not only capitalism but to the country itself. John F. Kennedy would later say: "Sociologists call the process of the melting pot "social mobility." One of the characteristics has always been the lack of a rigid class structure. It has traditionally been possible for people to move up the social and economic scale. Even if one did not succeed in moving up oneself, there was always the hope that one's children would. Immigration is by definition a gesture of faith in social mobility. It is the expression in action of a positive belief in the probability of a better life. It has thus contributed greatly to developing the spirit of personal betterment in American society and to strengthen the national confidence in change and future. Such confidence, when widely shared, sets the national tone. The opportunities that America offered made the dream real, at least for a good many; but the dream itself was in large part the product of millions of plain people beginning a new life in the

1 Elliott Gorn, p. 11

conviction that life could indeed be better, and each new wave of immigration rekindled the dream."[1]

John F. Kennedy said it all, with the exception that the dream depended on its ability to be passed on, and this is what *McGuffey Readers* did. The Readers passed on the hope, the faith, and dream to each boatload of immigrants. This was the common vision that allowed the tough living of the Industrial Revolution to be endured. These industrial immigrants were really not different than those who faced the rigors of the Western frontier. The industrial ghetto had similar challenges. McGuffey's Western vision proved just as valuable to the industrial worker as to the pioneer. It was the power of the dream that allowed capitalism to move forward with all its problems. Many might argue the late nineteenth century industrial family faced far more challenges than those of the eighteenth century frontier family. Workers opted for the dream over the political solution of Marxism. They opted for a slower democratic solution over the faster one of socialism. They maintained a moral compass while at times being exploited by the more powerful.

McGuffey's themes also rejected the idea of social Darwinism that cold-hearted competition was basis of capitalism. One of McGuffey's most powerful stories is found in the *Second Reader's* "Emulation without Envy." This is a story of two competing students, one the son of a wealthy farmer, the other a son of a poor widow. The two boys are competing for top honors. They competed week after week with the widow's son taking the lead just before the holiday break. "When they met again, the widow's son did not appear, and the farmer's son being next in excellence, could now have been at the head of the class." Instead the farmer's son went to the widow's home, only to find the widow could not pay for books and tuition. The rich farmer's son took money out of his pocket to pay for the poor boy's books and tuition. He would lose out to his rival, but note: "people of strong minds are never envious; that weak minds are ones filled with envy." This was typical of McGuffey's moral education. *McGuffey Readers* promoted fair competition, high rewards, and charity. Many McGuffey stories warned that there would be corruption and many that would abuse their privileges.

In fact, the only education of America's industrialist bad boy and capitalism's devil, Henry Clay Frick, was five semesters of *McGuffey Readers*. Henry Clay Frick often noted this humble education, and many have pointed him out as capitalistic evil generated by McGuffey. Frick, of course, is best remembered for his role in the bloody steel strike at Homestead in 1892. Henry Clay Frick, with all his love of money and art, had been touched about the need for charity. During a Wall Street panic, Frick heard of hundreds of children losing their Christmas accounts and replaced the money. He gave quietly to hospitals, children's homes, and parks. The real point, however, is the brief reading of the *McGuffey Readers* shows

---

1 John F. Kennedy, *A Nation of Immigrants* (New York: Harper & Row, 1964), p. 68

that charity was put above all other virtues and was hailed in the earliest stories. Another unfair linkage was the behavior of many of these industrialists towards immigrants, yet the *McGuffey Readers* only preached tolerance. Furthermore, in the 1857 edition, McGuffey included the "Song of the Shirt," which attacked the exploitation of factory workers in New England. McGuffey even advanced the claims that northern factories were no better than economic slaves.

McGuffey did, however, offer an insurance policy for these immigrants in common education. Lyman Beecher defines this insurance policy in the 1879 *Sixth Reader* lesson "Necessity of Education". In this lesson it talks of an American destiny and education: "Without the education of the head and the heart of the nation, they cannot be; and the question to be decided is, can the nation, or the vast balance power of it, be so imbued with intelligence and virtue as to bring out, in laws and their administration, a perpetual self-preserving energy. We know the work is a vast one, and of great difficulty; and yet we believe it can be." Europe offered nothing like the hope of America. With education, an American could jump the walls that imprisoned him in Europe. It could break down the rigid economic class system of Europe.

Property and the right of property ownership was another fundamental Western principle emphasized in the *McGuffey Readers*. The Romans called it *meum et tuum* or "that is yours and this is mine." The Scotch-Irish had migrated to own a piece of low taxed land that had been denied them in Scotland, such as the McGuffey family. Property rights were fundamental to the Scots-Irish and the Western frontier. Not surprising the British philosopher John Locke saw government's role as one of protecting property. Many early Germans came to America because inheritance laws diluted family land ownership. The Irish immigrants had their land taken from them in Ireland. Land had been the motivator of the great Western immigration of Eastern Americans. The right to own property had priority over everything in the Western psyche. Without the right of property, there can be no capitalism. Scottish philosopher Henry Kames put it this way in 1748, "It is a principle of the law of nature and essential to the well-being of society that men be secured in their possession honestly acquired." Scottish economist and follower of Kames, Adam Smith, argued all laws and government flow from the right of property. The concept of Christian roots goes back to the lawgiver Moses. Pagans such as Hammurabi saw property as the reason for moral order. And even atheists such as Robert Hume saw it as the foundation of society.

The cornerstone article and lesson for property rights was "Origin of Property" by Sir William Blackstone (1723–1780). The Blackstone essay originally appeared in the 1853 *Rhetorical Guide* and continued in the *Sixth Reader* through the 1879 revision. Richard Mosier noted: "To Blackstone, the McGuffey Readers give the difficult task of explaining the origins of property." Blackstone was a British capitalist, lawyer, and politician, and his ideas were often used in the writings of Alexander Hamilton. Thomas Jefferson was one of Blackstone's distracters. Blackstone sometimes disturbed point in the McGuffey essay was: "Necessity begat property; and, in order to insure that property, recourse was had to civil society, which brought along with it a long train of inseparable concomitants: states, government, laws, punishments, and the public exercise of religious duties. Thus connected together, it was found that a part only of society was sufficient to provide, by their manual labor, for necessary subsistence of all; and leisure was given to cultivate the human mind, invent useful arts, and to lay the foundations of science." Interestingly, while Jefferson often decried Blackstone view, he was the president that gave us the patent office to protect intellectual rights.

The McGuffeys had been part of the movement to move to the cheap land of the West, taking them from Eastern to Western Pennsylvania, and then to Ohio's Western Reserve. The West was always about land ownership. Like McGuffey's approach on politics, he went to the roots, not the issues, and at the heart of capitalism were property rights of the individual. Property rights were at the heart of their government and communities, and McGuffey put it at the heart of young minds. When McGuffey published his in 1838, property rights had been detailed in American laws, but McGuffey promoted a new respect for property. With stories in his *Second Reader*, like "The Honest Boy and the Thief," *First Reader* McGuffey taught the right of property. True to his Scotch-Irish roots, the right of property was paramount. His personal distrust of Andrew Jackson had come from Jackson's anticlericalism and his anti-property approach. Property rights were given by God to be protected by government and man. Many of McGuffey's closest friends such as Andrew Wylie feared men like Jackson would result in a Godless communal society. Their fear of Andrew Jackson proved unfounded because the nation too believed in property rights as fundamental to the American system.

Another story illustrating respect for property was the favorite McGuffey story of Teddy Roosevelt in the 1879 *Third Reader* — "Meddlesome Matty." "While seeking a young helper, an employer lets six boys into an empty room one at a time. Each of the six meddle or allow their curiosity to get the better of them, and are rejected by the employer for this reason. The seventh boy does not meddle, and as a result gets the job. He also receives a large legacy for his honesty upon his employer's death. A boy is taken for a tour of a beautiful garden. He is warned not to touch anything, and he obeys the warning strictly. While he is there, a bad boy knocks at the gate. The gardener refuses to let the bad boy in, since on the previous visit he had "meddled with what does not belong to him."

The strong linkage between McGuffey and Henry Ford has led many to believe the Readers had a subliminal message supporting capitalism. There is little evidence of such direct support for capitalism. McGuffey's support of American values and virtues did, however, allow for success in a capitalistic system. Many of McGuffey's stories extolled the relationship between hard work and material rewards. Accumulation of property was considered a right in the American mind. Likewise, laziness was pictured as a sure path to failure. Thrift and saving were also considered to be virtuous. Maybe the real impact was on the type of capitalism that evolved, more than McGuffey being a seed for capitalism. Paternal capitalism, philanthropic capitalism, and stewardship are themes in all of the Readers.

The research for this book had originally started to look for the link between great American capitalists and their McGuffey education. There is little evidence that the *McGuffey Readers* are the taproot of American capitalism as a theory. *McGuffey Readers* certainly did, however, have an impact on America's greatest capitalists. The support of capitalism by McGuffey may have not been so much in social and economic readings, but in something much different. The virtue of industry was promoted to all. McGuffey saw work as healthy and necessary to all. McGuffey held out a promise that you could go as far as your talents could take you, and that those talents would be further enhanced with education. Some believe that McGuffey even opposed industry because of the farm-based stories in the original series. The fact is that in 1837, the nation was basically agrarian. What industry that did exist such as iron making, wagon making and such was in support of agriculture.

In the 1843 edition of the *Third Reader*, there is a composition by John Aikin called "The Colonists," which deals with the various professions for the youth to consider. Farmers are considered primary, but mechanics, blacksmiths and other trades were considered next. Unavailable professions included lawyers, politicians, professional soldiers, and journalists. Lawyers, in particular, never get favorable representation in the series. In the original *Fourth Reader* there is an outstanding composition of the invention and workings of a steam engine. The lesson is proud in that the inventor Robert Fulton was an American. Later additions of the Fifth Reader included Henry Wadsworth Longfellow's poem "*The Village Blacksmith*," which was a favorite of Henry Ford. The 1879 edition of the series included more stories about inventors, which men like Henry Ford loved to read.

McGuffey's effort to promote free public education may well have been his greatest contribution to capitalism. Capitalism is not effective at distributing the wealth, and it can create inequities. What Lincoln called the "right to rise" was what helped American capitalism weather the storm of nineteenth century Marxism. Free education helped give everybody a fair start. Free education evolved in the West because equity was a basic principle on the frontier. William McGuffey and the "College of Teachers" did more than anyone for common schools. It was public education that allowed men like Andrew Carnegie, John

Rockefeller, Henry Ford, Charles Schwab, George Westinghouse, H. J. Heinz, and so many others rise from rags to riches. Common schools broke the monopoly of the aristocrats on education. It was this simple start that made the difference in the lives of these men. The *McGuffey Reader*, which dominated Western schools, became part of their memories of that education. These great American capitalists built schools, museums, libraries, and parks to foster the ability of all to rise to success.

McGuffey saw education as the great equalizer. This had always been the view of the West that education had to be available to all on an equal basis. The original Third Reader used the following: "Knowledge is power. It is the philosopher's stone, true alchemy that turns every thing it touches into gold."[1] The *Third Reader* further argued: "What raised Franklin from the humble station of a printer's boy to the first honors of his country? Knowledge. What took Sherman from his shoemaker's bench, gave him a seat in Congress, and there made his voice to be heard among the wisest and best of his peers? Knowledge. What raised Simpson from the weaver's loom to a place among the first of mathematicians; and Herschel, from being a poor fifer's boy in the army to a station among the first of astronomers? Knowledge." Without the equalizer of common schools, American capitalism would had faced more problems in the Gilded Age.

McGuffey's capitalism was a combination of the right of property, education, the right to rise in a democracy, and the virtue industry. We can see this in his own words published in 1834: "Look, on the other hand, at Ferguson, and Franklin, and Davy, and Henry, and Clay, and many others, both living and dead, who, without early education, and in the midst of the most pressing poverty, and the unceasing bustle of public life, have risen to an eminence in literature and science, and indeed in every department of human knowledge. On the other hand, we could, were not invidious, point out many who, with every advantage that the others did not possess, with equal talents, and not unequal ambition, began their descent from fame at the moment when their friends were applauding their maiden effort, and cherishing the fondest hopes of their future eminence. And why were these results so contrary to what was rationally expected? The one class, aware of their deficiencies, supplied them by their industry in after life; and in so doing, formed habits that remained with them while they remained upon earth. The other, presuming upon the superiority secured by their early advantages, suffered indolence, or pleasure, or perhaps dissipation, to break in upon those habits of patient thought, which were only in a forming state they left the halls of college, or the office of their professional instructor; and thus their former stores were soon squandered, and with them was lost that which

---

1 William McGuffey, *Electric Third Reader* (Cincinnati: Truman and Smith, 1837), p. 172

was far more valuable, the ability and inclination vigorously to apply themselves to mental pursuits."[1]

One theme above all others found in all four of the original Readers was the need for charity. "The Generous Russian Peasant" in the *Third Reader* is the classic lesson that charity is not only required by God but also rewarded. The majority theme in all of the readers was giving to the poor. Story after story teaches giving generously to the poor, and there are more stories on helping the poor than any other theme. He puts such charity ahead of work and industry. And McGuffey takes charity beyond virtue to the level of kindness. McGuffey saw charity as a duty. The poor were not only to be fed but just as important was the duty to educate them. Charity was the virtue that was linked to the stewardship as a responsibility of the rich. McGuffey's type of capitalism was moral based. Economists talked of paternal capitalism, but that is not a natural extension of McGuffey based morals. Paternal capitalism has many problems if the corporate father lacks the strong morals advocated in *McGuffey's Readers*. This was exactly why McGuffey believed aggressive moral based education was needed throughout the nation. In McGuffey's own view, man had a natural propensity to sin; and, therefore, any man-made system has a propensity toward corruption. For McGuffey, man's hope is in moral education.

McGuffey's principle of stewardship was based on Christian principles, but some capitalists such as Andrew Carnegie used it to justify the poor treatment of the worker. Carnegie's view was a distortion of McGuffey's teaching. Carnegie fostered the idea that as God's elect, capitalists knew best how to distribute the wealth. Carnegie's giving was legendary, but his quest for profit created industrial slums. Carnegie's capitalism was not paternal, but communal. Carnegie's giving to libraries and museums are gifts that are still giving to this day, but they were just as much the gifts of the mill workers of Carnegie who slaved at low wages. Carnegie clearly improved the culture of the nation, but critics can argue that the workers of the time would have benefited more from better wages. God's elect could even consider it redistribution of wealth. It was consistent in some aspects to McGuffey's idea of stewardship, but Carnegie's approach lacked the day-to-day pragmatic application of Christian principles.

Much has been made linking the ideas of Andrew Carnegie to McGuffey, but Carnegie only had part of it. Carnegie proudly talked of stewardship, but often McGuffey was much more Christian based. Richard Mosier put it clearly: "The McGuffey readers may have justified themselves by reminding the great stewards of wealth that their stewardship implied duties as well as rights, in accordance with the Pauline doctrine. It is clear that in the Gilded Age, as in the age of Jackson, the McGuffey Reader fell quite easily into the basic strategy of the business community. The conservative cause had been buttresses by both the legal and

---

1 William McGuffey, "General Education," *Western Monthly Magazine*, 1834

divine orders, which had identified themselves with natural order. Here we find all the basic ideas of the old conservative synthesis polished up for new and more vigorous service in the Gilded Age."

Andrew Carnegie's view of capitalism, other than his passion for giving, is not consistent with McGuffey. Carnegie's view of acquisition is truly a reflection of social Darwinism that Carnegie fully embraced. Carnegie even argued indirectly that the acquisition of capital was the result of God's elect, which was the one Calvinistic principle McGuffey had personally struggled with his whole life. The Carnegie view offered the strange twist of exploitation of the worker for his or her own good. There is always a danger of reading too much into McGuffey's reader selections. McGuffey was building a moral base; and while he had strong political beliefs, moral education ruled his selections. There is little evidence of an overriding hidden political agenda or even subliminal direction that trumped his moral goals. There are also better examples of McGuffey-educated capitalists in George Westinghouse and H. J. Heinz, who were both paternal in their acquisition and distribution of wealth. Still, American philanthropy by capitalists amazed an onlooking Europe and world.

McGuffey's concept of stewardship is spelled out in the 1844 *Rhetorical Guide*: "Were the divine principle of benevolence in full operation among the intelligences that people our globe, this world would be transformed into a paradise, the moral desert would be changed into a fruitful field." McGuffey hammered this theme of stewardship more than any other. McGuffey differed from Carnegie in that he believed stewardship to be a Christian imperative. He included biblical support for stewardship throughout his Readers. In his *Fourth Reader*, Catharine Beecher quoted: "thou shalt love the Lord thy God with all thy heart, and thy neighbor as thyself." It would be difficult for the young mind of the McGuffey student not to get the point.

McGuffey's foundational principle that it was the responsibility of the wealthy to help the poor had an impact on the Gilded Age. The *Oxford Guide to American History* noted: "The years from 1870 to 1900 saw an unprecedented burst of economic growth in the United States that generated vast wealth for new captains of industry, and in turn, opened a fresh chapter in the history of American philanthropy." No single theme dominated the *McGuffey Readers* more than charity and giving. As early as Lesson VII in the *First Reader*, a young reader is told to be kind to a beggar, and the first premise of the Golden Rule is introduced: "We should be kind to the poor. We may be as poor as this old man, and need as much as he." A few lessons later in the story of "*Little Henry*" is an even more powerful example of sharing: "John gave some of his cake to each of his school mates, and then took a piece for himself. He gave the rest to an old blind man." These are extremely powerful lessons for the young mind. These lessons continue as the student's reading progressed. In the *Second Reader*: "They did not ask for it, but she saw that they were in great need, which reminded her to share with them." In the *Third Reader's* story "The Way to be Happy," another plea: "I will give you an infallible rule. Do all in your power to make others happy. Be willing to make sacrifices of your own convenience to promote the happiness of others."

American capitalism, for the good or bad, was marked by McGuffey's moral education. American capitalism was much different than the paternal capitalism of the nineteenth century Germans. German paternalism was a self-serving approach to counter the socialism of the late nineteenth century. American capitalism proved much more charitable to society than that of Britain. American capitalism became philanthropic capitalism. Of course, many critics viewed it as welfare capitalism. In any case, it held capitalists responsible to giving back to society. It fulfilled the McGuffey lessons to take care of the poor through giving. It was far from perfect, and many argued that libraries were built on the backs of underpaid steel workers. Still, the philanthropy of American capitalists of the nineteenth and early twentieth centuries is legendary. This philanthropic capitalism went beyond the large corporations. Small business was asked to support community charities, and that tradition remains today.

McGuffey's foundational principles of capitalism are today overlooked, but it may demand a new look in today's globalized market. The plight of the worker during the Industrial Revolution eventually pulled the heartstrings of even the Robber Barons. The solutions took many paths, such as the patriarchic capitalism of Andrew Carnegie and Henry Ford, the welfare capitalism of J. P. Morgan, the unionization of Samuel Gompers, the paternal capitalism of George Westinghouse and H. J. Heinz, and the communal capitalism of Robert Owen. There were even political solutions, such as Communism and Socialism. McGuffey's points were clear. Capitalism and property rights were basic to American society, and the pursuit of wealth was consistent with Calvinistic principles. However, wealth came with responsibility to society and accountability to a deity. Giving was interrelated to the accumulation of wealth, and McGuffey taught this in the *First Reader*.

McGuffey's approach to Christian capitalism was pure Scotch-Irish. It was the very heart of the communities that he had grown up in. The frontier Scotch-Irish believed in making money free of government intervention and taxes. The Scotch-Irish had a strong sense of responsibility and duty to their fellow men and believed in community. Even in the frontier villages, the Scotch-Irish formed "poorhouses" to help the less fortunate. They gave money to build schools and roads. They welcomed the poor to their Sunday meals. Their concept of stewardship had more heart than that of Carnegie's. It had evolved from their Presbyterian predestination modified by their deep belief in the right of property and pursuit of happiness. It was truly Christian based and centered on the "Golden Rule." Carnegie's patriarchal approach lacked true Christian roots. The paternal capitalism of two true McGuffey alumni, George Westinghouse and H. J. Heinz, was more reflective of the McGuffey view.

With Westinghouse and Heinz, there was a true Christian based operating philosophy. The "Golden Rule" was applied in the workplace and the community. Both Westinghouse and Heinz supplied benefits and good pay, but pay was within Victorian norms, where women made half of that of men. Both of these McGuffey alumni practiced their Christianity in their management style. They believed, as McGuffey did, that God would direct and provide. Many have accused McGuffey of supporting capitalism directly. From McGuffey's basic principles, Christian socialism could be supported. His personal views, however, were with capitalism. McGuffey strongly opposed Christian socialistic communities in Kentucky and Indiana. The reason was his fundamental and uncompromising belief in individual property rights. McGuffey had often debated Christian socialist Robert Owen at Miami and the "College of Teachers."

Another unheralded contribution of the *McGuffey Readers* was through a common, although be it idealistic, vision of hope. It gave stability to struggling immigrants in a new industrial world. The 1870s to 1920s was a period of underlying concern. Labor and capital were struggling to establish their roles. Government was also developing its role. In the meantime there were striking differences such as opulent mansions of the managers and the industrial ghettos of the workers. Europe was turning to Marxism, but America never saw Europe as a model. Still, strikes and unrest were common across America by the 1870s. Radical socialists such as anarchists were promoting violence. Social reformers were getting frustrated with the slow pace of the Industrial Revolution. Capitalism was being tested by society. The Great Railroad Strike of 1877 left hundreds of strikers dead across the nation. Elliot Gorn summarizes: "Employees were killed by government troops, millions of dollars of property destroyed, and some people believed that America was on the verge of class warfare. Yet McGuffey persisted in their bucolic vision during, or perhaps in response to, this age of strife. The readers clung to a nostalgia that refused to accept the unpleasant realities of modern social and economic life. But by ignorance how the booming market economy destabilized so much of life, the McGuffey's softened the face of industrial capitalist society and helped it to escape criticism. Even as social protest and labor unrest mounted in the last decades of the nineteenth century, and even as growing numbers of children went to work in mines and factories, other children still read in McGuffeys that virtuous hard work was always rewarded." The railroad strike started the nation looking for stability.

The Great Railroad Strike put fear into the public. Labor historian Joseph Rayback described the effect best: "The Railway Strike of 1877 thoroughly shocked a large portion of the public. Not since slaveholders had ceased to be haunted by dreams of a slave uprising had the propertied elements been so terrified."[1] It was the perfect storm as the recession, heat wave, and strikers came together on July 21, 22, and 23. The country had never known such violence except in war and would never see such civil unrest again until the civil rights riots in the summer of 1967. The Great Railroad Strike touched the psyche of America, which was being industrialized.

On July 21st, Pittsburgh erupted in riots, and the state militia arrived. Tracks were torn up and cars burned. The unemployed and street gangs joined in the riot. Shooting broke out on both sides. By July 23, 1877, twenty had been killed, including the sheriff, with hundreds wounded lying on the sidewalks. Pittsburgh's Catholic Bishop Tuigg walked the streets giving last rites to the wounded, as another nine would die in the streets. Men, women, and children joined into the pillage. The Union Station was torched and freight cars of products were looted as citizens joined in. In all, 1,383 freight cars, 104 locomotives, and 66 passenger cars were destroyed at Pittsburgh. Damage came to over five million dollars. Chicago also had significant riots and property damage. In many cities the unemployed joined the strike and looting. A mob of over 20,000 terrorized Chicago. The riots traveled to the West coast by July 24. Americans had only read about such work related violence in Europe in the 1870s, but the European immigrants of the 1840s could well remember the unrest and riots caused by socialists.

Even the original Readers preached a type of economic stability in a number of lessons. Often McGuffey is criticized for his stories of accepting one's place in life, but it was always biblical based. The lessons were never meant to keep one in one place, but a type of true acceptance always balanced with large doses of hope. One of these was the lesson of "The Little Loaf," added in 1879. The lesson "The Little Loaf" depicts poor children accepting loafs of bread to get through a famine — "till God sends us better times." One girl takes the smallest loaf each time, until one day she finds silver coins in the loaf. This type of stories were increased in the 1879 after the Great Railroad Strike, which would lead to a fear of German socialists and anarchists into the nation. Another theme of the *McGuffey Readers* was to address the evil of envy in lessons such as "Emulation" in the *Fourth Reader* and "The Idle Boy" in the *Second Reader*.

Cynics, of course, might see *McGuffey Readers* as a cruel hoax on these immigrant children and their families. The facts, however, tell a much different story. Most of the sons and daughters of these workers moved up socially, and their kids would know the happiness of the American middle class. Immigrants of the cities proved even more resourceful than the characters of McGuffey. They rented out parts of their slum flats; all family members worked; they banded to-

1 Joseph Rayback, *The History of American Labor* (New York: Macmillan Company, 1959), 135

gether to create life insurance associations, planted gardens, and raised chickens and pigs in the streets. They saved money on subsistence wages! The movement up the class ladder was visual in the steel mill towns around Pittsburgh. New immigrants would enter into low rent districts and slums near riverbanks but below the railroad tracks that followed the rivers. Locals talked about those from "below the tracks." The slums were near the river and mill gates. Moving up in society meant moving "up the hill." The higher up the hill, the higher the level of society. The average stay in the slums was about a generation or less for these Pittsburgh steelworkers from 1890 to 1920. Some, such as the early Irish, used the illegal rackets; then the Italians followed them. More commonly, laborers moved up the skilled crafts ladder. Slavs and Germans tended to buy bars, saloons, and hotels to enter the middle class. Then, of course, there were the NBA-type stars of the period, men like Carnegie, Schwab, and others who started in the slums and rose to corporate offices. These stories were popular with many writers, but the odds were long. Still, upward mobility was the characteristic that gave the impetus of hope to these laborers.

Another theme of the *McGuffey Reader* was the economic manifest destiny. God had blessed America through its moral superiority. It was to be the light of the hill, and the economic and moral hope of the world. In the *First Reader* of 1837, the lesson "Duty of the American Orator" by Thomas Grimke (1786–1834) augurs the Gilded Age's belief in economic manifest destiny.[1] This passage is an example: "Let the American orator comprehend, and live up to the grand conception, that the union is the property of the world, no less than of ourselves; that it is a part of the divine scheme for the moral government of the earth, as the solar system is a part of the mechanism of the heavens; that it is destined, whilst traveling from the Atlantic to the Pacific, like the ascending sun, to shed the glorious influence backward on the states of Europe, and forward on the empire of Asia." This, of course, is also known as "American Exceptionalism." The term manifest destiny was properly avoided, as it was a political term of the 1840s.

Lessons on economic manifest destiny and American exceptionalism increased in every edition. The 1879 *Sixth Reader* in Lyman Beecher's "Necessity of Education" said it a little differently: "We did not, in the darkest hour, believe that God had brought our fathers to this goodly land to lay the foundation of religious liberty, and wrought such wonders in their preservation, and raised descendents to such heights of civil and religious liberty, only to reverse the analogy of his provision, and abandon his work." Only in America could civil war be seen as a manifestation of God's providence. In Europe, civil war would be seen as God's punishment by the religious, and a necessity social correction by the so-

---

1 Stanley W. Lindberg, *The Annotated McGuffey* (New York: Van Nostrand Reinhold Company, 1976), p. 143

cialists. There is no question that McGuffey's common vision helped the healing of the American Civil War.

Of course, critics of McGuffey and the Robber Barons of the Gilded Age can make aggregate assumptions as well. Typical of these criticisms is that of James Rodabaugh during the 1930s depression: "the period when McGuffey morality flourished was an age of individual and sectional strife which led to a bitter fratricidal war. Statesmen reared in the McGuffey atmosphere bled their Southern brothers in the Reconstruction Era and restricted their civil and political rights in order to retain radical control in Congress and to legislate on behalf of certain economic interests. It was men trained in the McGuffey school whose fame as captains of industry rests more on their unethical conduct than altruistic activities. It was men reared on *McGuffey Readers* that robbed the coffers of local, state, and national governments, and who deliberately misgoverned in behalf of themselves or other interests."[1] This type of cynical attack is still made today. It is the same argument used when the actions of a few of one religion are used to condemn the whole religion. It is a stretch to blame the failures of a few on the strongly and completely moral *McGuffey Readers*. McGuffey in many lessons pointed out that men can be expected to fall short of the moral standards, but these moral standards must still be held out. It might be held out that today's lack of moral and ethical education has increased the poor behavior in American business today. Ethics has been eliminated in most school curriculums today, and most business colleges have dropped their ethics courses in the last twenty years.

---

1 James Rodabaugh, Book Reviews, *Ohio Archaeological and Historical Quarterly*, Volume 46, 1936

Chapter 19. McGuffeyland Morals and Patriotism

> "Education is simply the soul of a society as it passes from one generation to another."
> — G. K. Chesterton

As noted, many politicians have used *McGuffey Readers* to support their views, and McGuffey had successfully kept his own political beliefs out of the Readers. Many historians have tried to define direct or sublime message in the *McGuffey Readers*. In the great political campaigns at the end of the nineteenth century between William McKinley and Bryan Jennings, both were lovers of the *McGuffey Reader* and had extreme opposing views. This would be typical in that both Democrat and Republican politicians would claim the importance of their childhood *McGuffey Readers*. This would be true for many decades after as well. But McGuffey was never about politics or economic theories. He believed that given a moral education, things would work out right. And that the problems of society were best solved by moral education versus radical, political, or social movements. The College of Teachers taught him to remain open to listening to all sides and stick to the overall objectives. As we have seen, he did not promote capitalism but helped change it to fit the American culture. His basic Christian views steered clear of dogma, uniting frontier Baptists, Methodists, Presbyterians, Congregationalists, and Unitarians. While an "Old School" Presbyterian, McGuffey was often asked to preach and pastor at Baptist and Methodist churches. His basic Christian principles even helped tramp down the rise of anti-Catholicism. He opposed slavery and drinking by moral teaching, avoiding radical political positions such as Abolition and Temperance societies. Many times he had friends on both sides of the issues, and he could find agreement by focusing on morals. This was

McGuffey's true genius. Taking out denominational dogma, McGuffey focused on Christian morals that had wide acceptability.

McGuffey's morals were rooted in biblical principles such as the Ten Commandments, the "Golden Rule," and the eleven beatitudes of the Sermon on the Mount. He sets the authority of the Bible in his *First Reader*: "The Bible says you must not use bad words. You must mind what the Bible says, for it is God's book." Remember that Bible quotes were not problematic in nineteenth century schools; in fact, they were considered part of education. Basically, the majority of students were Christian or accepting of Christian principles. The argument was over the injection of Christian dogma, not Christianity. Other *First Reader* biblical references include: "The Bible says that no drunkard shall inherit the Kingdom of God," and "remember the commandment which says, 'Thou shalt not steal.'" The *Second Reader* includes not only quotes but full biblical lessons such as "The Ten Commandments," "The Lord's Prayer," "Story about King Solomon," "More about King Solomon," "Story about Joseph," and "More about Joseph." The *Third Reader* continues with many lessons from and in the Bible, including the "Sermon on the Mount." The biblical base continued and increased in the 1857 editions, and McGuffey took the opportunity to add Jesus' words to the *Second Reader*'s Ten Commandments: "With all thy soul love God Above; And as thyself thy neighbor love." The 1879 editions significantly reduced biblical stories but the core lessons of the Sermon on the Mount and the Lord's Prayer remained.

McGuffey believed that morals had to flow from religion, as did most Americans of the time. McGuffey therefore built on the Ten Commandments, which were at the time universally accepted as a moral guide. At times his theology, while non-denominational, could be Puritanical as in the *First Reader* lesson, "The Sun is Up." McGuffey notes the following: "If God is with me, and knows all that I do, he must hear what I say. O, let me not, then, speak bad words; for if I do, God will not love me." Still, this is a rare slip for McGuffey; however, the nineteenth century reader would have no problem with the idea of eternal punishment to reinforce morality. Even the liberal Unitarian movement could accept a little fire and brimstone to keep the children on the straight and narrow. This would be especially true on the frontier where society tended to be on the rough side. McGuffey tended to be more positive in his approach, but morality had to be God based. Morality was part of salvation, not just a good way of living.

The heart and soul of McGuffey's approach to education was in morals. His Readers' literature, his spelling and reading techniques, and his innovative methods were all secondary to moral education. It was to that end, religion was used. McGuffey's view of moral education appears to go back to the 1693 book *Thoughts on Education* by John Locke. Locke believed that learning was of less importance than character and moral development. Locke also believed that religion was the basis of virtue and therefore plays a role in moral education. Locke was no promoter of Christianity, but he realized that "The aims of education are secular but not irreligious." This, of course, was consistent with McGuffey's Scotch-Irish heritage and McGuffey's approach. It must also be understood that McGuffey's approach was revolutionary at the time. School education focused on reading, writing and spelling. In addition, in New England religion was also the focus. McGuffey's true brilliance was in that he taught reading, writing, and spelling while teaching morals. His very *First Reader* imparted the evils of drinking and stealing, the importance of charity, obeying one's parents, and "honesty is the best policy." It was in this context that McGuffey hoped to improve America. Initially, McGuffey addressed some of the basic evils of his society such as slavery and drinking.

Temperance had been a fundamental belief of McGuffey. His family had come from the temperance-supporting sect of the Covenanters, yet the majority of his Scotch-Irish communities loved their whiskey. McGuffey didn't belittle or segregate from drinkers but held to his own personal course. He knew that all Scotch-Irish could find common ground on drunkenness and youths' drinking. Even the whiskey loving Scotch-Irish western Pennsylvanians hated public drunkenness. The effects of drunkenness were a moral issue that McGuffey attacked, not drinking per se. The same is true of the young drinking; he did not attack the drinking parent, but the parent that teaches a child to drink. It was the same moral approach he applied against slavery. The approach never polarized, but found a unity on the borders of an issue, and it was on the border that moral education could change things. For McGuffey the battle was won on the border without alienation of others.

McGuffey Readers were some of the nation's biggest indirect promoters of the temperance movement. Social chronicler and biographer of the *McGuffey Readers*, Richard Mosier, summarized: "it is clear that the compliers of the McGuffey readers fought intemperance throughout the whole history of the McGuffey Readers. Even in so early an edition as that of the original compilations by Dr. McGuffey, the readers carried lessons and stories vitriolic in their denunciations of the vive of intemperance, and the reasons for these strong denunciations of the vice of intemperance, as we shall see, were both Christian and social." The early teaching of the student on the evils of drinking had a much larger impact than that of Temperance Societies working with adult alcoholics.

In his *First Reader* of 1837, aimed at the first to second grader, he included two lessons on drinking — "*Don't take Strong Drink*" and "*The Whiskey Boy.*" In the first story McGuffey warns: "No little boy or girl should ever drink rum or whiskey, unless they want to become drunkards." The second story tells of the final end of "Whiskey Boy" in stark terms, as well as, addressing the parents: "He was found drunk one day in the street, and carried to the poor house, where he died in two weeks. How do you think his father felt after teaching him to drink whiskey?" In the *Second Reader*, McGuffey follows up in the story of George and Charles with: "All this misery flows from what? From the use of alcoholic drinks. Alas! How many have been ruined in the same way." Again, McGuffey appeared to be right on the curve of the Western mind. The temperance movement was embryonic in the 1830s but growing rapidly by the late 1840s. There is no question that McGuffey's early mind-setting lessons played a role in the temperance movement. In the 1853 edition of the *Third Reader*, a lesson by Lyman Beecher goes further: "My child will not be a drunkard! Cheering thought! How it swells the heart with emotions too big for utterance! What animating prospects does it open to the mind! Almshouses, and jails, and penitentiaries, and state-prisons, will then stand only as so many monuments of the vices of an age gone by." Another lesson, "Touch not—Taste not—Handle not" in the *Third Reader* warns further of the evil of drink.

In the story of Alexander the Great in the 1837 *Third Reader*, he states: "How shocking it is to think that a man who had subdued so many nations, should allow himself to be conquered by the sin of intemperance. It is a lamentable truth that intemperance kills more than the sword." For older students, McGuffey includes a vivid parody of drinking in his *Fourth Reader* of 1837 called the "The Venomous Worm." In this story drink is called the "foe of human kind," "the destroyer," and "the Worm of the Still." McGuffey used many lessons to warn the youth of drinking with great success that carried into adulthood. The temperance movement of the Gilded Age and beyond had no counterpart in Europe. It even went against the heart of the Scotch-Irish, who with the exception of the Covenanters, loved their whiskey. No single theme so dominates the first edition of the Eclectic Series as temperance. It's probably no accident that many of the Gilded Age industrialists such as George Westinghouse, Andrew Carnegie, Henry Ford, H. J. Heinz, John Rockefeller, Thomas Mellon, and William McKinley opposed drinking. McGuffeyland alumnus such as H. J. Heinz and John Rockefeller became advocates to eliminate youth drinking.

The temperance movement in the United States had its ups and downs through the 1920s, but the *McGuffey Readers* remained consistent in opposition to drinking. The temperance theme even survived the major 1879 revision. In that revision the *Third Reader* had a new story, "Beware of the First Drink." Temperance clearly was the longest and strongest theme throughout the history of the Readers. Many believe that *McGuffey's Readers* played a major role in prohibition. McGuffey's approach, as with other topics, was moralistic, not political. Slowly generations were converted on a moral basis. McGuffey personally avoided joining any political movement for prohibition or abolition.

Like abolition, McGuffey steered clear of public support of issue groups, which might politicize it. Yet many of his friends and family were advocates of temperance as noted by this letter from his sister Elizabeth Drake to his wife in 1842: "There is scarcely a limit to the success of the Temperance cause. Six or seven thousand have joined the Washington society and every week large numbers are added. Upwards of three thousand also, have joined the Female Temperance society. Not only in this city, but in many other cities and villages both East and West the good cause is onward."[1] Elizabeth Drake had joined the Methodist Church, which was a major supporter of the Temperance Movement, but even Presbyterian leadership such as Lyman Beecher had joined the temperance movement. William McGuffey's Covenanter principles of not mixing politics and morals proved correct with the Washington Society, as it died out in the late 1840s by moving into politics. McGuffey did more damage to intemperance and drinking by staying out of the movement, and attacking at the moral root of the problem.

Like temperance, abolition was a challenge to McGuffey. His refusal to more actively enter the political battle raised much criticism but was consistent with separating personal politics from the Readers. The majority of the "College of Teachers" were abolitionists. Many of his friends were part of the Underground Railroad and abolitionists who hoped McGuffey would take on abolition with the same vivid attacks made on intemperance. Many even felt he supported slavery because of his lack of public disclaimers. McGuffey clearly saw slavery was a moral evil. In his 1838 *Fourth Reader* in his story-"Character of Wilberforce," he states to his young readers: "The man whose labors abolished the Slave trade, at one blow struck away the barbarism of a hundred nations, and elevated myriads of human beings, degraded to the brute, into all the dignified capacities of civilized man. To have done this is the most noble, as it is the most useful work, which any individual could accomplish." Critics quickly point out that the story was removed in the 1844 and 1853 editions, but this was probably not McGuffey's decision. Truman and Smith were targeting Kentucky and didn't want to upset Southern readers.

The problem was that abolitionists represented a wide range of radical views. In the 1830s, some abolitionists wanted the North to break away from the South. Some wanted military intervention on plantation owners. Many abolitionists denounced the Constitution for permitting slavery. Other abolitionists believed in terrorism. Abolitionists of the 1830s and 1840s were divided on the direction to be taken. Many of the "College of Teachers" were abolitionists or moderate supporters such as the Beecher family. McGuffey is often criticized about not addressing slavery more directly, but had he taken such public support of political groups, the goal of a common school Reader would have been jeopardized.

---

1 Letter from Elisabeth (Drake) McGuffey to Harriet McGuffey, January 3, 1842, Miami University Archives.

Most complaints about McGuffey are rooted in his opposition at Miami University of abolitionist views in the church and classroom. He had opposed President Bishop in his efforts to inject abolitionist views into education. McGuffey's approach was consistent with his views of keeping politics, religion, and education separate. It was also consistent with his Covenanter roots of keeping politics separate. In his view, slavery was an evil best addressed by moral education. Personally, McGuffey was a believer in states' rights. While abolitionists supported war, McGuffey favored the parliamentary approach that had overthrown slavery in England. McGuffey was clearly aware of his friends' activity in the Underground Railroad, and he tacitly gave his support. McGuffey's brother Alexander did prove a bit more vocal, but out of concern for the Readers, also kept to the background. McGuffey's drift towards slavery or a liberal acceptance of it became more pronounced when he moved to Virginia and assimilated into Southern societies.

Another moral theme of the Readers, which was pure Scotch-Irish, was debt. No one virtue has been more linked to the Scotch-Irish than thrift. In a *Sixth Reader* essay on "Ironical Eulogy on Debt" defines the problems of debt: "Debt is the very highest antiquity . . . Society is composed of two classes, debtors and creditors." It is debtors that have the "sympathies of mankind." The irony is in the loss of freedom by the sympathetic view of others. In many respects, McGuffey was preaching to true believers. The frontier Scotch-Irish, German, and English Puritans all believed in thrift. It had been a premise in Benjamin Franklin's *Poor Richard's Almanac* and fully embedded in the nation's concept of the Protestant Work Ethic. It was at the root of their hatred of taxes and government. The role of the *McGuffey Reader* then was to pass this basic virtue on to the next generation.

The *McGuffey Readers* took on a number of moral issues that would be taboo today. Death was a popular theme probably because McGuffey faced so much of it in his life. Contrary to many popular views, McGuffeyland was not a fairyland. Death was addressed head on in the *First Reader* lesson "The Dead Mother," the *Third Reader* lesson "The Dying Boy," and the *Fourth Reader* lesson "What is Death." Death, particularly the death of children, was a common experience on the frontier. McGuffey's stories helped children deal with death in a Christian context. The heroic death of a boy with his father is even addressed in the *Fourth Reader* lesson "Casabianca." "Casabianca" was in the original first edition of the *Second Reader* and then moved up to the *Third Reader* in the 1857 revision.

McGuffey clearly built on the moral catechism in Webster's *Blue Back Speller* of 1824, which discussed the anti-virtues and virtues of humility, mercy, peacemakers, purity, of anger, of revenge, justice, generosity, gratitude, truth, charity, of avarice, frugality, industry, and cheerfulness. Two virtues represented the cornerstone of McGuffeyland: charity and honesty. We have seen how charity had changed the nature of American capitalists, but honesty was maybe just as 'important to the success of capitalism. McGuffey considered honesty to be the fabric of society. Honesty as a virtue addressed the commandment against stealing. McGuffey took on the virtue of honesty early with the child. One of the first sentences a child learns in the 1837 *Eclectic Primer* is: "If you tell a lie, you will be a bad boy." In another lesson in the Primer: "If God sees me, and knows all that I do, He must hear what I say." In the *First Reader*, McGuffey follows up with the stories of the Chimney Sweep. The lessons continue into the later readers. The virtue of honesty had deep Scotch-Irish roots in the overall respect for property. When the editors dropped the story of the "Little Chimney Sweep" in the 1879 revision, there was uproar. Eventually, the story was added again in 1885.

After morals and virtues, the most powerful theme of the *McGuffey Readers* was patriotism. McGuffey's selections were clearly nationalistic. McGuffey would espouse the view that America was the hope of the world, and she would lead the world.

This is a McGuffey composition in the *Fifth Reader* of 1857: "Be it then the noblest office of American eloquence, to cultivate, in the people of every state, a fervent attachment to the union . . . Nor is this all. Let the American orator comprehend . . . that the Union is the property of the world . . . that it is destined to shed its glorious influence backward on the states of Europe, and forward on the empires of Asia . . . Be it then the duty of American eloquence to speak, to write, to act, in the cause of Christianity, patriotism, and literature; in the cause of justice, humanity, and truth; in the cause of the people, of the Union, of the whole human race, and of the unborn of every clime and age." McGuffey further believed "the consequences of the independence will soon reach the extremities of the world." The Readers hailed American exceptionalism, manifest destiny, and America as God's country.

Certainly this type of patriotism was manifested in many McGuffey alumni such as Abraham Lincoln, William McKinley, Teddy Roosevelt, and Harry Truman. McGuffey chose the Puritan Fathers — Patrick Henry, John Marshall, Daniel Webster, and George Washington — to lionize. Critics see the patriotism of McGuffey as extreme nationalism. Certainly, McGuffey and many of his readers truly believed America superior to other nations. But it was not blind nationalism; McGuffey's moral approach addressed many of the evils of American society from a positive framework. McGuffey, like many people of the later Gilded Age, had a deep belief in American exceptionalism. McGuffey used biblical terms to describe leaders such as "Washington's sword and Franklin's staff." The nation was characterized as the "pillar of divine glory descending from God." Furthermore, McGuffey saw America as having a future mission to bring liberty and democracy to the world. Historian Richard Mosier described McGuffey's concept of an American mission: "America has a glorious destiny, a mission, which has been ordained by divine Providence. The flag, the constitution, the church —

these were the rocks on which the lusty patriots of the nineteenth century built their arguments."

It is fair to question whether McGuffey supported patriotism or nationalism, but the nineteenth century American did not make such distinctions that many make today. Many recent historians have tried to link McGuffey's patriotic writings to the expansionist policies of the Gilded Age, but McGuffey did not advocate war. McGuffey's stories opposed the very nature of war and remained true to his moral basis. McGuffey had infused the strong sentiments of the frontier pacifist Germans of Ohio's Western Reserve and Cincinnati. His hatred of war had been one of the reasons that McGuffey had personally rejected the radicalism of the abolitionists. McGuffey had opposed the practice of dueling, seeing it as immoral. He included a story "Criminality of Dueling" in his 1837 *Fourth Reader*. McGuffey consistently opposed war at all levels, even to the point of not using heroic soldier stories. The lesson "Horrors of War" appeared in the first edition of the *Fourth Reader*, then moved to the *Fifth Reader* in the 1857 revision, and finally dropped in the 1879 revision. It was dropped in the 1879 because of the wounds remaining from the Civil War. He also declared in another lesson: "War is the work, the element, or rather the sport and triumph of death." McGuffey, of course, was no pacifist either. He had many heroic stories of warriors including Washington, Napoleon, and Alexander the Great, but McGuffey tried to strike the difficult balance of a justified war. He certainly did not see justice in even the Civil War, so he set a tough standard.

Daniel Drake and the "College of Teachers" saw patriotism as having a role in the formation of a nation. Furthermore, patriotism and nationalism offered social glue to a divided and sectional country, and this was the basis of McGuffey passion for the nationalism of his Readers. On the frontier, it was necessary to blend the European immigrants into an American. Drake and the "College of Teachers" saw patriotism as a means to an end. In the West, the strings to Europe were culturally cut and the West needed a new source of culture. Daniel Drake prepared an 1838 *McGuffey Reader* essay "The Patriotism of Western Literature," which delineates the need and use of patriotism. Drake noted: "As a guiding star to the will, its light is inferior only to that of Christianity. Heroic in its philanthropy, untiring in its enterprises, and justly occupies a high place among the virtues which ennoble the human character. A literature animated with this patriotism is a national blessing, and such will be the literature of the West." Drake argues that patriotism is a requirement of the West because it serves to unite. Patriotism would serve also as a base for common schools.

In the first half of the 1800s, the nation and the West were highly polarized. The great Federalist tradition of George Washington had been divided by the politics of Thomas Jefferson and Alexander Hamilton. Then the Jeffersonian tradition divided among the supporters and enemies of Andrew Jackson. The feuds between the Jacksonians and anti-Jacksonians were every bit as heated as today. Slavery and tariffs divided North and South. It split churches, cut through nationalities, and eventually would even divide families. The popular politicians of the West such as Henry Clay and Andrew Jackson could not unite. McGuffey and his close friends saw Jackson as a demagogue, but avoided any direct political attacks. McGuffey saw very little in Jefferson as contributing to the moral character of America, and while some of Jefferson's writing were included in the Readers, he was a never held out as a founding father. If patriotism was to be injected into common schools, the current political divisions had to be avoided. McGuffey believed a well-educated electorate would not fall prey to demagogues. McGuffey believed that a strong belief in a Christian God would not allow one to fall prey to Jefferson's Deistic approach. Furthermore, he felt that America needed a hero of high moral standards to be used as a comparison. The West needed a heroic figure of old, and George Washington could fit the bill.

One of the key contributions to American nationalism by McGuffey was the crafting of the heroic George Washington. Some critics called it over the top hero worship or the "cult of Washington." McGuffey preferred to make a hero out of Washington than a Davy Crockett or Daniel Boone, which were popular folk heroes in the West. Washington was a real unifying figure for a nation. McGuffey certainly didn't want heroes such as Thomas Jefferson or Andrew Jackson; any national hero had to be Christian and of high morals. Daniel Webster added an essay for the 1838 *Fourth Reader* titled "Washington's Birthday." In this essay, Webster makes the point: "The ingenuous youth of America will hold up to themselves the bright model of Washington's example, and study to be what they behold. They will contemplate his character till its virtues spread out and display themselves to their delighted vision, as the earliest astronomers, the shepherds on the plains of Babylon, gazed at the stars till they saw them form into clusters and constellations, overpowering at length the eyes of the beholders with the blaze of a thousand lights."

Washington was one founding father that all could agree on. In his own essay McGuffey describes Washington as: "First in war, first in peace, and first in the hearts of his countrymen, he was second to none in humble and endeavoring scenes of private life. Pious, just, humane, temperate, sincere, uniform, dignified, and commanding, his example was edifying to all around him, as were the effects of that example lasting. To his equals, he was condescending; to his inferiors, kind; and to the dear object of his affections, exemplary." McGuffey took liberties in adding such virtues, as temperate, realizing Washington's love of Madera wine was legendary. McGuffey was not naive, he knew these were overstated, but he understood nation building, as did Daniel Drake. Washington offered the best piece of marble to start with. Jefferson's weak Christianity was a concern that would be difficult to mask, as would have been Benjamin Franklin's. The

McGuffey Reader promoted myths such as Washington cutting down the cherry tree. The 1838 *Second Reader* contained three lessons about George Washington — "The Little Boy and the Hatchet," "Story about George Washington," and "More about George Washington." And a fourth story about Lafayette included the person of George Washington. Thus, as a young student started to read, his first hero would be George Washington. It was a powerful statement and lesson, which McGuffey reserved for the tender minds of the *First* and *Second Readers*.

Much has been made of McGuffey supporting big business and the Gilded Age Republicans, but in fact, he died in 1873 a Southern Democrat. He clearly supported capitalism and republicanism over Jacksonian Democracy. He cared even little for most of Thomas Jefferson's views, preferring the views of Federalist Alexander Hamilton. He saw education as the enemy of Jacksonian Democracy and demagogues such as Jackson. Those of the Whig Party best describe McGuffey's personal politics. The Whig Party in the 1840s was a counter-revolution to that of Jackson. The Whigs united conservatives and religion, but not without problems. But again to McGuffey's credit, he kept politics out of the Readers. While the Whig Party would morph into the Republican Party in the 1850s, McGuffey did not. McGuffey could not support the pro-abolition stand of the new Republican Party. McGuffey favored essays by two of his favorite Federalists and Whigs — Daniel Webster and John Marshall. The McGuffey Readers favored Federalists and Whigs, but really the selections from these political figures are on more basic issues such as education, morals, and patriotism. Even the writings of Jefferson were included. Jackson seemed to be the one president that McGuffey avoided. In general, however, it is hard to make a case for a political view embedded in his Readers. The Readers were political only when moral values aligned with a party's political principles. McGuffey even added a lesson on always looking at two sides of an issue in the *Third Reader*.

Finally, McGuffey warned his students of the natural propensity of corruption in politics. In the *Fourth Reader*, the lesson Political Corruption makes the point: "We are apt to treat the idea of our own corruptibility as utterly visionary, and to ask, with a grave affectation of dignity — what! Sir, I speak what I have long and deliberately considered, when I say, that since man was created, there has never been a political body on the face of the earth that would not be corrupted under the same circumstances. Corruption steals upon us in a thousand insidious forms when we are least aware of its approaches. Of all the forms in which it can present itself, the bribery of office is the most dangerous because it assumes the guise of patriotism to accomplish its fatal sorcery."

CHAPTER 20. THE LEGACY OF THE MAN AND HIS BOOKS

"We are born for a higher world than that of earth; there is a realm where rainbows never fade, where the stars will be out before us, like islets that slumber on the ocean, and where the beings that pass before us like shadows, will stay in our presence forever."
— McGuffey High School Reader, 1857

The legacy of William McGuffey and his Readers are really two distinct topics, but they share a common vision. The Readers took on a life of their own, and they have often overshadowed the true legacy and accomplishments of McGuffey. McGuffey did much more than develop a series of Readers. He was the heart and soul of a true American movement birthed in Cincinnati's "College of Teachers." It represented a political counter-revolution as well as a cultural revolution. It changed our culture and the image of America forever. McGuffey more than anyone else started the implementation of common schools in America. His eclectic series of Readers was only one component of that effort. It was through the common opportunity of education for all that McGuffey created a revolution of his own. It was the common access of education that powered the American nation forward. The poor were no longer born to be poor, but could pull themselves up through education. Without this opportunity, industrial America could never have sustained capitalism but would have gone the path of social unrest found in Europe in the 1800s. Industrial America of the 1800s was a tough place, and it created many social evils; but with common education, it never lacked a large element of hope and ideals. The combination of common schools and the Readers laid the groundwork to assimilate millions of immigrants into American society between 1870 and 1920. Henry Ford said it best: "He was a great teacher who took the American nation into his class room."

McGuffey and his associates in the "College of Teachers" had a real vision of the future. Plato once noted that a society should ask only two questions. Those questions were — who will teach and what will they teach. These were the questions asked by a group of Western intellectuals who worried about the future of a young nation. McGuffey had a clear answer for those questions. It was that knowledge which allowed for the shaping of industrial America. McGuffey set the moral tone for teachers and students alike. The vision and tone gave direction to generations of new immigrants to this country. He modeled an ideal of what they and what America could be. *McGuffey Readers*, the "College of Teachers," and American teachers brought the spirit of the American Revolution to each new wave of immigrants. It proved Plato's words true that education defines a society, and a nation of immigrants was particularly dependent on education as a rite of initiation.

American immigrants had a sense of destiny for the next generation, often giving much to improve life for the next generation. These immigrants had a passion for education, but they were not interested in government control. Early American education as pioneered by the Puritans always had a religious element, but McGuffey reformed this by focusing not on dogma but religious values. When the descendants of these Puritans wanted public education to reflect their Protestant views, Catholic immigrants resisted. Early Scotch-Irish and German farmers also resisted and started their own schools on the frontier, collectively paying instructors. Later Irish, Slav, Hungarian, German, etc., would pay for their own schools out of their meager wages, but many lacked the resources and had to depend on public schools. McGuffey had held that common schools should be for all faiths and free to all. His Readers were honed over the years to be fair to all faiths. American immigrants wanted education as much as economic freedom. Education was a priority for most immigrants that had been withheld from them in Europe. Our immigrant communities were building many of our greatest colleges, but the country needed primary education that all could afford. Immigrants were just as eager to learn skilled trades, which had been withheld from them as well. The immigrants' desire for education changed America.

By the mid-1800s, America had more colleges than most of Europe. The lower and middle class of America were far better educated and had more opportunity than their counterparts in Europe. The amazing upward mobility of poor immigrants within one to two generations can be attributed to the access to education. The lower and middle class of America were far better educated and had more opportunity than their counterparts in Europe. The literacy rate was equal to that of Scotland as one of the world's highest rates. Upward mobility was proclaimed as an American right. The industrial ghettos were often a short stay for many immigrants. The average was less than one and half generations for poor working families to move into the lower middle class in the 1800s. The inability of the worker in Europe to move out of the ghetto created socialism as a path to help the oppressed workers. American immigrants, because of the opportunities available, rejected the equality of socialism for the upward mobility of capitalism. The very nature of our immigrants made them suspect of government, and the *McGuffey Readers* enforced the Whig idea of suspect government and taxation. Socialism had failed in the early colonies, and it would be rejected by later generations of immigrants. Immigrants didn't want equality as much as opportunity. The colonists' earliest grievances were economic, and the cause of immigration of the 1800s was economic as well. They understood that political and religious freedom was rooted in economic freedom. Immigrants had been held in economic classes in Europe by nature of their birth, and lack of educational opportunity. Often they fled poor economic conditions to find worse conditions in America, but they were looking for hope. There was a difference, however, through work, education, and saving; they could expect better life for their children.

Work, education, and savings were the very core principles of the *McGuffey Readers*, Much has been said of the great McGuffey alumni such as Henry Ford, William McKinley, Harry Truman and Teddy Roosevelt, but maybe McGuffey's greatest alumni were in the million unmanned immigrant middle class alumni. These were the people that truly defined American culture. It had never been McGuffey's goal to create great leaders and industrialists but to create a moralistic American culture. The virtue of industry was to be a middle class American virtue. Historian Richard Mosier put it best: "The middle class faith was held by the overwhelming majority of Americans in the last three decades of the nineteenth century. No purer statement of its doctrines could be found than those in the *McGuffey Readers*." A story entitled 'Advantages of Industry,' for example, tells of a Charles Bullard who worked hard and successfully during his days in schools. His idle and careless classmate, George Jones, is amazed at the rewards that Charles' industry brings him." *McGuffey Readers* did not promote a cult of success but a moral code that had roots going back to Benjamin Franklin's *Poor Richard's Almanac*. It was through the moral ethic of work that one would find success.

Furthermore, McGuffey never put success as a goal in itself. McGuffey saw happiness in giving and helping. McGuffey did not invent American middle class virtues. He often merely borrowed these virtues from the middle class. He found them in our history and founding fathers. These were the virtues of our first immigrants. McGuffey preserved these founding principles in his Readers to pass them on to new generations. He held George Washington out as a role model for immigrant Italians, Hungarians, Slavs, and Poles. He made American citizenship something to desire and aspire to. He gave them hope, not opium, as Karl Marx would have called it. Another part of the McGuffey legacy was its ability to reso-nate with the average middle class kid.

These young people were not lovers of school and books, yet somehow the *McGuffey Readers* touched deep. Henry Ford and his school buddy Edsel Ruddi-man were typical kids. They were known to have carved their initials on the wooden desks. They played pranks on fellow students. They were average stu-dents. Henry Ford was in the middle of the class, not a scholar. Still, he found a deep love for the lessons and stories, and this was the magic of the *McGuffey Readers*. Many have tried to explain the phenomena of the Readers, and it doesn't seem any one thing, yet no textbook in the history of the world has had such a following. How many people today can remember their grade school textbooks of many years ago? And if they can, how many of those are fond memories?

The real lasting stories and lessons were not pure rages to riches, but those of family values, kindness, giving, and thrift. It was clearly a Victorian model. Re-searcher Frank Davidson in a 1935 survey explored the McGuffey favorites. The top stories and poems were "I love, you Mother," "Waste Not, Want Not," "My Mother's Hands," "Rock Me to Sleep," and "Hugh Idle and Mr. Toil." McGuffey alumni reported the ability to recall many lines from memory and noted a deep impact on their lives. What is striking is the strong image of family created by the *McGuffey Readers*. Richard Mosier painted the image Thus: "This prescription for a happy family life were not enough, we are given a picture of the ideal home life for the McGuffey students. Both children, Harry and Kate Brown, have done well in school. After supper the whole family gathers around the table, reading and doing the little domestic chores that make home life so comfortable. 'Harry and Kate read a story in a new book, the father reads his newspaper, and the mother mends Harry's stockings.' Accompanying this picture of domestic bliss is the question, 'Do you not wish that every boy and girl could have a home like this?'" Kate and Harry were from the *Second Reader* story, "Evening at Home." McGuffey set the ideal, but 1950s sitcom character types were not the only citizens in McGuffey-land. There were bad kids, drunken fathers, and other evils to provide contrast.

There are, of course, many critics that argue that the Age of McGuffey gave us the abuses of the Robber Barons. Still it is a stretch to find some inherent lessons in *McGuffey's Readers* that promoted such evils. A fairer statement of the legacy was given in the *Austin Chronicle*: "His *Reader* helped establish education as we know it (or knew it), but for most of his students it didn't inoculate against committing genocide, slavery, Jim Crow, child labor, the suppression of women, bigotry of all kinds . . . the list goes on and gruesomely on. I believe it is not only legitimate but necessary to expect education to be at least an antidote to, and a means to fight, atrocity and oppression. Yet it is also true that most of the people who learned how to fight these immoralities, from the 1830s into the 1930s, were people who developed, in large through reading, and who had, in effect, learned to read at McGuffey's knee, as part of an educational movement, unique in history, of which the *Reader* was a crucial element. And a result was implicit in the *Reader* from the start. McGuffey was a mixed blessing to be sure, but a blessing nonetheless."[1]

Another part of the McGuffey Reader legacy is that revolutions might best happen in America's classrooms. Such a conclusion offers both hope and a warning. McGuffey had initially envisioned a counter-revolution to the Jacksonian era, which he believed lacked moral backbone. The classroom revolution of McGuffey proved highly successful. If education can take power away from demagogues as McGuffey believed, demagogues such as in Nazi Germany can also use it. If *McGuffey Readers* created a moral revolution, some future text may create an unwanted shift in society. The "College of Teachers" demonstrated what Plato had believed — that society is determined not by politicians and constitutions but by teachers and through textbooks. Common schools can build a nation as McGuffey demonstrated, but common schools can also destroy a nation. The McGuffey revolution showed the inherent power of the educational system.

One part of the McGuffey legacy is the devotion to the Readers over the years. Societies and clubs dedicated to the Readers started to appear in the twilight years of the 1920s. There had been even earlier informal clubs throughout the Midwest. In 1918 a group of devotees formed the Fifth Reader Club in Columbus, Ohio; later in 1921, the group was incorporated as the McGuffey Society of Columbus. Chapters soon spread throughout Transylvania in such places as, Akron, Youngstown, Pittsburgh, Lexington, Louisville, Chicago, Cleveland, Indianapolis, Oxford, and Portsmouth. By the end of the decade there were groups throughout the Unites States including California. In 1930, the Akron membership was 1,100, the Indianapolis was 1,000, and Columbus had over 600 members. The Annual Columbus Club Dinner had 300 in 1930. Henry Ford attracted a crowd of over 15,000 in 1934 for the dedication of a granite memorial near McGuffey's birthplace in Washington County, Pennsylvania. Ford had invested thousands to assure the legend of McGuffey and "certify" official sites and artifacts.

By 1935, the "National Body of McGuffey Societies" was incorporated. The first National Convention was held in 1936 at Oxford, Ohio, the two major financial supporters being Henry Ford and Dean Minnich of Miami University. Henry Ford hosted the 1938 National Convention at Greenfield Village. At the same time Henry Ford started an experimental McGuffey school at Greenfield Village. Over the years, Ford found much happiness in going to Greenfield Village to sit in on these classes. While not a McGuffey school, Greenfield Village maintains a high school. Students are selected by a lottery from the Detroit area. McGuffey continues to be memorialized. As recently as 2004, the Peter Kole–William McGuffey

1 Michael Ventura, "McGuffey Eclectic," *The Austin Chronicle*, October 23, 2008

endowment was established at Idaho State University. The Kole–McGuffey prize will give $10,000 plus annually to graduate students whose "thesis or research project explores a concept revolutionary to the delivery of education."

In 1927, the *McGuffey Readers* were the subject of a *Saturday Evening Post*: "Viewed from any standpoint, the *Rhetorical Guide*, the *Fourth*, *Fifth*, and *Sixth Readers* — were remarkable literary works, and they probably exerted a greater influence consciously upon the literary tastes and unconsciously upon the morality of the United States than any other books, excepting the Bible. In any edition of the *Sixth Reader* there are seventeen selections from the Bible, and no one could make seventeen better choices from a literary and poetical standpoint, nor seventeen that would give less cause for compliant from any creed that might oppose Bible reading in these schools."

Part of McGuffey's legacy is his giving family values to a struggling nation. McGuffey taught more than just obedience of parents; the Readers promoted marriage, temperance, thrift, honesty, and fidelity. McGuffey historian Stanley Lindberg noted: "Marriage was often recognized in popular literature of the West as a desirable civilizing influence, a virtual social institution. Furthermore, having a large family was important on the frontier — almost a necessity if land were to be successfully managed — since children growing into extra workers were always needed." But this was far more integral to the infrastructure of America than just the frontier. The industrial immigrants of the later 1800s depended just as much on the family as a social, economic, and moral unit. In the 1890s, the immigrant families of mill workers at Carnegie's steel mills worked truly as a unit. The wife did sewing and cleaning jobs for others, the boys worked selling vegetables and small labor jobs, and the daughters worked in the nearby Heinz or Westinghouse factories.

The lessons in the Readers were at times hard and difficult. In McGuffeyland, there were fathers who gave their kids whiskey, husbands who became alcoholics, children gone bad, children treating others and animals poorly, and mothers who died. There were tough lessons. In one story in the 1857 *Fourth Reader*, a child refuses his mother her last request for a glass of water (only in fun). The next day he finds his mother dead. And of course, there were many lessons of rebelling children. The popular story "Hugh Idle and Mr. Toil" was typical of these. A young boy refuses to learn in the school of Mr. Toil and runs away. Later Mr. Toil disguises himself as a wanderer and proposes to wander with him. The journey had painful lessons, driving Hugh to cry out, "Take me back to school!" Mr. Toil then identifies himself.

One criticism of McGuffey and his Readers was that they addressed country values, not those of the city and the nation's immigrants. Such critics miss the point that family values crossed those lines. Yet many of America's immigrants were in the factories of Pittsburgh, Cleveland, Detroit, Cincinnati, and Buffalo.

Their environment of smoke and coal dust was a stark contrast from the fields of the Midwest, but the values were the same. Family, faith, and country were the core values of all. They found common ground with McGuffey's moralistic and nationalistic approach. McGuffeyland was a moralistic ideal, not the American farm. McGuffey painted the picture of the American family in the minds of youth before they read the *Saturday Evening Post.* Immigrants found strength in family and faith. Ohio Chief Justice noted the influence of the Readers: "The Third, Fourth, and Fifth and Sixth Readers in their total of more than three inches of thickness contain more character building material than any five-foot shelf of books. The precepts in those old volumes have influenced me more than any others. And it is true that they influenced those of my day who went to school more than any other books."

In an 1839 advertisement in the *Common School Advocate*, William McGuffey and publisher Winthrop Smith clearly defined their Platonian goals: "Finally — the fine moral the effect the whole series is designed to produce. This should be ranked among their most prominent merits. An education is not completed until there is united with the thorough discipline of the mind, a corresponding culture of the heart and affections. The Eclectic Series unite in much greater perfection, this intellectual and moral education of the pupils, than any other series with which we are acquainted, and is thus admirably adapted to make good children as well as scholars." They more than achieved this initial goal!

Rudolph Reeder summarized the legacy of McGuffey best in 1903: "The McGuffey series has probably attained the largest sale and widest distribution of any series yet produced in America. In range of subject matter, it swept almost the entire field of human interest — morals, politics, literature, history, science, and philosophy. Many a profound and lasting impression was made upon the lives of children and youth by the well-chosen selections of this series and valuable lessons of industry, thrift, economy, kindness, generation, honesty, courage, duty, found expression in the lives of millions of boys and girls who read and reread these books, to the influence of which lessons were directly traceable."[1]

---

1 97 Rudolph Rex Reeder, *The Historical Development of School and Methods in Teaching Reading* (New York: Columbia University Press, 1903), p. 56.

BIBLIOGRAPHY

Arnold, James. "A Biography of William Holmes McGuffey." PhD dissertation, University of Cincinnati, 1967.

Badger, Catherine. *Teacher's Last Lesson: A Memoir of Martha Whiting*. Boston: Gould & Lincoln, 1855.

Beecher, Catherine. *The Duty of American Women to Their Country*. New York: Harper, 1845.

Buck, Solon and Elizabeth Buck. *The Planting of Civilization in Western Pennsylvania*. Pittsburgh: University of Pittsburgh Press, 1939.

Butler, Joseph, Jr. *History of Youngstown and The Mahoning Valley, Volumes I and II*. Chicago: American Historical Society, 1921

Cameron, W. "The Mind of McGuffey." A talk delivered at Miami University, July, 1937, Benson Research Center Archives.

Crain, Patricia. *The Story of A*. Stanford: Stanford University Press, 2000

Crawford, Benjamin. *The Life of William Holmes McGuffey*. Delaware, Ohio: Carnegie Church Press, 1974.

Davidson, Frank. "The Life and Moral Influence of William McGuffey," Master Thesis: The Ohio State University, 1935.

Dolch, E. "How Hard Were The McGuffey Readers?" *The Elementary School Journal*. 1945

Filler, Louis, ed., *An Ohio Schoolmistress: The Memoirs of Irene Hardy*. Kent: Kent State University, 1980.

Flanagan, John. *James Hall: Literary Pioneer of the Ohio Valley*. Minneapolis: The University of Minnesota, 1941.

Fullerton, Hugh. "Who Was That Guy McGuffey," *Saturday Evening Post*, November, 1927.

Good, Harry and James D. Teller. *A History of American Education*. New York: The Macmillan Company, 1973.

Gorn, Elliott ed. *The McGuffey Readers: Selections from the 1879 Edition*. New York: St. Martins, 1998.

Havighurst, Walter. *The Miami Years*. New York: G. P. Putman's Sons, 1958

Jennings, W. *Transylvania: Pioneer University of the West*, (New York: Pageant Press, 1955)

Herman, Arthur. *How the Scots Invented the Modern World*. New York: Three Rivers Press, 2001.

Kauffman, Henry. *The American One-Room Schoolhouse*. Morgantown: Masthof Press, 1997

Kennedy, John, F., *A Nation of Immigrants*. New York: Harper & Row, 1964).

Knepper, George. *Ohio and Its People*. Kent: Kent State University Press, 1989

McGuffey, William. "Conversation in a Classroom," *Monthly Chronicle of Interesting and Useful Information*, March, 1939.

Minnich, Harvey. *William Holmes McGuffey and His Readers*. New York: American Book Company, 1936.

Mosier, Richard. *Making the American Mind: Social and Moral Ideas in the McGuffey Readers*. New York: Russell & Russell, 1965

Nietz, John. "Why The Longevity of the McGuffey Readers," *History of Education Quarterly*, Vol.4, No. 2, June, 1964.

Olson, Sidney. *Young Henry Ford*. Detroit: Wayne State University Press, 1963

Reeder, Rudolph. *The Historical Development of School and Methods in Teaching Reading*. New York: Columbia University Press, 1903.

Richard, Carl. *The Battle for the American Mind*. New York: Rowman & Littlefield, 2004.

Rishel, Joseph. *Founding Families of Pittsburgh: Thee Evolution of a Regional Elite*. Pittsburgh: University of Pittsburgh Press, 1990.

Rudolph, Emanuel. "Daniel Drake as a Nineteenth Century Educational Reformer," *Ohio Journal of Science*, Volume 4, 1985, pp 148-153

Ruggles, Alice McGuffey. *The Story of the McGuffeys*. New York: American Book Company, 1950.

Rusk, Ralph. *The Literature of the Middle Western Frontier*. New York: Columbia University Press, 1925.

Saunders, D. A. "Social Ideas in McGuffey Readers," *The Public Opinion Quarterly*, Vol. 5, No. 4, Winter, 1941

Sullivan, Dolores. *William Holmes McGuffey: Schoolmaster of the Nation*. Fairleigh Dickinson University Press, 1994

Sullivan, Mark. *Our Times*. New York: Charles Scribner's Sons, 1903

Theobald, Paul. "Country School Curriculum and Governance." *American Journal of Education*. Volume 101, Feb. 1993.

Wade, Richard. *The Urban Frontier: The Rise of Western Cities, 1790-1830*. Chicago: University of Illinois, 1959.

Weisenburger, Francis. *A History of the State of Ohio, Volumes 1-4*. Columbus: The Ohio Historical Society, 1941.

Woody, Thomas. "Country Schoolmaster of Long Ago," *History of Education Journal*, Volume V, Winter, 1954.

Wyllie, Irvin. *The Self-Made Man in America*. New York: Free Press, 1954

Vogt, Helen. *Westward of ye Laurall Hills*. Parsons: McClain Printing, 1976.

Source of McGuffey Readers

Henry Ford's personal collection of McGuffey Readers was used for reference. These books are currently available at The Henry Ford-Benson Ford Research Center, Dearborn, Michigan

INDEX

D

Davis, Jefferson, 54
Dayton, 62, 72, 116, 119, 123-125, 136, 148
Drake, Daniel, 3, 54, 60, 63, 73, 76-79, 81-88, 90, 92-93, 95, 104, 106-107, 112, 117, 119-120, 122, 125, 132, 169, 173, 176, 188-189, 202, 224-225, 236
Drake, Elizabeth, 3, 78, 86, 106, 117, 123, 221

E

Eclecticism, 97
Emerson, Ralph W., 12, 127, 158

F

Ford, Henry, 1, 3-5, 7-10, 13, 37, 149-150, 175, 193, 197, 207-209, 212, 220, 228-231, 236-237
Franklin, Benjamin, 31, 44, 77-78, 176, 222, 225, 229
Franklin Reader, 44, 70, 152
Frick, Henry Clay, 1, 10, 29, 197-198, 205
Fullerton, Hugh, 154, 235

G

Goodrich, S. S., 152
Gravel Hill farm, 39
Greenfield Village, 1, 4, 9, 231
Greensburg Academy, 46

H

Hall, James, 63, 71, 80, 82, 84, 86, 153, 235
Hamilton, Alexander, 5, 7, 28, 30, 41, 121, 167, 176, 198, 207, 224, 226
Havighurst, Walter, 59, 123, 236
Heinz, H. J., 1, 4, 8, 197, 209, 211-213, 220, 232
Hepburn, Andrew, 125-126, 135-136
Hepburn, Henrietta McGuffey, 123
High School Reader, 115, 158, 227
Honesty, 11, 42, 96, 200, 207, 219, 222-223, 232-233
Hughes, Thomas, 46

I

Income and prices of the day, 53-54, 147, 159

Industry, 2, 5, 8, 11, 13, 40-42, 44-45, 47, 52, 83, 89, 103, 113, 131, 151, 163, 190, 197-201, 203, 208-211, 216, 222, 229, 233

J

Jefferson, Thomas, 48, 77, 120, 122, 127, 135, 153, 163, 191-192, 207, 224-226
Jefferson College, 30, 36, 48, 166, 192

L

Lewis, Samuel, 81, 86-88, 106, 142, 148
Locke, John, 90, 165, 167, 176, 189, 206, 218
Lord's Prayer, 146, 161, 218

M

McGuffey family
    Attitudes towards slavery, 14, 34-35, 37, 42, 47, 49, 52, 59, 64-65, 71-72, 78, 83, 85, 88, 93-95, 115, 117, 121-125, 129-132, 156, 173, 188, 193, 204, 206, 210, 214, 217, 219, 221-222, 225, 230
    McGuffey, Alexander (father), 3, 18, 29, 32-33, 37, 39, 45, 62, 81, 86, 91, 102, 106-107, 111, 117, 121-125, 129, 132, 198
    McGuffey, Anna Holmes (mother), 17, 19, 37
    McGuffey, Anna (daughter), 37, 125, 130
    McGuffey, Charles Spining (son), 123-124
    McGuffey, Edward Mansfield, 64, 76, 90, 95, 104, 106, 117
    McGuffey, Harriet Spining (first wife), 62-63, 106
    McGuffey, Henrietta (daughter), 123-124
    McGuffey, Laura Howard (second wife), 124-126, 135
    McGuffey, Mary Haines (daughter), 63, 106, 117, 123-125
    McGuffey, William Holmes Jr. (son), 64
McGuffey, William Holmes
    arrival at Oxford, OH, 7, 56-58, 62-64, 66, 72-73, 91, 231
    as President of Ohio University, 106
    at Miami University, 3-4, 15, 30, 53, 56-58, 61, 64-67, 73, 76-77, 84, 91-92, 94, 101, 108-109, 112-114, 119-120, 122-123, 126, 134-136, 155, 175, 182, 195, 221-222, 231, 235

S

Sargent, D., 133, 159
Sargent, Wilson and Hinkle, 159
Scott, John Witherspoon, 64
Sermon on the Mount, 2, 161, 218
Smith, Adam, 5, 23, 165, 167-168, 187, 189, 206
Smith, Winthrop, 96-97, 103-106, 113-116, 129-130, 153, 156-159, 177, 180, 193, 233
Speller, 30, 43-44, 53, 70, 76, 91-92, 102, 105, 149, 151, 153, 156-157, 171, 175-178, 180, 199, 203, 222
Spining, Isaac, 62
Stewart, William, 125
Stowe, Calvin, 66, 76, 86-87, 170, 172-173, 176
Stowe, Harriet, 76, 81, 186
Sullivan, Mark, 14, 236

T

Temperance, 80, 83, 87, 91, 217, 219-221, 232
Ten Commandments, 13, 155, 218
Thrift, 5, 11, 13, 42, 154, 166, 187, 200, 208, 222, 230, 232-233
Truman, Harry, 12, 223, 229
Truman, William, 103, 229

V

Vail, Henry, 3, 133, 160

W

Washington College, 30, 36, 48-49, 52-53, 56, 64, 67, 119, 123
Washington, George, 10-11, 14, 25-26, 34, 36-37, 121, 153, 176, 223-226, 229
Winthrop B. Smith and Company, 96-97, 103-106, 113-116, 129-130, 153, 156-159, 177, 180, 193, 233
Webster, Daniel, 8, 60, 65, 94, 121-122, 127, 153, 173-174, 176, 186, 223, 225-226
Webster's Dictionary, 7, 44
Western College Teacher's Institute, 76, 121, 169
Western Reader, 68-71, 82, 152-153, 209
Westinghouse, George, 1, 8, 29, 197, 209, 211-213, 220
Wick, William, 40, 43, 45
Worcester, Samuel, 96, 153, 176
Worcester Readers, 96
Work Ethic, 197, 200-201, 203, 222, 229
Wylie, Andrew, 48-50, 73, 100, 207

5169238R0

Made in the USA
Charleston, SC
09 May 2010